THE BEATLES
Extraordinary Plagiarists

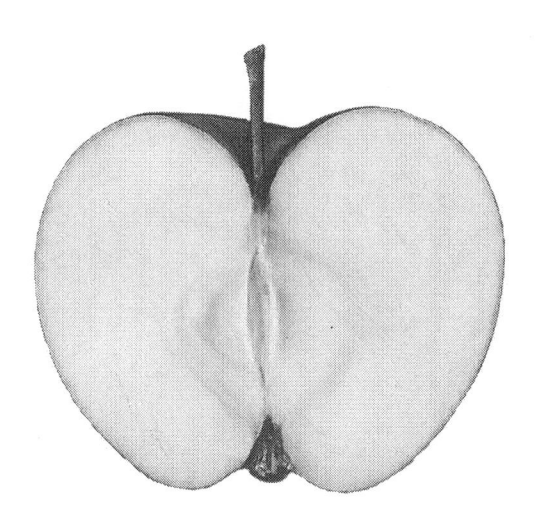

By EDGAR O. CRUZ

THE BEATLES: *Extraordinary Plagiarists*

By EDGAR O. CRUZ

DESIGN BY EDGAR O. CRUZ
LAYOUT BY MARK JUSTINE S. ISIDRO
DISTRIBUTION BY JUSTIN JOHN MATA

PHILIPPINE COPYRIGHT © 2009
THE NATIONAL LIBRARY
MANILA, PHILIPPINES
ISSN A2009-2138, ISBN 978-971-94954-0-6

PUBLISHED IN MANILA, PHILIPPINES
BY EXOM PUBLISHING HOUSE
CONTACT PARTICULARS:
ADDRESS: 2213 BEATA STREET
PANDACAN, MANILA 1011
PHILIPPINES
LANDLINE: (632) 561-4435
MOBILE: (632) 0939-502-5338
E-MAIL: exom.ph@gmail.com

ALL RIGHTS RESERVED.
NO PART OF THIS PUBLICATION MAY BE REPRODUCED,
STORED IN A RETRIEVAL SYSTEM, OR TRANSMITTED IN
ANY FORM OR BY ANY MEANS, ELECTRONIC, MECHANICAL,
PHOTOCOPYING, RECORDING, OR OTHERWISE, WITHOUT
PERMISSION IN WRITING.

FOR REMEDIOS O. CRUZ

THANKS TO

ROSS CELINO, JR. • ETHEL RAMOS • RICKY LO • SHEIK MOHAMED ALFADL • ROSARIO GARCELLANO • JORGE LLANES • JR MERCADO • EMMY VELARDE • IMELDA CRUZ-WOOD • ENRICO SANTOS • THELMA SIOSON SAN JUAN • ERNIE LOPEZ • DINAH VENTURA • NANCY REYES LUMEN • WILLIE REVILLAME • EDITH FIDER • JACK KIDWILER • ATTY. JOJI ALONSO • BABY PACHECO • KANKAN RAMOS • JOYCE PILARSKY • JUSTIN JOHN MATA

Contents

Introduction

1 White Negroes

2 Reinventing rock 'n' roll

3 The song is the message

4 Beyond recognition

5 Rejecting the communal ownership

6 The shift

7 Art and artifice

Glossary

Introduction

George Harrison once said that the Beatles reshaped the Sixties to "mini-Renaissance" proportions. Music critic Eric Zalsman, in a piece for the *Stereo Review*, echoed this thought: "They were, in effect, the first poets of the technological culture, the first to strum the mass media as their instrument, to tune their lyres to 60-cycle hum, to take inputs from the Global Village and turn them into messages for our time." Psychedelic drug guru Dr. Timothy Leary had a similar, though more fantastic, view: "I declare that the Beatles are mutants. Prototypes of evolutionary agents sent by God, endowed with a mysterious power to create a young race of laughing freemen."

Crew John Lennon, Paul McCartney, George Harrison and Ringo Starr did it through a relentless barrage of song discourses about love. Out of the 213 songs officially released by the Beatles in the United Kingdom, 163 -- or about three-fourths of their total song output -- are about love: romantic love, illicit love, gay love, kindred love, materialistic love, universal love, love for music, and love for animals -- practically all permutations of normal and sometimes aberrant love. The Beatles' creativity was mind-boggling, but not beyond comprehension. Tracing their root and artistic influences provides a better understanding of how this creativity was honed and developed.

The Beatles began as mere Elvis Presley wannabes who started writing songs ignorant of the rudiments of music. Yet despite this artistic illiteracy, they developed into the most commercially viable songmakers and musicians of their generation. Their phenomenal success even led behavioral scientist Dr. Joseph Crow to compare their accomplishment to the feat of inventing the A-bomb without knowledge of the laws of Mathematics or Physics.

Crow, often referred to as America's "Number One Expert on Musical Subversion" by members of the John Birch Society and other right-wing Christian evangelists, wrote: "Some of the newer Beatle songs...show an acute awareness of the principles of rhythm and brainwashing. Neither Lennon nor McCartney was a world-beater in school, nor have they had technical training in music. For them to have written some of their songs is like someone who had not had physics or math inventing the A-bomb...Because of its technical excellence it is possible that this music is put together by behavioral scientists in some 'think tank'...I have no idea whether the Beatles know what they are doing or whether they are being used by some enormously sophisticated people, but it really doesn't make any difference. Its results that count, and the Beatles are the leading pied pipers creating promiscuity, an epidemic of drugs, youth class-consciousness, and an atmosphere for social revolution."

Lennon and McCartney, the songmaking tandem that steered the Beatles to this unparalleled level of artistry, were praised and ranked by some music critics and pop historians such as the London *Sunday Times'* music journalist Richard Buckle ("The greatest composers since Beethoven.") and writer / producer / broadcaster Tony Palmer ("The greatest songwriters since Schubert.") at par with the genius of classical composers. Harrison -- yes, George Harrison of the Beatles -- and Lennon himself ("Beethoven is a con, just like we are now. He was just knocking out a bit of work that was all.") were more down-to-earth with their assessments.

Why the extreme variation?

These contradicting perceptions of the genius of the Beatles had bred -- and continues to breed -- a number of critiques and studies both in the realm of popular music and the academe. At the same time, these diametrically opposed descriptions of the Beatles pushed music enthusiasts to ask: Is the Beatles' body of songs art or artifice?

Media sensationalism and critical intellectualization of every Beatles song at the peak of the Fab Four's popularity practically removed the simple auditory pleasure that gave the three-minute pop song the complexity and richness of a Stravinsky symphony. It was probably because their songs had tremendous influence on the rise of fanaticism and how they affected the behavior of the youth that the pervasive power of the Beatles' songs and images had been given due and/or undue importance.

Such contradicting views reveal a polarity between the real Beatles and the way they were perceived by the public, both fans and critics alike. With the renewed and undying interest in Beatles songs, this year being the 40th year of the group's break in 1969, these opposing views remain unresolved.

To allow a systematic discussion in this book, the Beatles' creative cycle shall be described, explored, and analyzed here using the albums released during the period including the singles before and during the issuance of such albums, thereby providing a better view of how the Beatles wrote their songs:

Period	Albums covered
Birth	*Please Please Me* and *With the Beatles*
Growth	*A Hard Day's Night, Help, Rubber Soul,* and *A Collection of Beatle Oldies But Goldies*
Maturity	*Revolver* and *Sgt. Pepper's Lonely Hearts Club Band*
Decline	*Magical Mystery Tour* and *The Beatles*
Death	*Yellow Submarine, Abbey Road* and *Let It Be*

Removed from its time, devoid of the period's sentimentality, the sources and methods of the Beatles' creativity can now be revealed and analyzed in retrospect. This book attempts to provide an in-depth, comprehensive, and extensive analysis of the Beatles' creativity. It also aims to give the readers a chance to journey back and revisit the phenomenal rise to fame of the Fab Four from Liverpool, England. songs that John and Paul write, they're all right, but they are not the greatest.") and revisit the phenomenal rise to fame of the Fab Four from Liverpool, England.

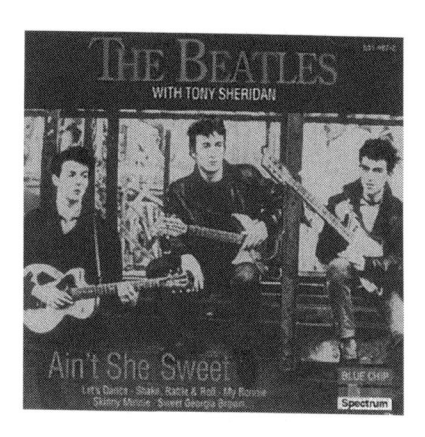

Chapter 1

White Negroes

"If I could find a White man who had the Negro sound and the Negro feel, I could make a billion dollars."

- Sam Phillips

Norman Mailer put forward the idea of the rise of Whites who imitated the music and manners of Black Americans in his 1957 essay *The White Negro*, which is about his encounters with middle-class Whites who had dropped out of mainstream society and got to be known as the Beat generation. "So there was a new breed of adventurers... who drifted out at night looking for action with a Black man's code to fit their facts. The hipster has absorbed the existentialist synapses of the Negro, and for all practical purposes could be considered a White Negro," wrote White man Mailer.

Whites, reasoned Mailer, imitated Blacks out of a psychological anxiety that the latter are a freer people and, being slaves in the past, whatever the future holds for them would just have to be better. On the other hand, writer Ned Polsky explained, "The White Negro accepts the real Negro not as a human being in his totality, but as the bringer of a highly specified and restricted 'cultural dowry,' to use Mailer's phrase."

That kind of mindset led to the creation of the Beat Movement, which centered on the White Negroes' pleasure-seeking view of life and involved choosing the excitement of the present over worrying about the future and its dreary prospects Jack Kerouac, Allen Ginsberg, Neal Cassidy, and William S. Burroughs, a bunch of male White friends who were considered the leaders of the Beat Movement, expanded their group consciousness of anti-collectivism and pro-individualism. According to Mailer, it was the Beat Movement's search for meaning, inspiration, and a better future that drove Whites to adopt Black culture: to turn themselves into White Negroes. These "hipsters" started a cult of imitation.

White Negroes in the United States

In the United States, musicologists single out Elvis Presley as the White Negro who successfully "inter-married" rhythm-and-blues with country music and popularized the hybrid music that came to be known as "rock 'n' roll."

Rock 'n' roll was the race music, which the older generation of Whites disliked because it was initially considered as Black music and had strong associations with sex. Presley was perceived as a White who sang like a Black -- and he would eventually be adulated by the Whites precisely because he sounded and moved like a Black. Presley's ascent to massive popularity began when Sam Phillips, head of Sun Records in 1954, produced for him "That's All Right," a country song popularized by Arthur Crudup, giving it the rougher idiom of rhythm and blues. Disc jockey Alan Freed gave this hybrid music a name: "rock 'n' roll," which means to dance and have sex (roll was an abbreviated form of jelly-roll, a Black euphemism for sexual intercourse). All the wiggling and writhing with the song repelled parents and church leaders -- but not the White youth, the target market for Presley's albums.

But what gave Sun Records the idea of making a White like Presley record a country song with a palpable texture of rhythm and blues more associated with Black singers?

The recording company learned that an increasing number of young Whites were buying blues and rhythm-and-blues records popularized by Black musicians. Blending the appeal of a White singer in Presley and the popularity of rhythm and blues, record executives thought of a better way to capture both markets by getting a White singer to churn out songs associated with Blacks. The outcome of this marketing strategy became Elvis Presley. Presley turned out to be the crossover singer with an infinitely larger commercial potential because of his good all-American appeal.

From that point on, there was no doubt that the White Negroes' popularity was rising in meteoric proportions. Black singers themselves were benefiting from the oxymoronic tag. Chuck Berry, a Black singer, received the dubious label of a White Negro after writing songs intended for the White market. As a songwriter, singer, and guitarist, he shaped rock 'n' roll as we know it today. He converted rockabilly into the now 4/4 rock 'n' roll beat and installed wordplay as a standard lyricist's tool. He revamped the hillbilly tune "Ida Red" into the massive hit "Maybelline," inspired by the leading brand of cosmetics. As a Black playing White music and doing it by supplying fresh verses to old favorites, creating the middle's 24-bar guitar solo in the process, and performing them with showman-like flair, he gained crossover appeal, embraced by Whites and Blacks alike.

If Presley provided rock 'n' roll its imagery, it was Berry who was the genre's musical genius. Berry is credited for having established rock 'n' roll's White Negro code. But the songs unwittingly -- and alarmingly -- promoted sexuality that parents and church leaders continued to find repulsive, along with the kind of lifestyle that it bred. Two other White Negroes led at the peak of their popularity: Jerry Lee Lewis married his minor cousin, while Little Richard capitalized on his homosexuality for that rock 'n' roll difference. With such negative role models, who would not fear the "devil's music" as they denigrated rock 'n' roll at the time? Seeing how the young were being affected by it, more authorities began wishing for the craze to end -- or if this was not possible, for a "safe" version to turn up.

Lennon and being hip

Meanwhile, on the other side of the industrialized world, in distant England, the stage was being set for the emergence of the biggest White Negroes of them all: the Beatles.

Being a White Negro is founded on being hip. And to be hip then meant being aware of what was happening in the environment and adopting certain beliefs, styles, and practices before they could become mainstream mores and manners. John Lennon, acknowledged founder and leader, manifested this hipness while growing up in working class Liverpool, and became inordinately attracted to rock 'n' roll.

In the 1980 *Playboy* interview, he talked about this hipness as a boy, "... There was something wrong with me, I thought, because I seemed to see things other people didn't see. I thought I was crazy or an egomaniac for claiming to see things other people didn't see. As a child, I would say, 'But this is going on!' and everybody would look at me as if I was crazy. I always was so psychic or intuitive or poetic or whatever you want to call it, that I was always seeing things in a hallucinatory way."

This had a creepy effect, "It was scary as a child, because there was nobody to relate to. Neither my auntie nor my friends nor anybody could ever see what I did. It was very, very scary and the only contact I had was reading about an Oscar Wilde or a Dylan Thomas or a Vincent van Gogh -- all those books that my auntie had that talked about their suffering because of their visions. Because of what they saw, they were tortured by society for trying to express what they were. I saw loneliness."

At 11, Lennon received a copy of Lewis Carroll's *Alice's Adventures in Wonderland* (commonly shortened to *Alice in Wonderland*) as a birthday present. The surreal, fanciful volume left a lasting impression. Lennon noted, "I was passionate about *Alice in Wonderland* and drew all the characters. I did poems in the style of 'Jabberwocky.' I used to love Alice..."

By the time he was 15, Lennon was wishing he could write something like *Alice in Wonderland*. Though Lennon did eventually publish several volumes of nonsense in the style of Carroll, his connection to Alice would surface later.

He then realized he was not insane. He explained, "I belong in an exclusive club that sees the world in those terms. Surrealism to me is reality. Psychic vision to me is reality. Even as a child. When I looked at myself in the mirror or when I was 12, 13, I used to literally trance out into alpha...But I would find myself seeing hallucinatory images of my face changing and becoming cosmic and complete. It caused me to always be a rebel. This thing gave me a chip on the shoulder; but, on the other hand, I wanted to be loved and accepted...But I cannot be what I am not."

He was ostracized, "Because of my attitude, all the other boys' parents, including Paul (McCartney's) father, would say, 'Keep away from him.' The parents instinctively recognized what I was, which was a troublemaker, meaning I did not conform and I would influence their kids, which I did. I did my best to disrupt every friend's home I had. Partly, maybe, it was out of envy that I didn't have this so-called home. But I really did. I had an auntie and an uncle and a nice suburban home, thank you very much."

He would, however, stress that his not having parents had good effect on him. "I was free from the parents' stranglehold. That was the gift I got for not having parents. I cried a lot about not having them and it was torture, but it also gave me an awareness early," he confided.

Lennon's hipness manifested early in his life and greatly sprang from his desperate search and deepest need for role models to replace his parents, who abandoned him as a child. His unfulfilled need for love resulted in emotional instability. Old enough for independent action, he expressed his anger at having been deprived of a family by attacking the families in his neighborhood with truancy and vandalism. At the age of eight, he formed and headed a gang that engaged in shoplifting and hooliganism. Breaking rules expressed his distrust of authority and rejection of convention -- both of which were hallmarks of being hip. To escape the unverbalized pain of a dysfunctional childhood, he organized the Quarry Men at the age of 17 from among gangmates and played skiffle, the musical craze in England popularized by Lonnie Donnegan in the '50s with the self-composed song, "Rock Island Line."

Quarry Men was named after Quarry Bank High School where the members were enrolled but it had an unintended meaning. With the Latin motto "From this rock, you will find truth," Lennon must have thought it cool as it suggests their type of music and in an unconscious way as expressed later on in their songs, a search for truth.

The jug-band method of skiffle, an offshoot of traditional jazz and country music, is a do-it-yourself beat music based on a three-chord style. The band kept Lennon and his friends off Liverpool streets and the delinquency those streets bred.

Then, too, and soon enough, skiffle brought Lennon and McCartney together. At a garden party, McCartney turned up and saw Lennon's Quarry Men playing. After the show, he amazed the drunken Lennon with his guitar wizardry by playing "Twenty Flight Rock." McCartney resembled Presley and could, in fact, imitate his singing voice perfectly. Quietly considering the benefits of having

McCartney in his band, Lennon eventually took him in as a member -- for his own benefit, not for McCartney's.

In one live performance of the Quarry Men, George Harrison tagged along with friend McCartney to see the group play. Harrison met Lennon, befriended him and girlfriend Cynthia Powell. One time they went to the house of Lennon's Aunt Mimi, a sister of Lennon's mother (Julia) to whom her mother had entrusted him when she left Liverpool. Harrison's pink shirt and winkle picker shoes appalled Lennon's aunt. For this, Lennon decided to recruit Harrison as a member of Quarry Men as the latter proved hip enough -- a White Negro in-the-making -- to repel older people.

One day, Lennon went to the Liverpool cinema to watch the movie *Blackboard Jungle*, a scene of which features juvenile delinquents smashing their professor's vinyl records as Bill Haley and The Comets' "Rock Around the Clock" played to the end credits. Lennon expected spontaneous dancing and vandalism to break out, similar to American reaction during the screening of the same film. To his dismay, no mayhem materialized.

A budding White Negro, Lennon threw the question he lifted from *Blackboard Jungle*: "Where are we going, fellows?" at disgruntled members when their singing career was leading nowhere. In false American twang, a manifestation of their developing ambition to be Afro-Americans, they would answer back, "To the top, Johnny." And he would retort, "Where is that, fellows?" They would chime back, "To the toppermost of the poppermost!"

First father figure

Hearing Presley's "Heartbreak Hotel" for the first time, however, helped Lennon set his mind on becoming a rock 'n' roll singer. Lennon admitted, "It was Elvis who really got me buying records. I thought that early stuff by him was great. The Bill Haley era passed me by, in a way. When his records came on the wireless, my mother used to hear this, but they didn't do anything for me. It was Elvis who got me hooked on beat music. When I heard 'Heartbreak Hotel,' I thought 'this is it.' And I started to grow sideboards and all that gear..."

This was the single decisive moment in his artistic development: consciously wanting to be a White Negro.

At that very moment, too, Lennon found his first father figure: Elvis Presley.

Lennon and his guitar; McCartney's musicality

Lennon's truancy decreased when he began to believe that his guitar could express his individuality and attract the attention he needed. With the death of their respective mothers, Lennon and McCartney gravitated towards rock 'n' roll as a more sophisticated form of beat music. Lennon's idolization -- and adulation -- of Presley was a cultural encounter that etched itself in Lennon's psyche as he unconsciously sought to express his individuality in small-town Liverpool. The urge to express himself soon led to his forming a rock 'n' roll group with McCartney.

In reality, however, Lennon could not really do without McCartney. Being the better musician between the two of them at the time, McCartney taught Lennon real guitar chords in place of the banjo chords the latter learned from his mother. Together, they learned chord formations and vocal deliveries, grappling with their abilities to play the guitar and sing. They tuned in to Radio Luxembourg to hear the latest Afro-American rock 'n' roll songs. American beat songs provided adequate materials to practice, eventually giving them self-assurance as singers and guitarists.

As a primary tool of hipness, Lennon and the boys adopted the Teddy Boy look, displaying their non-conformist nature. The Teddy Boy was a juvenile dressing code that adopted drainpipes, black leather jacket draped over T-shirt, slicked back hair with "DA" ("Duck's Arse") and crepe-soled shoes made conspicuousby bright socks. From such outlandish outfits, they learned that non-conformity attracted peers and repelled adults.

The Teddy Boy look, however, served Lennon in a different way. Underneath his Teddy Boy exterior, he hid the vulnerable person, the real Lennon: emotionally scarred, lonely, and confused. With that put-on look, he called attention even as the look was calculated to give a brave impression that was different from the person underneath.

In need of a name to propel them to popularity and to assume a brand name in the record market, Stuart Sutcliffe suggested calling the band the "Beetles," a conversion of the name of Buddy Holly's back-up group, the Crickets. It immediately appealed to Lennon. In a streak of wordplay, he blurted "Beatless" as a joke. He changed the double "e" to "ea" to connote beat music. It was fast becoming the "in" music in Liverpool at the time, drawing droves of overeager followers. In doing so, he unwittingly aligned his band with the Beatniks, as adherents of the Beat movement were called, forging the band's artistic and psychological ties with the White Negroes of America.

Since Holly wore black-framed spectacles, he made it okay for Lennon to wear glasses to correct his poor eyesight at the same time. Lennon's conversion into a White Negro was completed. He even shamelessly boasted, "I'm Buddy Holly!"

As Victor Hugo put it, it was an idea whose time had come. Thus, the name "Beatles" was born, prefiguring the essence of their being White Negroes, an imaginative visualization of novelty and dissension.

Turning into White Negroes

With their three-guitar format -- Harrison, 17, on lead; Lennon, 19, on rhythm; and Sutcliffe, 20, on bass, plus McCartney, 18, on piano, and Pete Best, 19, on drums -- the pre-fame Beatles adopted ensemble-playing and recreated standard and newly released rock 'n' roll songs. Sutcliffe was Lennon's close friend at the Liverpool College of Art. Though Best had a defective drumming technique, he got into the group because his mother, Mona Best, owned the Casbah, the club in Liverpool where the boys played regularly. During their regular gigs there, they fleshed out traditional materials with their deft interpretations of modern techniques. Soon enough they started playing in more venues and the rounds of Liverpool music halls.

Their hipness intensified in Hamburg, which lived up to its dubious distinction of being the Liverpool of Germany when they went there in August 1960. But Hamburg was tougher. At the Indra club, they had to relate to the rough-and-tumble environment with their songs expected to pull in customers. To do so, they resorted to "mak show," the German pronunciation of "to make a show," which means performing while singing, to sustain audience attention. They did this by staging madcap performances, mainly improvised, with loud music and gimmickry. They made no distinction between the stage and the audience area, and even between the performers and the audience. The Beatles sometimes attended to their extreme personal necessities in full view of their audience, even while talking to them.

In the process, they developed a tight sound with a hard-driving edge to survive the arduously long sets of eight straight hours. To sustain their high level of energy for the grueling performances, they learned to ingest slimming pills, known as Predulin, to prop up their adrenaline -- the second important step in their developing hipness. They met Astrid Kirchherr, a member of the Hamburg-based group of black-clad intellectuals known as the Exis, a contraction for the noun "existentialist."

The Exis subscribed to the humanistic philosophy of Existentialism as propagated by Pierre Teilhard de Chardin. They fostered the belief that man is responsible for himself and has free will, enabling him to oppose the hostility of the environment. Kirchherr noted that when the usually uptight Lennon was under the influence of Predulin, he loosened up and opened up to others.

The group was eventually booted out of Hamburg. Harrison, McCartney, and Best were deported: Harrison for being underage and working without a permit, McCartney and Best for accidentally setting the quarters they were holed in on fire. Lennon and Sutcliffe's work permits were also revoked. They returned to Liverpool as dejected and battered rockers, but they left with a distinction: they had an urban cowboy look and a hard-driving style their Hamburg audience adored.

A month passed without any contact among the members. When they did meet, they celebrated it by executing elaborate handshakes and by breaking into joyful dancing that ended in hugs. It was a behavior that signaled early on their forthcoming dependence on each other, drawing individual identities from one another, thus losing their own identities when they lost touch for a period of time. That's why when they finally reappeared at the Casbah in a show billed as "Direct from Hamburg," the Beatles played in their wild Hamburg-style, occasionally causing riots among the audience.

In other occasions, they played as Little Richard's front act when the gaudy Afro-American artist, one of their icons, appeared in the Cavern. Although their performances were mostly uneventful, their stint at the Cavern with Little Richard gave them their first real encounter with White Negro culture. Lennon worshipped Little Richard like a hero, and as the American idol who willingly taught McCartney his holler, "*Ooooh! Ooooh!*"

They returned to Hamburg with Little Richard in March 1961, this time legally. Being cooped up with him increased their hipness via cultural osmosis. To them, he was the epitome of rock 'n' roll success.

Capitalizing on his androgynous personality, Little Richard gained popularity utilizing the three rules for achieving rock 'n' roll fame: a different kind of record, an unusual singing style, and gimmickry.

Beatles and the moptop

Kirchherr, who had gotten romantically involved with Sutcliffe, cut his hair in the style common among Hamburg youth. She brushed his long hair down into a fringe and snipped bits off above the eyes before tidying it up. When Lennon, McCartney, Harrison, and Best saw Sutcliffe's new hairstyle for the first time, they ridiculed him. But when they recognized its novelty, long hair being an oddity in the '60s, they adopted the one-of-a-kind, but quirky, 'do. Best opted out.

The trip to Hamburg in 1962 also resulted in a long-playing album (colloquially called as LP) with the Beatles providing back up to London vocalist and guitarist Tony Sheridan. Sheridan met the Beatles during their first Hamburg trip in 1960. He helped Harrison master the guitar so that during the Beatles' second trip to Hamburg, Harrison had become accustomed to playing with them. They recorded "My Bonnie," a version of the traditional song "My Bonnie Lies Over the Ocean," as the Tony Sheridan and the Beat Brothers flipsided by "The Saints," a version of "When the Saints Go Marching In" and released as a single in August 1961 in Germany under the German Polydor. They had to change their name, at least temporarily, as Beatles sounded like "peedles" when pronounced by the Germans. And "peedles" is the German street word for penis. "My Bonnie" is the first recorded vocals by the Beatles, which the group sung as a march rather than the original soft version by Gene Vincent.

The album entitled *Ain't She Sweet* from which they were culled included the songs "Why," "Cry For a Shadow," "Take Out Some Insurance On Me Baby," "Nobody's Child," "Sweet Georgia Brown," and, of course, "Ain't She Sweet."

Wearing what had become known as the Beatle moptop (everything they had done thus far were being copied), they returned to Liverpool for their eventful recording test with Parlophone on June 6, 1962. As a symbol of juvenile rebellion, the Beatle moptop became a sensation that completed the uniqueness of the group.

Before this could be fully realized, however, there was a turnover of members. Sutcliffe decided to stay in Hamburg so he could be with Kirchherr, paving the way for McCartney to shift from guitar to bass.

Substantially hip, the Beatles did not follow individualism as required by the Beatnik code: they pursued, instead, a "collective independence" from what sociologist Dr. A.D. Buckmeller termed "the strictness of adult society." While the Beatles deviated from the mores of their elders, they expressed this in collective difference and indifference -- in effect, by being White Negroes.

Collective identity, communal ownership

In the ritual passage to adulthood, a teenager usually rejects the trappings of childhood and turns his attention toward adult role models. The Beatles expressed this rejection in a collective manner that was classless within their group. Adopting a peer group mentality, they manifested the rejection of adult society through loyalty to the group -- as opposed to loyalty to individual members -- and communal ownership's predilection for their own kind of uniformity.

With their improved hip quotient, the Beatles further closed ranks with the concept of the art of derivation. The term is applicable to the Beatles in its two meanings: first, as a group, the Beatles operated as a self-sufficient artistic entity; and second, as an artistic entity, they were not constrained in the pursuit of individual artistic expression. This allowed them to shake off the shackles of status quo, thinking and becoming what they wanted to be within the concept of the Beatles. For better or worse, derivation would truly become their art form.

The Beatles would eventually become the entity that would transfer its hipness to the youth of the '60s, and, perhaps, beyond. The four boys, of course, were also young men themselves at the time. The Beatles was a costume that four individuals wore to prevent detection of their real selves. They strove to be different as a way of ensuring their viability, their unique propositions on which they banked their products: the Beatles songs.

Possessing inadequate individual talents, they instead collectively fashioned themselves as the best musicians of their generation by believing that talent in its real sense was not necessary for success. Talent, especially for Lennon, was subscribing to the belief that one can do something. Despite the many defeats and misfortunes they individually and collectively experienced, they pursued their ambition with a momentum that bred action. They did not follow the mainstream trends of their time, but instead went to the extent of debunking them.

Their hipness assured them of a means to progress with their brand of music with such an ease that surprisingly overcame lack of self-confidence. With their continuous reinvention of themselves, they became a formidable force that was visually and aurally exciting -- hip and mod to the '60s *lingua franca*. This increased the quartet's strength more than fourfold.

Art of derivation

Derivation starts with the collection of information and sensory impressions known as input. This input can be mentally and mechanically stored. The creative act is the formation of ideas, the selection of input, and their adaptation in an orderly, sometimes disorderly, manner to produce the output.

Adaptation is the creation of an output -- with minimal or without variation -- that closely resembles the input from existing source/s. The simplest adaptation is copying the input and integrating it with other similarly copied input or with original ideas, while a complex adaptation is an attempt at imaginative association that results in variance and distinction from the model/s. In adaptation, there is an attempt to alter the input to make it suitable for the desired output. This connotes a semi-determined attempt to present the input in an altered form or in a new combination that makes the output deviant from the input. Adaptation is actually the art of derivation.

Artists, even practitioners of other fields, use these basic processes in the art of derivation. Derivation can take place outside the creative act. The conscious or unconscious recognition of artistic input, natural, artificially induced, or a combination of both, is the beginning of the process of derivation. In the case of the Beatles, the art of derivation employed any or a combination of the following techniques, which are classified into the following:

Conversion is the process of making input appear different or take a distinct form by adding and combining existing ones. The varying inputs are changed to a suitable form, transformed to a different output that assumes a new meaning, sense, or application.

Inversion is the opposite of conversion, reversing the input.

Modification is taking something away from the input by reduction or by elimination. The rule of opposites applies here. Modification involves the process of applying the input to its opposite contrary meaning, sense, or application.

Exaggeration is the process of combining inputs, whether by conversion, modification, or the combination of both, to give the outputs a greater magnitude or appear in an unusual way. It transforms the inputs into an unrecognizable output, but still maintains the characteristics of the inputs.

Distillation is originality, the real creation, and the refinement of all input into an original output. It involves the breakdown of the inputs to one or more elements and their subsequent reformation into a new form.

By shamelessly appropriating their musical style from all sources through cultural osmosis and adapting them to the Beatles, Lennon and McCartney installed the concept of communal ownership by deciding to write songs collaboratively. They used the art of derivation when it was time to write songs. They patterned the form and content of their earliest songs from Berry -- down to the key of A, which they mistook to be his key signature. When they discovered he wrote in diversified keys, they corrected themselves by doing the same. Since Berry rehashed songs, Lennon and McCartney took that Berry habit as a patent liberty to do the same. The Beatles' imitation of Berry was so base that the question of originality was academic, since there was none.

Lennon and McCartney crafted the greater part of their early songs in a crude way. They skipped classes and hid at a relative's house to take those initial steps that would take them to the popularity that they had begun to seek more consciously: they wrote songs by whistling to one another. During the press interview for the first American tour in 1964, the Beatles was asked, "Is it true none of you can read or write music?" McCartney replied, "None of us can read or write music. The way we work is like, we just whistle. John will whistle at me and I'll whistle back at him."

Neither had formal musical education. Thus they could be considered "primitive" musicians. This so-called "primitiveness" defined their style and fixated them to that style. Likewise, this lack of formal knowledge on the fundamentals of music and composition caused them undue losses as they failed to note the songs they wrote, forgetting them in the process.

The Beatles' creative process followed a loose, free-wheeling procedure. Either Lennon or McCartney would craft the main structure while the other would contribute in terms of additional lyrics. They would pluck individual lines or phrases from songs by other singers or groups that intrigued them. Then they would pick out the most memorable riff, usually an interesting beat or captivating words and phrases.

McCartney recalls: "I'm always taking a little of this and a little of that. It's called being influenced. It's either called that or stealing. And what do they say? A good artist borrows; a great artist steals -- or something like that. That makes us great artists then, because we stole a lot of stuff. If anyone ever said to us, 'Wow! Where's that from?'...We took a lot of stuff, but in blues, anyway, you do: People lift licks. It's part of the fun of being alive, too. You hear somebody's incredible riff and you go 'Oooh.' You hear a new chord somewhere and you go, 'Oh, my God, that's it!'"

At that phase in their creative cycle, they were driven to learn and to excel. McCartney reveals: "We used to travel miles for a new chord -- literally -- in Liverpool. We used to take bus rides for hours to go visit the guy who reputedly knew B7. None of us knew how to finger it. He was like the guru. We went to his house, and we sat there, and he played it a few times. Then we all said, 'Brilliant, thanks!' and we went home and practiced it. Yeah, we lifted a lot of stuff from Motown, but quite unashamedly. I'm happy to have done it."

Lennon and McCartney identified this as a most effective technique: combining song elements and expanding them with their own input. Giving prominence to the beat by repetition, they magnified the tune with more instruments and more voices, exposing the idiosyncrasies of their style.

A union of strengths...and weaknesses

Co-writing Beatles songs was a necessary decision since both Lennon and McCartney had miniscule talents and minimal musical training. But their gargantuan aspiration belied what they really were as individuals before they consented to forge a partnership: deficient and lacking in direction. Thus, they agreed to credit their songs as "Lennon-McCartney" compositions.

The agreement was a wedding of strengths, a melting of two talents compensating for each other's weaknesses. They wanted to be like Gerry Goffin and Carole King, who masterminded a string of smash rock 'n' roll and rhythm and blues songs, such as their first hit, "Will You Still Love Me Tomorrow" performed by the all-girl group The Shirelles, whom both Lennon and McCartney idolized. Sealed with a gentleman's agreement, any song composed by Lennon and McCartney, either separately or in collaboration with one another, automatically became a "Lennon-McCartney" composition by credit. They, of course, decided on this at a time when their vision far exceeded their talents.

Lennon and McCartney further explored the concept of communal ownership by turning their backs on the idea of having the Beatles conform to the lead singer- backing group format, the trend during the period. This made the roles within the group interchangeable. The members became composers, singers and instrument players. The Beatles became a self-sufficient creative entity with overlapping artistic functions.

Although Lennon was regarded as the group's leader, this was somewhat in a loose sense because he shared leadership equally with the others in making decisions pertaining to Beatles issues. As country boys in urban London and foreigners in their overseas destinations, they created a tight bond as a deterrent for the frequently hostile environments that personal appearances brought. They developed their own system of communication and relied on one another for emotional support. A common observation about the group was that they took a distinct personality that excluded everybody around them except for some favorite people.

The concept of communal ownership became the strength of the Beatles while they believed in it. Its combined effect gave greater result than the totality of its individual parts. Established by a system of congruent relationships with the element of correct timing, the Beatles were on their way to success. This concept was a self-made one, a solution for the weaknesses that existed within the group and posed as a hindrance to their objective of superlative renown.

They retained their individuality, but only in a collective sense. They did this by subordinating differences for the collective benefit. They became one entity; their tightly sealed bonding made their music appear always evolving as an expression of their hipness. Their songs were not the product of inspired creativity as they were the end result of their ability to adapt at their convenience. This explains the prolificness, the wide diversity, and the fast evolution of Beatles songs.

At the turn of the '60s, the field of popular music in the US was thrown wide open for conquest as a result of the sidetracking of rock 'n' roll. It proved to be the perfect time for the Beatles to lay their claim on popularity with their loud-stomping music and hybrid songs: an amalgam of styles, borrowed bits, and reprocessed collection of American R&B styles thrown together. The Beatles absorbed and synthesized their influences, thus lending to their music a compositional newness and a sophistication all their own.

But the communal was not enough to be magical; it needed the chemistry of relationships to make it work. When Brian Epstein, George Martin, and Richard Starkey entered the communal relationship, their admission completed the formula that would eventually lead to Beatlemania.

Two great backroom Beatles

Jewish merchant Brian Epstein, who operated the successful record store called NEMS, got wind of the Beatles supposedly when a young customer named Raymond Jones was looking for the Beatles' single "My Bonnie" in his store. This turned out to be the "My Bonnie" recorded in Germany in 1961 when the Beatles played backup singers to Tony Sheridan. This prompted Epstein to look for the group until he found them singing in the dingy club Cavern. Recognizing their economic potential, and the fact that homosexual Epstein got sexually attracted to Lennon, he offered them a business management agreement. The Beatles gladly accepted, realizing that a respectable businessman had finally taken an interest in them.

Epstein recounts this incident in his ghostwritten autobiography *A Cellarful of Noise* about the early years of the Beatles. But *Mersey Beat* publisher Bill Harry contends that it is an Epstein fabrication. He reasons out that his record store was about 100 meters away from the Cavern and it was impossible for him not to be aware of the emerging makers of what would eventually be called as "noise music." He even reveals that the boys were his regular customers. He also distributed *Mersey Beat*, which was nothing more than a Beatles fanzine.

But this kind of myth-making would be an important tool for Epstein to make the Beatles appear larger than life, a key element in the early success of the White Negroes. By presenting them for what they were not, he started to compensate for the group's deficiencies that contributed immensely in starting them off as a commercially viable entity. In an economic sense, however, this would have a greater effect on the psychological make-up of the group as artists. This caused Lennon and McCartney to strongly form their belief that image could be enhanced, magnified, or altogether changed. This further amplified their shameless notion that things could be improved or invented, perking up their mindset that they could do anything as White Negroes.

Having a flair for showmanship, Epstein eventually sanitized the rough-and-raw projection of the Beatles image by cleaning up their White Negro character. He made them shed their hip get-ups for the collarless suits that Pierre Cardin designed for them. He stopped them from smoking on stage and also toned down the cuss words that littered their language -- all for monetary gain. The Beatles were aware that dance hall promoters rejected them for their thug image. Epstein, in an unspoken collusion with McCartney, wrestled the free-spirited Lennon into observing the cleaned-up image. Successful to a certain extent, he made them take a synchronized bow after each show, endearing them to the public.

Epstein did his best to peddle his boys to record companies. There were no takers. Rejected by Decca Records, the group had a similar fate at Pye,

Columbia and HMV. Polydor had also rejected them because, according to Artist & Repertoire man Bert Kaemfert, "They had talent but did not know how to use it." These rejections stuck to Epstein's and their minds as torment.

With the persistence that became their most potent tool, Epstein approached his Electric and Musical Industries (EMI) connections and pulled George Martin, incharge of artists and recording of EMI's Parlophone label, to agree to hear them play.

As EMI's Artist and Repertoire head, Martin oversaw artist selection, development, and management since 1955. At the time the Beatles applied with Parlophone, he was scouting for a rock 'n' roll group to establish a pop category at EMI. Martin became the Beatles' most important musical resource, next to their dependence on Lennon and McCartney for song materials. Trained as a classical pianist at the Guildhall School of Music, he played the oboe. His taste in music was a study in contrasts. While he was steeped in light orchestral music, his penchant for comedy revealed his taste for what was popular. At EMI, he produced comedy records, achieving success with Charlie Drake and Peter Sellers, Flanders and Swann, and scoring a top hit with "You're Driving Me Crazy" by the Temperance Seven. Lennon relished the idea of making records with the man responsible for his favorite, *The Goon Show.*

The rightful "fifth" Beatle

Martin can very well be regarded as one of the unseen forces behind the success of the Beatles. As producer of majority of Beatles' songs, he captured the raw market for raw talents like the Beatles and propelled them to prominence. Martin told the *Irish Times* about the producer's role: "The producer is the person who shapes the sound. If you have a talent to work with -- a singer together with a song -- the producer's job is to say, right, you need to put a frame around this, it needs a rhythm section to do this or that, and so on. He actually decides what the thing should sound like, and then shapes it in the studio. He may also be an arranger, in which case he may write the necessary parts. He shapes the whole lot. It's like being the director of a film." As such, Martin crafted the song structures, organized beginnings and endings, harmonies and solos for the Beatles.

But Martin's role turned out to be more than that of a record producer. He became an artistic collaborator, rightfully the fifth Beatle, the invisible and invincible person responsible for shaping Beatles music as we came to know it. His educated ears compensated for the musical deficiencies of the group members. If the Lennon-McCartney songwriting union was born out of expediency, Martin was the nursemaid who brought the union to an auspicious start, and nurtured it -- for as long as the White Negroes allowed it.

Although he rarely contributed to the lyrics of Beatles songs, Martin heavily influenced and shaped their aural aspects. He concretized the concept of the early Beatles sound. By his act of selection, determining the best manner to record songs, he organized and refined the disparate elements of Lennon-McCartney compositions into a song concept that enhanced its qualities.

Initially, Martin required the Beatles to submit songs for recording. The initiation of Lennon and McCartney to the creative field of songmaking served both as an opportunity and a burden. While it gave them chance to grab the long-awaited opportunity to break into the field of popular music, recording posed the burden of risk and hazard as their abilities failed to match the required output. Lennon and McCartney recognized its make-or-break nature, so they tried to compensate through musical intensity predicated mainly on bravado.

In 1962, Lennon and McCartney presented a batch of self-penned songs like "Love Me Do," "Please Please Me," and "Ask Me Why," including a reworking of "Besame Mucho." The test records disappointed Martin, who was unimpressed with their sluggish tempo and manifest derivation. But then his recognition of a vital energy distinct and manifested during the Beatles' live singing made him subordinate his poor critical evaluation of the group to their market potential and proceed to sign them up as Parlophone recording artists in January, 1962.

Chapter 2
The birth phase

Reinventing rock 'n' roll

"A work of art is always a forgery."

- Paul Valery

The creative act is a process, undergoing the stages of preparation, execution, and finalization. Derivation takes place in varying degrees in any stage of the creative cycle. It begins with the birth phase, progressing to a growth period, achieving maturity during which the best output are realized, and undergoing a stage of decline before the terminal phase, the death cycle.

Certain works are keys to the art of the artist during a phase of the creative cycle. These key art works establish the dominant style of the artist for a given and more or less identifiable period. It is usually the finest output that best exemplifies an artist's style. In turn, an artist's key output in a given period determines this viability. The best output does not just materialize in the birth to maturity periods, but also comes out during the decline period as an exception.

In relation to the Beatles, the creative cycle recognizes that the art of the artist evolves in inverse relationship with derivation. Change is a means of existence which an artist has to learn to live with. An artist's body of work undergoes ways to interpret reality, the artist tends to produce outputs of varying degrees of derivation.

State of the art

From 1958 to 1962, rock 'n' roll stars kept the greater part of the globe shaking and rolling with their raucous songs which seemed to emanate from harmless dingy garages or out of tin cans. Their freewheeling attitude got them involved in various incidents, however, invariably booting them out of the music scene and opening it wide to sweeping changes.

Jerry Lee Lewis' song "Whole Lotta Shakin'" reverberated in the music market with record-breaking sales. Yet when he committed bigamy by marrying his 14-year-old second cousin that shocked the prevailing sensitivities of the establishment, the US Church condemned his gross violation of its tenets. Thus, when his minor wife accompanied him to Britain for singing engagements, the reaction of the press bordered on outrage, the bad publicity forcing the cancellation of 34 concerts.

In a terrible twist of fate, Buddy Holly, Ritchie Valens and The Big Bopper were all killed when the Beechcraft Bonanza plane rented to transport them to their next singing engagement crashed in a corn field minutes after take-off. Holly's guitarist Tommy Allsup surrendered his plane seat to Valens while bassist Waylon Jennings gave his to The Big Bopper for them to take a much-needed rest. As it turned out, such rest was to be eternal.

Little Richard succumbed to the "evil" label of his music. He turned a gospel singer in 1960 after surviving an airplane's engine fire, considering the accident as an act of condemnation from God.

Berry started to serve a three-year conviction when he transported a 14-year-old female Apache Indian from Texas to Louisiana to work in his club. Unknown to Berry, the minor worked as a waiter-prostitute when hired, thus violating the Mann Act.

Tin Pan Alley vested interests and politicians charged Freed for accepting illegal payments to play records known as payola. His persecution left him off the airlane.

The US Army drafted Presley, removing him from the rock 'n' roll mainstream for two years. He was assigned in a base facility in Bremerhaven, Germany as a driver of the platoon sergeant. When released from duty in March, 1960, he abandoned rock 'n' roll to wallow in the sentimentality of the ballads.

As a popular sign that rock 'n' roll had been subverted, teen fluff singer Frankie Avalon pinch hit for Holly in the aborted singing engagement with Valens and The Big Bopper. Paul Anka, late '50s teen idol and songwriter, began to dominate the musical charts with such maudlin ballads as "Put Your Head on My Shoulder," "Puppy Love," and "Hello Young Lovers." Pop/country singer Connie Francis released the patriotic song "God Bless America" in the year rock 'n' roll suffered its worst turnmoil. She also recorded materials culled from traditional sources. Mitch Miller, producer of Easy-Listening artists like Ray Coniff, became rock 'n' roll's avowed enemy. Sentimentality ruled the American airwaves, leading to the conclusion that decency and order had returned among the youth.

It became apparent that the conspiracy to kill rock 'n' roll had succeeded.

But not for long.

Rise of the masters of derivation

Their conscious use of the derivation technique was the single, most decisive aspect in Lennon and McCartney's artistic development.

Based on the principle of being "hip," the art of derivation gives a semblance of innovation, or even originality, when applied by the non-conformist and received by the greater population, particularly in different environmental application.

The art of derivation is actually a hoax, as these non-conformists did not conceptualize it. As such, credit for the innovation could not be granted. Any claim of innovation for adapted practices is definitely a deception. In this context, Lennon and McCartney were rehashers -- like many great artists before them.

During the birth period, the Beatles were merely song providers and musicians particularly in the *Please Please Me* album. Martin produced all aspects of that album with strict supervision, from material selection to mixing. He used the songs presented by Lennon and McCartney and recorded them with an ear for quality and saleability. He was aware that the initial Beatles songs that would reach the market would make or break them, and that recovering lost ground from an initial failure would be difficult. The Beatles was dependent on his artistic judgment and technical competence.

Martin polished the raw Lennon-McCartney songs and introduced the duo to the technology of record making. As Lennon himself once admitted, "George (Martin) was in there quite heavily from the beginning." This dependency, however, did not translate to an absolute relationship. In the question of artistic direction, Lennon maintained a firm grasp of musical issues.

"Love Me Do," tradition-breaker

"Pretty poor" was George Martin's unflinching verdict of Lennon and McCartney's self-penned songs when he required them to submit materials for their recording test. "Love Me Do" is "the best stuff they had," opined Martin. It was one of the 100 songs McCartney claimed they wrote and the only one that got published. But then "Love Me Do" somehow gave the Beatles a breakthrough. Martin just had to admit: "Those songs weren't very good because we were reading the music papers and trying to find the next new sound. The *New Musical Express* (now called *NME*) was talking about calypso, and how Latin rock was going to be the new thing. The minute we stopped trying to find the next new beat, and went back to our own things like 'Love Me Do,' the newspapers said...we were the 'next big sound.'"

Martin's low regard for the duo's songwriting ability did not deflate their egos into submission to his complete artistic judgment. Actually, before the song finally got recorded, Martin offered instead that they do Mitch Murray's "How Do You Do It" as a replacement.

Before the Beatles changed the practice, British musical acts were asked by their recording companies to shop for song materials at the innumerable music publishers on Denmark Street, London's Tin Pan Alley, after inking a recording contract. In the US, a handful of performers did self-pen their materials in a particular style that kept them fixed to such style, while others relied on external creative sources.

The use of off-the-cabinet materials was an industry practice, and any deviation was sneered at for its non-conformist ambition. So when Lennon and McCartney handed their banal songs to Martin, it was a courageous step at challenging the status quo. They recorded "How Do You Do It" so lamely that they ensured it would be rejected. The offer was retrieved.

The duo's outright refusal of Martin's well-meaning substitution spoke of their unflagging determination that would prevent the Beatles from sharing the fate of popular groups during their time: they remained only as viable as their last hit song. These popular groups' dependence on external songwriters more or less assured limited creativity and viability.

"How Do You Do It" eventually became a top hit for Gerry and The Pacemakers, giving credence to the validity of Martin's judgment. The duo's flat refusal, however, wrestled control for the group's materials. In the process, it established Lennon and McCartney as songwriters and gave momentum to the important rethinking of industry practices. As the duo showed in this initiative, they unwittingly started the trend for rock 'n' roll groups to sustain their viability by producing their own materials.

Doing so, in effect, successfully installed them as songwriters. It started the important redirection of industry practices, igniting the revival for British beat groups to produce their materials, assuring their perpetuity as a self-contained artistic entity. (Note: In the case of the Lennon-McCartney composing tandem, capital letters indicate the name of the partner more or less responsible for composing the song. Also, the listing of singles and albums here is based on their U.K. release dates, though the U.S. release is used where necessary.)

Best out, Starr in

The Beatles recorded "Love Me Do" as an incohesive band. Lennon fired Best just before recording the song. Realizing his personal attachment to the longtime buddy, Lennon had to ask Epstein to serve the firing notice. Martin served as scapegoat. The Beatles were afraid an inevitable ramble would ensue if they confronted Best themselves. Best's inadequate drumming technique, characterized by defective timing, besides being perennially unavailable, posed as a development hindrance for the Beatles as a tight band.

On Harrison's suggestion, Lennon recruited Richard Starkey, who used to fill in whenever Best was sick, to take over Best's slot. Starkey was the formidable drummer of Rory Storm and the Hurricanes and was nicknamed "Ringo" because of his predilection for finger bands. When he joined the Beatles, he was renamed Ringo Starr.

Martin, however, harbored reservations about Starkey's drumming technique, preferring the show-drumming style. This led him to recruit another drummer, Andy White, for the recording session of "Love Me Do." White took over the drum set; Starr was relegated to the less complex task of jangling the maracas. Though humiliated, the latter's charming disposition made him take it in stride. As a compromise, Martin recorded another version, with Starr and White exchanging instruments. But there was no marked difference between them.

Starr did become the Beatles' regular drummer, and he solidified the group's sound and provided additional charm that softened the members' rough edges. By this time, Epstein had repackaged the group's offending crudity to delightful roughness. He also pursued a policy of creative isolation for his wards to devote their time to music-making with single-minded purpose. Starr, on the other hand, took on the role of collaborator, which compensated for their musical inadequacy. He was taken in to complete the communal ownership, but not without undergoing baptism: They clipped his surname to "Starr" so that when he did a drum exhibition with the group, it could be introduced as "Starr Time."

"Love Me Do" / "P.S. I Love You" single

The quartet issued the love songs "Love Me Do" and "P.S. I Love You" as their first single on October 5, 1962.

"Love Me Do" (Lennon-MCCARTNEY) is the product of a fledgling 16-year old aspiring to be a songwriter. McCartney labored on the verse while Lennon took care of the middle eight. Lennon was supposed to sing it during recording,but the lead vocal was given to McCartney because Lennon was assigned to play the harmonica. The inclusion of the harmonica in their recording was copied from American singer Bruce Channel's "Hey Baby," which was a big hit when McCartney converted it into "Love Me Do."

Delbert McClinton plays harmonica in "Hey Baby." As he was touring England with Channel when the Beatles were to record "Love Me Do," the task of instructing Lennon how to play the harmonica cross-harp style fell on McClinton. As the harmonica blast is the first thing you hear in the song, filling in with the words during the break and taking the instrumental solo in the middle, harmonica playing would become a major factor in the early Beatles' success on record.

On the other hand, the melody of "Love Me Do" closely resembles Presley's "Wooden Heart," a popular hit included in their repertoire during their Hamburg stint, a song they performed partly in German. By abbreviating the stanza's first two lines of "Wooden Heart" (*'Can't you see I love you*") to "Love Me Do's" "Love, love me do," rehashing the second line (*"Please don't break my heart into two"*) to "*You know I love you,*" and approximating the syllable counts of the third and fourth lines (*"That's not hard to do / 'Cause I don't have a wooden heart"*) to "I'll always be true / So please love me do," the duo diffused their model's essence.

To approximate the eight syllables of "Wooden Heart's" last line, melisma is used in "*please*" by assigning three-syllable counts ("*plea-ea-ea-ease*"). The accordion accompaniment of Presley's song gives way to the harmonica in some passages.

Music reviewer Henrik Doktorski noted that before "Love Me Do" became popular, "the accordion was the number one instrument taught at private music schools. But after the Beatles hit the scene, young people in droves abandoned the accordion for the electric guitar." Electric guitars were the primary instruments with which the Beatles achieved their impending global fame.

Lennon and McCartney, on the other hand, based the two-part harmonies from The Everly Brothers' first number one record, "Cathy's Clown."

In retrospect, McCartney rated it as the Beatles' "greatest philosophical song."

McCartney converted The Shirelles' 1962 surprise R&B hit, the cheerless "Soldier Boy" into the gloomy **"P.S. I Love You"** (Lennon-MCCARTNEY) as Lennon revealed, an answering song. During the period, it was common for another artist to reply to another artist's song. On the part of the Beatles, doing an answering song was an early sign of how they coped with their deficient creativity, for sure, a White Negro trick.

They removed the introduction and made the melody fluider through McCartney's smooth vocals, turning out an improved variation. The talent of the Beatles was "*take a sad song and make it better*" as McCartney would reveal in a later phase of their recording career. At this stage, it was often done by removing the original's "garage recording" quality, often with poor acoustics.

McCartney wrote it for girlfriend Dot Rhone, who visited him during their first Hamburg trip, along with Cynthia Powell, who was Lennon's girlfriend then. Hanging out in a houseboat, McCartney wrote the song to tell Rhone how much he loved her. But the relationship was not meant to last. As soon as they returned to Liverpool, McCartney broke up with her, claiming immaturity on his part to be in a serious relationship. The title came from the favorite postscript in love letters of the time.

This initial single established the theme of most songs of the Beatles: love. They sang about juvenile romantic relationships and aspirations. These are songs that used the first person to attest to their source-to-receiver nature, directly communicating ideas, instead of narrating stories, and dealing with only a singular subject: love.

A typical Beatles song made evident pronouncements of their need to reach out to their listeners, a translation of the group's personal appeal exuded in stage performances. This established performer-listener contact, the furtive factor for their improved appeal. More crucial than the artistic implication, the love-themed songs allowed the Beatles to cover a greater portion of the music market, unconstrained by geographical boundaries that live performances dictated, through record purchase, radio airplay, and the media hype that went with every record release. The record became the communication medium between the Beatles and the youth.

The Beatles' first single turned out to be a mild sensation in Liverpool, their home turf, which its cocky natives unabashedly claimed as the musical capital of North England. Epstein attempted to create a false demand by purchasing 10,000 units that pushed it up to a decent number one in the *NME* chart.

"Please Please Me" / "Ask Me Why" single

The Beatles issued "Please Please Me" and "Ask Me Why" as their second single on January 11, 1963.

An adaptation of American singer Roy Orbison's falsetto sound, Lennon wrote **"Please Please Me"** (LENNON-McCartney) when he heard Orbison's song "Only the Lonely" played on the radio as sang by Presley. As a child, Lennon's mother used to sing the Bing Crosby song *"Please"* to him, which has the lyrics *"Oh please / Lend your little ear to my pleas / Lend a ray of cheer to my pleas / Tell me that you love me too."* Intrigued by the alliteration of "please" and "pleas," he translated these words as the song's title and lyrics *"please please me."*

However, "Ain't Nothing Shakin'," part of their standard repertoire during the Cavern days, has the same phrase. As Lennon once put it, "Please Please Me" was "a combination of Bing Crosby and Roy Orbison." The use of *"ooooooooh"* and the quadruple *"come on"* was an imitation from The Isley Brothers' "Twist and Shout."

The duo presented the song to Martin with a strong Orbison flavor: slow tempo and bluesy vocals. He rejected it as a first-single material, but used it for the group's second single by removing these characteristics and speeding up the original tempo, thereby tremendously improving its quality. This single act by Martin earned him the Beatles' respect and confidence.

The *NME* bestowed "Please Please Me" the distinction of being "the single that created pop music as we know it today. Even now it charges like a bull elephant from the speakers, cocky and raw as hell."

Lennon nicked the guitar phrase of **"Ask Me Why"** (LENNON-McCartney) from Smokey Robinson and The Miracles' "What's So Good About Goodbye." But the authors wanted the Beatles to be the first band to adopt the emerging calypso beat trend. As rock 'n' roll fame was predicated on the Sun Records formula of new sound-new kind of singing gimmickry, the Beatles wanted to beat the rest in coming out with their interpretation of the new sound. This act by Lennon and McCartney was important because it confirmed their White Negro roots and it was an act which they would repeat in future songs.

This second single immediately jumped to the top of the charts, which burst Beatles' entry into the US national musical scene. Their progress was simply amazing. The Beatles achieved this feat through the art of derivation, nearing perfection when they recorded this single. As soon as they had established the personal and professional relationships that catalyzed their art, they became the most economically successful and globally recognized musical group after Presley, as earlier predicted by Epstein.

Please, Please Me album

As was to be expected, their songs were not original, but derivatives. For the *Please Please Me* album tracklist, Martin picked songs from the Beatles' first two singles ("Please Please Me", "Love Me Do," and "P.S. I Love You"), American rock' n' roll songs which were part of their repertoire ("Anna [Go To Him]," "Chains," "Boys," "A Taste of Honey" and "Twist and Shout"), and some new songs, the most impressive of which was "I Saw Her Standing There."

"I Saw Her Standing There" (Lennon-MCCARTNEY) is a conversion of the style of their pre-fame rock 'n' roll repertoire such as "September in the Rain," Berry's "Sweet Little Sixteen," and particularly Bill Haley's "The Saints (When the Saints Go Marching In)." It was McCartney's best copy of Little Richards' demented vocals. During their live set and as a back-up band on Tony Sheridan's recording of the song, the Beatles performed "The Saints (When the Saints Go Marching In)." As pointed out by Beatles song analyst Allan W. Pollack, the melody and chord of "I Saw Her Standing There" run largely parallel with "The Saints (When the Saints Go Marching In)." This is readily discernible in the first and second verses:

Lennon-McCartney rehashed the first two lines of "The Saints (When the Saints Go Marching In)" (*Oh when the saints when the saints / Go marching in, marching in*) to "I Saw Her Standing There's" *"Well she was just seventeen / And you know what I mean."*

The duo did the same for third verses of each song: *"And the way she looked was way beyond compare / So how could I dance with another oh / When I saw her standing there"* to *"When the saints go marching in/I want to be in that number When the saints go marching in."*

Lennon changed the first verse's sophomoric line as written by McCartney *"Never been a beauty queen"* to rhyme with *"seventeen"* into *"Do you know what I mean?"* giving it a colloquial and in-the-know attitude. What does it mean? According to McCartney, "Absolutely nothing!"

McCartney nicked the bass line from Berry's 1961 song, "I'm Talking About You." He admitted, "It's a great riff. And most of the people we played for didn't know the song, so we were pretty safe."

Martin dubbed the thriller intro, *"1, 2, 3, 4,"* from another take to give it a "live" appeal. Martin originally wanted to record the Beatles first album live at the Cavern where the group had created the reputation of being livewire performers, a local phenomenon. Time put a block so he recorded them at the Abbey Road studios. Epstein encouraged Lennon and McCartney to write songs not only for themselves, but also for other artists as a promotional gambit. They whipped up

Written for Helen Shapiro, **"Misery"** (Lennon-McCartney) was based on the Motown sound of various groups of the period. But her management rejected it, showing how other managers had substandard regard for the duo's compositions.

But Lennon and McCartney were learning songwriting fast. They changed the song's original introduction, *"You've been treating me bad, misery"* to *"The world is treating me bad misery"* to give it international appeal, a reason for the wide acceptability of Beatle songs.

"Misery" is the first Beatles song in which a basically sad song takes the opposite character of being "cheerful" (to use a description by critic William Mann). This was a result of Martin's practice of speeding up the tempo of Lennon-McCartney compositions, a practice which he started in "Love Me Do" to improve its appeal to speed-crazy youth.

A breakthrough act, this song started the practice of an artist writing material for another artist. Even if it did not chart, Kenny Lynch released it as a single.

R&B artist Arthur Alexander originally recorded **"Anna (Go To Him)"** (Arthur Alexander). Since Lennon and McCartney could not cope with the demand for new song materials, the Beatles resorted to the use of American beat music, true to their White Negro character. What they did was pick up the obscure B-sides of hit singles that were not yet popular with the British music market. While the *Please Please Me* album included eight original Lennon-McCartney songs, it had seven cover versions of American rock 'n' roll songs. While the album's thrust was to present the "new" sound of the Beatles, it also capitalized on the diversity of styles provided by the American cover versions.

Referring to their practice of using obscure songs to copy from, McCartney further revealed, "All the other bands knew the hits; everybody knew 'Ain't That A Shame.' Everybody knew Bo Diddley's 'Bo Diddley.' But not everybody knew [Bo Diddley's] 'Crackin' Up.' Hardly anybody knows 'Crackin' Up' to this day -- it was just one of his B-sides that I loved. I don't know how dynamite it is, but I like it. We used to look for B-sides -- a good, smart move, too! -- and obscure album tracks, because if we were turned on by them enough to bring something special to them just by being in love with them, you sing them good. John, for instance, used to sing 'Anna' on the first Beatles album. And that was a really obscure record that we'd just found, and guys would play in the clubs. We'd take the record home and learn it. We learned a lot of songs like that: 'Three Cool Cats,' 'Anna,' 'Thumbin' A Ride' -- millions of great songs."

The R&B trio The Cookies originally recorded **"Chains"** (Goffin-King). The Beatles added a harmonica section to be different from the original.

"Boys" (Luther Dixon-Wes Farrell), a song by The Shirelles extolling the delights of boys, became known as "Ringo's Theme" because he would sing it live during early performances to please his diehard followers. As if demonstrating how amateurish the Beatles were during that time, nobody bothered to correct the wrong male gender (it must be female) they were singing about.

"Boys" served as a model for Lennon-McCartney self-penned songs such as "Ask Me Why." The verse is constructed with a two-line narrative followed by scat chanting and ricochets around the subject that draws its emotional content from scat chanting.

The Beatles issued "Ask Me Why" / "Please Please Me" and "Love Me Do" / "P.S. I Love You" as singles.

As a display of McCartney's fondness for girl groups, the Beatles covered **"Baby It's You"** (Mack Davis / Barney Williams / Burt Bacharach), an original recording by The Shirelles.

Lennon picked the motive of **"Do You Want To Know A Secret"** (LENNON-McCartney) from a variation of a song from the 1937 Walt Disney movie *Snow White and the Seven Dwarfs* which his mother, Julia, used to sing to him as a child. In an opening scene, Snow White is working as a kitchen maid. Standing by the castle's well, she sings to the doves. He recounted that this was "*Wanna know a secret? Promise not to tell? We are standing by a wishing well.*" Lennon rehashed this as "*Listen, do you want to know a secret / Do you promise not to tell?*" But there are no such line in "I'm Wishing/One Love" which is Snow White's scene with the doves. There's also no song in the soundtrack called "Wishing Well" which most Beatles websites claim from which this song was based. Lennon's mother must have rephrased her remembrance of the lyrics or Lennon could have erroneously recalled.

Harrison, however, squealed the song was hacked from the melody of The Stereos' doo wop hit "I Really Love You." To hide the derivation, Martin sped up its tempo. The secret Lennon is talking about? That he loved Cynthia Powell. Having made his girlfriend pregnant, he would be a father soon. This pregnancy turned out to be Julian Lennon.

Lennon, however, let Harrison sing his composition, breaking the house rule of the songwriter taking lead vocals. The logic: "It only had three notes and he wasn't the best singer in the world." Clearly showing in the recording, Harrison strains his voice to hit the high notes. Lennon and McCartney wrote songs for Harrison and Starr in the beginning to allow them to take center spot during performances. Regardless of its derivation and quality of singing, it is innovative for not repeating the opening phrase and remarkable shift in tone.

Forced to sing standard ballads by their Hamburg and Liverpool live audiences, they compromised by doing **"A Taste of Honey"** (Scott-Marlow), the theme song of the Acker Bilt starrer released in 1961.

"There's A Place" (LENNON-McCartney) is a fine example of Lennon's ability at derivation. A heartfelt introspection, he adapted the song's melody from The Miracles' "Way Over There" as written by Smokey Robinson. Lennon nicked the title from Leonard Bernstein's *West Side Story* song, "There's A Place For Us (Somewhere)." The song has reckoning theme which makes them vaguely similar. Lennon infused the track harmonica blasts to give it a distinctive personality. It supposedly shows Lennon's better understanding and control of theme, an indication of his improvement as a songwriter. This assessment is, of course, misleading as it was a simple case of using an expressive song to derive from.

If Lennon's lead vocal had a demented quality in **"Twist and Shout"** (Bert Russell / Phil Medley), that's because he screamed to sing this Isley Brothers hit. The album's one-day marathon recording session gave him a sore throat so he ended up shouting the lyrics to make up for his weak voice.

The *Please Please Me* album proved to be a wisely conceived collection of original Lennon-McCartney songs and cover versions of American rock 'n' roll. The album also established what would become the standard format of a Beatles album, which always began and ended with a fast song. This format arouses the curiosity of listeners at the start and makes them clamor for more in the end. The format encourages active listening. The succeeding songs alternate from slow to fast to keep the listeners engrossed and prevent interest from lagging.

The songs use familiar experience written in the first person, with a simplicity of language that makes it seem as if the singer intended it exclusively for the listener, thus, establishing an emotional bond between singer and listener.

The sophomoric and derivative nature of Beatles songs clearly manifests the group's ambition rather than genuine artistry. Although bright, pleasant, and uncluttered with embellishments, the songs' characteristics signify technical naiveté as songwriters and musicians rather than an intended effect. The rehashed songs of Lennon and McCartney were lethargic -- and gained energy only after they passed through Martin's genius.

In this birth phase of the Beatles, Martin became more entrenched in giving concrete input for the group's songs, aside from discharging the specific duties of a producer. For instance, he began to play instruments during recording and overdubbing sessions. He contributed musical parts to their most memorable songs. His valuable contributions practically gave him member status as much as Harrison and Starr had as members of the Beatles.

Short of doing a vocal part in a Beatles song, Martin formulated and reformulated ideas and concepts with Lennon and McCartney. Equal status marked their collaboration, bouncing song possibilities that made the final product more important than who contributed its elements. This undeniably qualified Martin as the fifth Beatle, although he disagreed with this classification.

During this period, Martin exercised the function of quality controller, besides being an artistic collaborator. He determined the essential nature of a song, its quality as a separate work and as it relates to a collection of songs. He utilized the standard of fully realized work that required completeness and unity of the highest type. As a way to finish a song, he did not resort to abbreviation. He went through the tedious process of improving details and their impact on the totality. Every decision was a major one. He did not stop until he achieved what he and the Beatles wanted.

As a collaborator, Martin had enormous knowledge of classical and popular music that the other popular singers did not have access to. He was a strength the Beatles fully exploited when their intrinsic intentions remained unmuddled by false aspirations. In hindsight, it could be said that being a Beatles collaborator was a role that Martin perfected. The collaboration between him and the boys was an unparalleled meeting of minds and energies.

"From Me to You" / "Thank You Girl" single

The quartet released "From Me to You" and "Thank You Girl" as a single on April 11, 1963.

Lennon and McCartney converted "From You to Us," the title of the letter column of the *NME* to "**From Me to You**" (Lennon-McCartney) by reversing it. McCartney explained, "It could be done as an old ragtime tune…especially the middle-eight. And so we're not writing the tunes in any particular idiom."

When Lennon and McCartney were making it up, singer Kenny Lynch who was with them in the coach they were writing it in heard them singing "ooh." He remarked, "You can't do that. You'll sound like a bunch of f----- fairies." McCartney did not find the song strong enough so he wanted to rewrite it in 1964. They decided not to touch it.

Martin suggested the opening lick *"Da da da da da dum dum da"* which convinced the Beatles of his "enormous musical sense," as EMI producer Ron Richards put it. McCartney and Harrison's naughty scat chanting, *"tit tit tit tit tit / tit tit tit tit"* recalls the airy abandon of "*Arat-tat-tat-tat*" of the Berry song "Almost Grown."

"**Thank You Girl**" (Lennon-McCartney) is "a silly song," as McCartney himself once put it, which they did as an exercise at becoming songwriters. Lennon and McCartney recorded it as a duet, adapted from the Everly Brothers' style. The singing style might have been derived, but it expresses a genuine gratitude to female fans that patronized them.

The critical comments by the Beatles of their songs quoted or paraphrased here were mostly made after the group disbanded in 1969. The songs of the birth and growth periods were generally unsophisticated as they were still learning to be composers and musicians, frequently lacking the time to refine them. As such, they tend to be overly critical of the earlier songs as they were necessarily comparing them with songs of the maturity period, even the decline and death periods.

"She Loves You" / "I'll Get You" single

The moptops issued "She Loves You," flipsided by "I'll Get You," as a single on August 23, 1963.

"**She Loves You**" (Lennon-McCartney), the first Beatles song released as a Lennon-McCartney composition, is the final stroke in the reinvention of rock 'n' roll. While keeping the short verses and the hard, repetitive, driving choruses, often raucously shouted, "She Loves You" and the other self-composed songs by the Lennon-McCartney tandem removed rock 'n' roll's out-and-out sexuality. Since rock 'n' roll offended parents and older people, making them to want their children and relatives to avoid such songs, the Beatles removed the anti-social element, making it a sanitized form of rock 'n' roll. By removing this offending crudity, the Beatles made rock 'n' roll a safe form of music, becoming known as "rock & roll."

McCartney recalled the circumstances they crafted the song, showing the technique their White Negro practice during the period: "There was a Bobby Rydell song out at the time 'Forget Him' and, as often happens, you think of one song when you write another. We were in a van up in Newcastle-Upon-Tyre. I'd planned an answering song where a couple of us would sing 'She loves you' and the other ones would answer 'Yeah yeah.' We decided that was a crummy idea but at least we then had the idea of a song called 'She Loves You.' So we sat in the hotel bedroom for a few hours and wrote it; John and I, sitting on twin beds with guitars."

McCartney based "She Loves You" on the idea of the "call-and-answer" song. He sings "*she loves you*" and the rest of the Beatles answer back. Lennon persuaded McCartney to drop the hackneyed idea and to use McCartney's idea of the triple "yeah" as a counterpoint. It was not a novel idea at all. American and French beat songs previously used a double "yeah." "She Loves You" took its novelty by magnifying the use of "yeah" by tripling it ("*yeah, yeah, yeah*"). Thus, the overflowing use of scat chanting gave it new appeal. McCartney took the "*oooooooh*" idea from the The Isley Brothers' "Twist and Shout" and appended everything like Presley's use of "*uh, uh,*" "*oh yeah*" and " " in "All Shook Up."

"She Loves You" relied on the novelty of "*yeah, yeah, yeah.*" "Yeah" is a standard colloquialism in rock 'n' roll. In Europe, rock 'n roll is known as "ye-ye," French for "yeah, yeah," meaning beat music. Lennon and McCartney exaggerated the use of "yeah" by repeating it three times with an energy that pulsates with youthful concurrence, a reflection of peer group mentality.

Why the "she" and "you" instead of "me" such as in the title of "Love Me Do," "Please Please Me" and "From Me to You?" They had to! They had been doing "me" songs and wanted to veer away.

"She Loves You" was about McCartney's Liverpool girlfriend Iris Caldwell. He based the melody, for sure, on Rydell's "Forget Him."

First used by Glenn Miller and his orchestra, it ends with the use of the sixth chord, unusual by pop music standards. Lennon and McCartney demonstrated how they could use borrowed music to their advantage. Martin originally did not like it, but agreed to keep it once he realized the chord fit perfectly. He explained, "I told them it was corny. I told them Glenn Miller was doing it 20 years ago. But they said, so what? That was what they wanted."

"She Loves You" propelled the Beatles as a group every British female can aspire for romantically. Unconscious of the distinct appeal of their individual personalities, Lennon regarded McCartney's appearance as weak, Harrison as taciturn, Starr as venial, and himself without appeal. He calculated that their group offered a diversity that female fans would find appealing.

With the chart success of "She Loves You," the Beatles used this diversity to their advantage during live performances. In the adoration of musical personalities as expressions of latent sexuality, the Beatles served as subliminal opposite-sex partners or, more correctly, models of partner aspiration in a heterosexual context. With their songs addressed to the listener, the association turned transparent, converting every listener into a diehard follower in this exercise of empathy building.

"I'll Get You" (Lennon-McCartney) is an early indication that *Alice in Wonderland* would be used extensively in Beatles songs. Joan Baez's version of "All My Trials" inspired the G to E9 chord change in the bridge to break the word "pretend." The lead guitar is reduced to a second rhythm guitar with McCartney's bass and Lennon's harmonica as dominant instruments.

With an advance order of 310,000 units, the "She Loves You" / "I'll Get You" single topped the UK charts with 1.3 million copies sold. This remained the fastest selling British single until the Wings' "Mull of Kintyre" (McCartney) dislodged it in 1977.

And mass hysteria kicks off

By then riots were taking place with regularity wherever the Beatles went, and it was the first real indication that the Beatles had become popular. One clearly documented event of them getting mobbed was when they made their television debut on ITV's high-rating show *Sunday Night at the London Palladium* on October 13, 1963 as the top bill.

Recalling America's love affair with Presley after his first performance at the *Ed Sullivan Show* seven years before, the British public took the Beatles to their hearts following the TV appearance. The fans went into hysteria outside the Palladium. The next morning the Beatles became headline news. The press reported the incident and coined the term "Beatlemania" to mean mass hysteria created by the Beatles' presence.

The Beatles became household names. Their charisma, a personal mark that allowed them to impress their personalities on their followers and influence them in the process, had taken a firm grip among their British fans. Removing the barrier of gender, the girls screamed at them in adoration, making them objects of their yearnings, while the boys applauded in admiration, turning the Beatles into models of their aspirations.

As a group, the Beatles' individual persona exuded different appeals, which made the adulation even more individualistic. Even when a married Lennon was photographed crawling out of a Swedish whorehouse in late 1963, they exuded an innocence that made them safe idols, even if the elders were still repulsed by their boisterous packaging.

Chance art

Chance art is part of the art of derivation, permeating all artistic fields. It is founded on the belief that having made the selection of what to derive, the resultant output becomes the artist's own. In chance art, this is an accepted principle, as art remains an illustration of reality. Art reflects reality, an interpretation of the world where the artist interacts with its elements. This basis makes all art derivatives, from the primitive artists who drew the animal illustration in the cave in Provence, France, to Pablo Picasso's assimilation of the basic line of an ancient stone figure Into Cubism.

Most art works are derived from other art works. What may be perceived as imitation is usually termed by artists as "inspired" and "influenced" by the work/s of other artist/s, sometimes describing such derivation with the edifying label of being a parody. When these artists use the derivation technique in startling new ways and express it with a high degree of refinement, their works take the semblance of breakthrough art.

In chance art, the stature of the artist is immaterial as it reflects nothing more than a refined ability at the art of derivation. The separation of great art from what is mediocre or pedestrian in variety does not rest on the question of originality. Great art is a product of the persistence to realize a vision of reality expressed in a particular medium and shared generously by the creator with his audience.

With the Beatles

For the group's second album, *With the Beatles*, issued on November 22, 1963, the Beatles adopted a new two-stage recording technique, which allowed them to maximize the advantages that a recording studio could offer. As it was fairly simple, the process was highly flexible.

The composing member came in to the recording session with a finished or partially completed song that underwent a process of refinement as the group collectively transformed it from concept to recorded form. Relying on the other Beatles and Martin for input, the song's composer presided the recording sessions. Recording sessions took longer to complete, from several days to several weeks, and, in some cases, even several years. The key factor here was the composer's belief in the song's potential. McCartney, however, did not use their regular recording procedures to record songs several times because he was driven to continue and/or finish recording in the fewest number of sessions possible.

The Beatles rehearsed the basic rhythm in one track as many times as necessary to perfect that track to the degree of their collective satisfaction. As EMI artist, the Beatles was allowed unlimited use of the recording studio -- and charge-free. The Beatles took advantage of this arrangement by rehearsing songs with the tape machine running the whole time.

During the rehearsals, at a later time during this period, the Beatles explored the various possibilities of melody and lyrics, the delivery of lead vocals and the combination of harmonies, relying on improvisations, and chance input. Each rehearsal was assigned a take number, and the rehearsals could have as many takes as the song's composer desired or until he felt satisfied with the quality of the rhythm track. From among these numbered takes, the Beatles later on decided on the best take, which would become the basis of overdubbing.

Relying on incidental decisions, the songs became the product of chance art. In many cases, they would allow so much time to pass before they resumed work on an unfinished recording. They might not have been aware of it, but they relied on the subconscious to percolate new possibilities for the song.

With the instrumental backing takes safely recorded on one track, other vocal or instrumental elements would be individually or collectively recorded in the remaining three vacant tracks. The Beatles overdubbed or "dropped in" extra sounds onto the tape at will. They could superimpose overdubs of vocals, instruments, or effects onto an existing take. They did this to improve the existing track, remove an improper element, enhance instrumentation, or whatever they felt was necessary to exploit the song's full potential.

The process is known as a reduction mix, which involves vacating recording tracks by mixing together existing ones and transferring them to a lesser number of tracks on a different tape. This process is a series of additions or deletions until the music takes the shape of what the artist or songwriter intends it to be. This process allowed the Beatles practically unlimited ways to create a final version of a song, as each overdubbed version was assigned a new take number.

The products were then matched. The Beatles carried on this formula-led approach to song crafting for the larger segment of their career.

Although their second album may be regarded as a major improvement from their debut collection, it did not involve top-quality creativity. Steeped with the influence of Smokey Robinson and the Miracles, the Beatles seemed to be content in doing cover songs and making them better than the original. While they were becoming more skillful musicians at playing their respective instruments, the Lennon-McCartney tandem continued to rely on patching together elements from different sources and covering up the imitation to make them sound like their own -- with, of course, tons of help from Martin. It was in the vocal aspect that the Beatles greatly improved -- besides starting to dictate the music and fashion norms of the time, eventually turning themselves into cultural icons.

With the Beatles opens with **"It Won't Be Long"** (LENNON-McCartney). Beatle song analyst Pollack found the opening lick similar of "Beethoven's 5th." He wrote: "The opening lick is strangely reminiscent of Beethoven's 5th in its hammering insistence, and ends unusually with the downward leap of a perfect 4th; sing it aloud and notice what doing so physically pulls out of you…I insist, the parallel is extraordinary…"

It uses *"yeah,"* for sure, to capitalize on the novelty created by "She Loves

You." Lennon opens the chorus with the hook line "*It won't be long,*" followed by a successive exchange of "*yeah*" by Lennon and backing harmonies by McCartney and Harrison. This is a conversion of the technique used in "She Loves You," indicating peer group concurrence at the singer's uncontained excitement about a girl's return.

But "It Won't Be Long" has another significant meaning for Lennon: his chance discovery of double tracking by manually recording his voice twice, thus giving it a fuller body. Lennon had always considered his voice inferior to that of McCartney, and was thus always finding ways to improve it at least in the recording studio. Eventually, he did not have to literally record his voice twice as Artificial Double Tracking (ADT) would be invented, and he would take advantage of this technological innovation to improve his voice, at least in their albums.

"**All I've Got To Do**" (LENNON-McCartney) is a conversion on a faster beat of the Tamla-Motown sound of Smokey Robinson and The Miracles' "(You Can) Depend on Me." According to McDonald, they are similar musically and lyrically. The Beatles' version expanded the refrain section from Robinson's four lines to six. Although it avoided the repetition used by Robinson's hook line, the phrasing remained the same. Its last two lines, "*You just got to call on me, yeah / You just got to call on me*" betray this similarity. This song was intended for the American market as clearly shown by the untypical practice of calling a girl by telephone. This was an unimaginable practice for British youth when it was written.

"**All My Loving**" (Lennon-MCCARTNEY) is a song for Jane Asher, McCartney's girlfriend by the time he wrote it. It may be considered a breakthrough song for McCartney if only because for the first time, he wrote the lyrics first before coming up with the melody. The song's lyrics are actually taken from a poem he wrote for Jane.

During this birth period, Asher served as a major theme in McCartney's songs, which reflected his age and need to be loved. He met the actress when the Beatles invited her to the Royal Court Hotel, where they were staying, after the concert at the Royal Albert Hall. As the representative of *Radio Times*, a British Broadcasting Company magazine, she was supposed to do the show's review. Her encounter with the Beatles, however, ended up with McCartney badly smitten by her and "interviewing" her to get to know her better. After that first meeting, they started to date, and by the end of 1963, he had moved into a room in Asher's house on Wimpole St. as a friend of her brother Peter, who was one-half of the Peter & Gordon vocal duet, which was also famous at that time.

Asher's influence on Beatles songs instilled in McCartney a fondness for love songs. McCartney, on the other hand, heavily associated himself with the genre because he believed it was "a very serious subject." He believed it would expand the Beatles' rock 'n' roll medium.

Music-wise, Lennon adapted the rhythm guitar from The Crystal's "Da Doo Ron Ron." Harrison played a guitar solo influenced by Chet Atkins.

Reluctant to write songs for the Beatles, Harrison composed **"Don't Bother Me"** (Harrison) while bedridden in a Bournemouth hotel. Bill Harry, founder and editor of the *Mersey Beat*, insisted that he write a song, to which he answered by telling the editor not to bother him. He had the motive for a song, his first which the Beatles recorded for this album. He did not have a high regard for its quality, but he thought it was a good initial attempt that placed him in the league of Lennon and McCartney.

"Little Child" (Lennon-McCartney) is a filler written for Starr's customary *once* song per album. According to Pollack, the first verse recalls *"One After 909's"* *"move over once, move over twice"* phrase, while the second verse rehashed earlier songs "Ask Me Why" and "There's a Place." McCartney admitted nicking the line *"I'm so sad and lonely"* and part of melody from British folk singer Elton Haye's "Whistle My Love" while Lennon played the harmonica in the style of Cyril Davies of Blues Incorporated.

The Beatles lifted **"Till There Was You"** (Meredith William), Peggy Lee's minor hit in the UK, from the Broadway musical *The Music Man*. They would belt out the song to chill off the crowd in their live performances when the scene got heated up with all the shouting and pushing. Why is McCartney so fond of this standard song? Older cousin Bett Robbins used to play it to the McCartney brothers, Paul and James, when she babysat them. It embedded in McCartney's mind that would reappear as a song in the early Beatles repertoire. More than the partiality, it gave the Beatles' repertoire an out-of-the-box personality that played not only rock 'n' roll numbers but standard as well.

The Marvellettes originally recorded **"Please Mister Postman"** (Dobbins / Garrett / Garman / Brianbert) in 1961, the group's first hit. Lennon liked it so much he made sure it was included in this album. Lennon's lead vocal with McCartney was manually double-tracked, while Harrison and McCartney backed him up a la The Shirelles. The Shirelles' ensemble singing style is particularly noticeable in the chorus and coda sections.

The Beatles recorded **"Roll Over Beethoven"** (Chuck Berry), a Berry hit. They loved it so much that they had been performing it since their early club appearances. Harrison did lead vocals.

"Hold Me Tight" (Lennon-MCCARTNEY) is an adaptation of Carl Perkins' "Sure to Fall (In Love With You)." McCartney removed its country music flavor and gave it a rock 'n' roll inflection. He modified Perkin's chorus *"So hold me tight "* to *"So hold me tight (me tight)."* He abbreviated *"Oh Darling, don't ever let me go / For loving you is a natural thing to do"* to *"Let me go on loving you."* And used repetition and melisma, *"Tonight, (tonight) / Making love only to you / So hold me tight, tonight, (tonight) / It's you, you you you – oo-oo – oo-oo."*

Melody-wise, McCartney copied the style of The Shirelles, the first girl group to hit number one in the US music charts. Intended for the *Please Please Me* album, it was bumped off for its weak quality, but was later included in this second album.

The Beatles' fondness for the Motown sound became apparent when they decided to cover **"You Really Got a Hold on Me"** (Smokey Robinson), a hit song by Smokey Robinson and The Miracles. Lennon and Harrison alternated in the pleading lead vocals while Martin played piano.

Originally written for the Rolling Stones, the composing duo converted the feel of The Shirelles' "Boys" and the dragged out *"mannn"* from the chorus of Benny Spellman's "Fortune Teller" in **"I Wanna Be Your Man"** (Lennon-McCartney). With Decca pressing for a new release for the Rolling Stones, Lennon and McCartney went to work and created the song, giving the Rolling Stones their first hit and Starr his customary song for this album.

Lennon recounted to *Playboy* how he rehashed the song: "We were taken down by Brian (Epstein) to meet them at the club where they were playing in Richmond They wanted a song and we went to see what kind of stuff they did. Paul had this bit of a song and we played it roughly for them and they said, 'Yeah, OK, that's our style.' But it was only really a lick, so Paul and I went off in the corner of the room and finished the song off while they were all sitting there, talking. We came back and Mick and Keith said, 'Jesus, look at that. They just went over there and wrote it.' You know, right in front of their eyes. We gave it to them. It was a throwaway."

And the Rolling Stones seemed to have never realized that the song was a mere derivation. "I Wanna Be Your Man" was, of course, an absolute proof that Lennon and McCartney had perfected the art.

Harrison took such a liking to the all-girl group Donays' **"Devil In His Heart"** (Drankin) that he picked it for the Beatles to record. They had no choice, of course, but to convert the song to the masculine gender, but then the indiscriminate adaptation of a female group's song necessarily imparted an effeminate character to the Beatles as exemplified by this cover song. The Beatles' conversion usually dispenses with logic, portraying men as dependent on women, thus contradicting the chauvinistic attitude of Liverpool men like the Beatles. One line in the Beatles' conversion is *"She'll never hurt"* -- as if women typically hurt men.

"Not A Second Time" (LENNON-McCartney) begins with *"You know you made me cry,"* which Lennon sings in the style of Mike Smith of the Dave Clark Five. According to McCartney, Lennon adapted the "trapped in a controlling relationship theme and rambling melody mainly from Smokey Robinson and The Miracles' "You've Really Got A Hold On Me."

Critic William Man of *The Times* observed the Aeolian cadence of Lennon's vocals at the song's end and the same chord progression appears at the end of the final movement as Gustav Mahler's "Song of the Earth." No matter how Lennon disliked the idea, admitting "I have no idea what [Aeolian cadences] are. They sound like exotic birds,".it was the first time a well-known music critic analyzed a Beatle song in classical terms. While it showed Lennon and McCartney's growing sophistication as songwriters, it did not fail to trace their White Negro character. It might have been unconscious on their part or unintended, but the similarity is there, an unavoidable fact.

The *With the Beatles* album closes with the Barrett Strong original, **"Money (That's All I Want)"** (Berry Gordy-Janie Bardford), which the Beatles improved, mainly by Lennon's manic vocals definitely a style he picked up from Little Richard.

"I Want To Hold Your Hand" / "This Boy" single

The Beatles released "I Want to Hold Your Hand" and "This Boy" as a single on November 29, 1963, at the same time as the *With the Beatles* album.

Lennon and McCartney converted the raw vitality of Bobby Freeman's "Do You Want to Dance," another song performed regularly by the group during their Cavern days with the brief handclaps patterned after Holly, to **"I Want to Hold Your Hand"** (Lennon-McCartney). The Beatles recorded the latter using four-track technology for the first time.

Four-track technology afforded them greater flexibility during recording because it allowed the combination and recombination of sound elements, which, in turn, they could shape with as much texture and color as their creativity and time availability would allow. This lent to the recorded song clarity of sound elements as this new-fangled technology prevented leakages from other elements and unacceptable ones could be corrected by overdubbing. As a final benefit, stereomixing, which is a basic feature of four-track technology, allowed panning that gave extraordinary depth and combination to this clarity. Song elements could alternately pan on the right and left ears, imparting to the song exceptional texture and vitality. Four-track technology also allowed the Beatles to adapt Phil Spector's song production process known as the "Wall of Sound."

The Beatles' use of four-track technology converted the recording studio into a workshop as it took them more time to finish a song recording, entailing a corresponding increase in recording-related expenses. The flexibility offered by the technological advances, however, allowed the Beatles to record as many as three songs per eight-hour recording stretch. Despite the pre-set rules of the Abbey Road studio (such as pre-determined maximum equipment settings and loads to prevent equipment abuse), four-track recording paved the way for the Beatles to meet Martin's exhortations for more experimentation. Since the Abbey Road rules and regulations were preventing the Beatles to go beyond what they had been doing in the recording studio, they decided to circumvent those rules.

"It was John (Lennon) trying to do Smokey (Robinson)," said Harrison about **"This Boy"** (LENNON-McCartney). He converted its "I've Been Good to You" with similar chord changes, melody and arrangement according to Harrison. Lennon, McCartney and Harrison sing a three-part harmony. Lennon tried to imitate Robinson's singing style in the middle eight.

These early Beatles songs manifested the potency of their American beat music models with all its emotional outbursts, but minus the anger. American beat music was based on actual emotions and experiences, but then the cultural transfer from American White Negroes to the Beatles reduced its experiential contents into poor duplicates, thus also removing the sociological implications of those experiences. The Beatles confused American beat music's narrative for a personal level of storytelling that centered on adolescent relationships. But then the confusion removed the sexual connotation of their models that gave their songs a distinct air of innocence. The British sense of uprightness as imposed by Epstein and Martin obliterated much of rock 'n' roll's sexual connotation in the interplay of borrowed White Negro riffs. In turn, the obliteration made rock 'n' roll evolved into a safer form of beat music as rock and roll.

"Can't Buy Me Love" / "You Can't Do That" single

The moptops released "Can't Buy Me Love" and "You Can't Do That" as a single on March 20, 1964.

McCartney started the use of the swing idiom in **"Can't Buy Me Love"** (Lennon-MCCARTNEY). It seems inevitable that he would resort to it since he grew up listening to jazz, his father's favorite type of music which was popular in the '40s and '50s. Popularized by George Gershwin and Ella Fitzgerald, swing is a form of jazz that has a four-to-the bar rhythm and was performed by the big bands of that era.

Martin specified that "Can't Buy Me Love" must be upbeat and should start with a chorus as a follow-up single for "I Want to Hold Your Hand," which was a big hit in the U.S. He noted this song was a significant departure from the standard Beatles song arrangement, indicating Lennon and McCartney's improved ability as composers.

McCartney denied in 1966 that "Can't Buy Me Love" is about prostitutes. He clarified, "The idea behind it was that all these materials possessions are all very well, but they won't buy me what I really want." Later, he stated it should have been titled "Can Buy Me Love" considering fame and money had brought them.

Lennon adapted the structure of **"You Can't Do That"** (LENNON-McCartney) after the R&B sounds of Memphis and the structure from the Wilson Pickett style. It has kilometric sentences, a first for a Beatles song since the members were not highly educated young men capable of long, involved sentences. For sure, the use of long sentences in a Beatle song was an early influence of Bob Dylan on Lennon. Take a look at this song's lyrics: *"Well, it's the second time I've caught you talkin' to him / Do I have to tell you one more time I think it's a sin."*

Harrison used a 12-string Rickenbacker guitar for the first time. Rickenbacker manufacturer and distributor F.C. Hall presented a Rickenbacker 360/12 FG electric 12-string guitar worth $900 in New York for the *Ed Sullivan Show* series. Having two sets of strings, the Rickenbacker made him sound as if his guitar was double-tracked; the ultimate effect was to have a fuller and chiming sound. The Rickenbacker was used first in "Can't Buy Me Love" but was lost in the mix.

By this time, the introduction of new technology into a Beatle song usually caused it to evolve. As true-blue White Negroes, the Beatles actively pursued new ways of doing things, often copying them from other artists, to keep themselves a viable act.

Creative theory

Is there a single theory that shows where the Beatles based their art of derivation, the basis of their creativity?

Edward de Bono's Random Input theory comes to mind. De Bono is the scholar and doctor who hypothesized the Lateral Thinking theory in the early '70s, a few years after the Beatles ended their musical revolution. Through the Random Input, a powerful Lateral Thinking technique, De Bono proved possible the artificial means of generating new ideas on demand without having to wait for inspiration.

Random Input involves the association of a word which generates new connections in the mind, often stirring instinct and producing insight. Either through words or images, the brain organizes new connections out of them.

In the case of the Beatles, Random Input came in the form of other artists' riffs, lyrics, or music-playing techniques. Another technique was formulating a nonsensical statement and examining it to see where it would lead. Among the Beatles' techniques was using incomplete or substandard lyrics during a song's composition or recording phase with the intention of finalizing them later.

But then the Beatles based these derivation techniques from chance art, not exactly from the De Bono theory.

Chapter 3
The growth phase

The song is the message

"The song is moral by being itself."

- Bob Dylan

A fresh, new and exciting period, the growth phase is a time for the artistry to blossom.

The *Ed Sullivan Show* was the cultural barometer of post-war America, when households were not affluent enough to own multiple television sets. A single TV set at home assured that children and parents would have the communal pleasure of watching shows together as a family. As the most popular Sunday variety fare, The *Ed Sullivan Show's* appeal rested mainly on Sullivan's credibility as host. Whenever he said the viewer was about to see the greatest act ever, he delivered. Those acts could be anywhere on the brow scale, as its something-for-everybody format accepted anything from the low brow animal acts to the high brow art of Bolshoi Ballet. Their common denominator was the act's ability to pull the viewers' intent gaze to the small screen.

New artists made the show the mecca of their first national appearance, and having done so, they could claim they were already made, and had become national idols. The appearance of the Beatles in the show ensured access to its 30-million audience base. Epstein's shrewd decision to make the Beatles perform three sets was calculated to disprove the American perception that British musical groups were largely poor copies of their own.

Cowering from the thought of a negative reception since some American interests labeled them "ugly," the Beatles were ambivalent about what was awaiting them. Due to the dismal state of rock 'n' roll that no American wanted, Lennon questioned himself about this predicament. On their way to the U.S., while on board a Pan Am jet flight 101, McCartney cynically asked the legendary record producer Phil Spector, "Since America has always had everything, why should we be over there making money? They've got their own groups. What are we going to give them that they don't already have?"

When the jet landed, a throng of welcomers, estimated at 10,000, was waiting at the airport. Harrison thought they were the well-wishers of an important foreign leader. To their amazement, the welcomers were mostly hysterical adolescent girls, frantically calling out their names. These young girls accorded them a reception befitting an important celebrity.

The local media, however, were not impressed. In fact, the media covering the event treated them with skepticism, as evident in the press conference that followed. To commence it, Lennon shouted "Shurrup" to the shocked journalists. Lennon asked Cousin Burcie about the hostile attitude they were being accorded. He replied, "They're taking the role of the parents: 'Rock 'n' roll is the tool of the devil and it'll grow hair on your hands.'"

Fortunately, their innate charm and irreverence equipped the Beatles to counter the hostile attitude of those scribes. Their humorous and off-the-cuff replies during the conference pulled the media's defenses down. While Lennon, McCartney, and Harrison answered the questions matter-of-factly, Starr charmed the jaded coterie with off-the-cuff and self-derisive answers. Thrown a query about his height, Starr retorted without blinking an eye, "Two feet, nine inches."

Seventy-three million Americans watched the first *Ed Sullivan Show* appearance of the Beatles, even if it meant propping up Harrison with a huge dose of amphetamines for his flu. America stood still during the program's timeslot as everyone from all walks of life sat glued to their black-and-white TV sets. No juvenile misdemeanor transpired when the Beatles played rock 'n' roll music. And Sullivan's shrewdness paid off: his show received its highest audience share in its 25-year history.

A hysterical mob again received the Beatles when they arrived in Washington State by train. On a revolving stage with 20,000 fans in unabated screaming, the Beatles played their first full-blown concert at the Washington Coliseum in Washington, D.C.

The moment Lennon, McCartney, Harrison and Starr stepped on the revolving stage, the fans started pelting the quartet with jelly beans. During the live performance, the magic of their presence made the audience even crazier. The hysterical shouting obliterated the singing; even the apparent errors barely mattered. This magic, created mainly by the boyish charms of McCartney and Starr, made the female audience drool in instinctive awe. McCartney's pixie smile and Starr's hawk-shaped nose and multi-ringed fingers exuded an appeal that the fans hopelessly adored. Starr's charm played its wonder to the American audience, making it a major influence in their early success.

Performing songs from their LP, Lennon played a California-made Rickenbacker rhythm guitar with a round prominence. He vamped in the style of the rhythm guitarist of the Shadows' Bruce Welch, providing ample support to Harrison's lead guitar. McCartney played a left-hand Hofner bass guitar in the pumping style of Carl Perkins. German-made, the Hofner is made from balsa wood and is violin-shaped. Its lightness allowed for comfortable motion and gave a resilient snap to the entire sound combination.

Harrison used a Gretsh lead guitar that permitted dexterous finger movement and aptness. This gave the Beatles greater chord flexibility that exceeded the limitations of the I-IV-V chord progressions. It was also capable of producing delicate melodic embellishments where it was unworkable before.

Starr used a Ludwig drum kit composed of one snare, one rack tom, one floor tom, one bass drum, one hi-hat and two cymbals. Known for spare hydraulic drumming, the Ludwig kit allowed Starr full drumming flexibility that economically cut to the heart of the rhythm.

Starr did not play the drum in the conventional way: instead, he developed a distinct style. With a preference for heavy tom-tom drumming, he reversed the standard drumming sequence which begins on the left. He disliked drum solos and was incapable of doing rolls. To compensate for his inability to play his drum kit around, he accentuated his drumming with fills.

Aside from its feisty beat, Starr had a hidden motive for his fondness for the Ludwig kit. He was gifted with a mini kit, which gave him greater audience visibility -- an advantage considering his short stature.

For the lead vocals, Lennon and McCartney alternated, depending on song authorship. The partner who conceptualized the song took center stage to deliver it. It was their way of recognizing individual contributions. The rest provided the strident vocal harmonies. The Beatles sang to the fullest of their vocal ranges and the requirements the song allowed. Their voices were flexible and expressive, allowing them a wide range of musical possibilities.

The English-made Vox amplifiers reproduced the collective sound, both vocals and instrumental, with fidelity. Giving the greatest impact to their music, its simple sound gave prominence to its loudness, exceeding the standards of rock 'n' roll.

The Beatles, however, knew the live performance must approximate the sound reproduction of their recorded songs. The realization led to limited musical possibilities and affected the quality of their songs. Aside from their regular instruments, Lennon could only use a harmonica. This limited the reproduction possibilities of their songs.

With the primitive amplifiers used, they found out later this did not make any difference because the hysterical shouting during the concert obliterated the performance. The chaotic swarm of girls covered their ears to be able to scream. This overshadowed the music of the Beatles even if they played the best instruments and played them in the best way possible. Even the apparent errors hardly mattered. After the show, McCartney quipped that when the screaming got too loud, they stopped singing and mimed the song's lyrics to rest!

In time with this 15-day blitz, Capitol Records released the *Meet the Beatles* LP. Due to the one-year difference of the Beatles introduction to the U.S. market in relation to their U.K. debut, it became imperative for the U.S. to catch up with this phenomenon. The Beatles' U.S. distributor, Capitol Records, released their first and second U.K. LPs with a different title as a strategic move. It released *With the Beatles* in the U.S. as *Meet the Beatles!* Billed in America as the "first album by England's Phenomenal Pop Combo," the album became the fastest selling LP since the emergence of the 12-inch format.

Returning to New York City, the quartet performed two sold out concerts at Carnegie Hall and reappeared at the *Ed Sullivan Show* televised from Florida. Pandemonium broke out upon their arrival at the Miami International Airport and clashes of pro- and anti-Beatles interests marred the show. The Beatles returned to Britain on February 22, 1964.

This first U.S. concert could be described as a "cultural transfer." Overcoming American resistance to British musical groups with the Beach Boys as its leading musical group, The Beatles successfully uprooted American popular culture and transplanted the seeds of the Anglicization of the American youth. Every American teenager aspired to become a copy of their favorite Beatle by starting to grow their hair into moptops. Adapting the Carnaby Street fashion of bell-bottoms to Cuban-heeled Beatle boots, the American youth ditched Presley and his greased hair and adapted the Beatles and their free-flowing manes as their image of rebellion. The Beatles finally hurdled the imitator status of British musical group's *vis-à-vis* their American counterpart. Though America is the source of rock 'n' roll, the Beatles resurrected it by repackaging it as a form of music that transcends the color of the skin, despite its predominant British attitude.

Breakthrough act

Undoubtedly, the Beatles, at this point had gained recognition as a musical force of consequence. The public started to expect eagerly song releases from the group to relish their relatively new sonic pleasure. The commercial success of Beatles inspired a creative spirit unknown in proportion before them. Soon enough, the group realized the significance of its mission of developing their music to its highest potential to become the most influential musical force of their time. Various relationships forged a union to exploit this end.

Unschooled as songwriters, Lennon and McCartney relied extensively on spontaneous decisions and input for song materials. At this point, Lennon and McCartney songs had become a reflection of their environment and how that environment changed their lives.

The two were not practitioners in the traditional school of songwriting where the composer writes the song based on music theories before it is performed and/or recorded. But, then, being composers and performers at the same time allowed Lennon and McCartney a great degree of flexibility in the songmaking aspect. This constantly involved the entire process, from conception to song recording. The unstructured approach of decisions and input provided natural and appropriate spontaneity.

Lennon and McCartney did not limit themselves to a finite source of input. Everything was a potential source. They read, listened -- and remembered. They drew their materials from a myriad of sources, schools of thoughts, and influences. The media became their primary source of input -- radio, movies, newspapers, magazines, books -- and provided stimuli from where they drew bits of music and lyrics or even used them in songs absolutely unaltered. They relied on their remembrances of things past to put nostalgia and local color into their songs' hearts. Even the unconscious mental level became a source of indiscriminate input.

They were a short distance away before a musical trend, giving a semblance that they started the trend when in fact it was derived from the developed styles of established and emerging musicians. They mingled with underground personalities who were fertile sources of innovative ferment. They were to refine this ability into an art that adequately served their need to self-actualize.

Lennon, the book author

Lennon's art of derivation did not start at this stage. As a boy, he compiled his writings and drawings into albums, which he considered as "books." As the young Lennon stuck his ears to the radio with the same passion as waiting for American beat songs to air, he tumbled hilariously to Spike Milligan and Harry Secombe's clever use of voices. Stanley Unwin was a gobbledygook linguistic comedian, who converted the King's English into gibberish.

Relying on chance art, Lennon produced a book of collected drawings, humorous pieces, poems and satirical sketches: *In His Own Write*. The compiled materials were actually first submitted to *Mersey Beat* for which he was a regular contributor. Lennon's friend brought the compiled materials to Cape Publications, which immediately published it in 1964 to cash in on Beatlemania. This compilation capitalized on word play, without which a greater part of its wit dissipates.

A Spaniard in the Works followed as a second volume where Lennon collaborated with McCartney in a short story titled *In SaFairy With Whide Hunter*.

Using the same art of derivation of Beatles songs, Lennon transposed its techniques to a literary application. These books based their materials on *Alice in Wonderland, Winnie the Pooh,* Stanley Unwin and *The Goon Show*. Produced by Martin before signing the Beatles to the Parlophone label, Lennon regularly followed the radio program *The Goon Show* as a boy.

He used Carroll's sentence construction and jumbling of images and Milligan and Secombe's verbal punning in the surrealistic poems *Jabberwocky* and

The Hunting of the Snark. With Joycean punning about human deformities and illustrations in Thurberesque doodles, Lennon's vision was crude, something like making Snow White a hunchback, all covered with hair in the wrong places, and dotted with warts. Lennon described its humor as a manifestation of personal "hidden cruelties." He abhorred religion, the capitalist system, obesity, and deformities, deriding cripples as social opportunists. Aside from poking cruel fun at the protagonist's misfortunes and drawing bitter humor from them, Lennon terminates existence through death in the denouement.

Critics took the slim books seriously. *The New York Times'* Harry Gilroy described the first volume as "inspired nonsense." They accorded the first volume with favorable reviews while the next one, which was nothing more than a repetition of the original, received mixed opinions, some of them derisive such as "a collection of 20th century British rubbish."

These books reflected the dark side of Lennon's psyche, largely unexpressed in Beatles songs until this point. Lennon had a latent ability for introspection, even in its extreme manifestation, such as chauvinism. But then the need to cross over was not as immediate as constricts of image and self-censorship. Lennon diverted this negative introspection to his non-musical output. This experience made him realize that their mass audience could appreciate introspection, no matter how reactionary.

To Lennon, the books represented an accomplishment beyond being the Beatles' songmaker/singer. While he collaborated with McCartney in writing songs for other singers or groups, a Beatle broke away from the group's song format for the first time and received recognition. While the books' commercial and critical success remained anchored on the Beatlemania phenomenon, the books stood as a personal glory for him, an important output outside the Beatles.

The books manifested Lennon's unconscious striving for a distinct personality. The success reaped with the Beatles and by himself satisfied Lennon, instilling a creative security in him most of all. Nurturing an ego with a deep-seated need for emotional stroking, Lennon required constant superlative assurance about his ability for his creative energy to manifest itself in equally optimum expression.

Dispensing with the concept of originality and adopting derivation as the standard creative tool and reorienting it as a mass-production mill, Lennon's books had the same artistic pretension that made him proclaim his aspiration to be a novelist at mid-life. Failing to recognize the fact that his publisher marketed the books as artifacts of Beatlemania, Lennon's naiveté led him to believe its false premise. As incontrovertible evidences of Lennon's ability to write, these books asked the readers to suspend judgment about literature being the least prone to rehashing among the arts. If it is anti-literature in the Dadaist sense, Lennon's silence about this issue made it a valid assumption.

It also gave Lennon the basis of a style for writing lyrics, which he would use later in his songwriting career.

As White Negroes, the Beatles' recognition of public taste made chance relationships meld to their advantage. The recognition of opportunity was the first important step. Their sensibilities were not better developed; the necessity for sensory impressions urged them to be vigilant in finding styles to imitate. They cultivated their faculties, as there was always the next opportunity to apply them. This required being White Negroes all the time, a requirement that had them continually searching for materials to imitate.

Thus, the Beatles became both the visualization and the commentary of their times.

The Extended Play record

Besides the 45rpm and long-playing album, the Beatle also released songs in Extended Play (EP) format, usually containing four songs. Among the Beatles songs not released in 45 rpm and LP album in the UK was an EP called "Long Tall Sally," first issued on June 19, 1964 containing the songs "Long Tall Sally," "I Call Your Name," "Slow Down," and "Matchbox."

McCartney recorded **"Long Tall Sally"** (Enotris Johnson / Richard Wayne Penniman / Robert Alexander Blackwell), a Little Richard hit, in a single take with no overdub. It has so much style and energy the imitation exceeds the original, quality-wise. The first song McCartney performed publicly in 1957, Lewisohn calls it his "greatest ever Little Richard impersonation." For sure, McCartney had turned out into an impeccable White Negro.

Originally written by Lennon for Billy J. Kramer and the Dakotas, "I Call Your Name" (with "Bad to Me" on the flipside) landed number one in the British music charts in 1963. It was an early attempt to introduce *ska*, the Jamaican beat which the "it" music in Britain by mid-'65. But not for long. As soon as the Beatles released

"I Call Your Name" (LENNON-McCartney) with Lennon doing the lead vocal, it dislodged Kramer from the top slot.

Lennon did the lead vocal of the rocker **"Slow Down"** (Larry Williams), which Martin superimposed with piano. Originally released in 1958, Larry Williams' single has "Dizzy Miss Lizzy," another non-original song recorded by the White Negroes, on the flipside.

Best used to sing White Negro Carl Perkins' **"Matchbox"** (Perkins) in the Hamburgh live performances, which Lennon took over as soon as Best was fired from the group. Starr eventually got to do the lead vocal when he joined the White Negroes. Perkins, of course, was the Beatles' White Negro hero. In this track, Martin played boogie-woogie piano.

A new high from Bob Dylan

In their second U.S. tour in August 1964, the Beatles finally completed their Americanization. The cultural osmosis rubbed on the quartet the liberal American lifestyle, as initiated by a meeting with Bob Dylan, which imprinted their psyches with new possibilities and highs. The effect of marijuana did not immediately surface in Beatles songs except for some telltale signs that obscured their conversion from uncomplicated moptops to sophisticated potheads.

By imbuing political sense in his hybrid style of folk music, Dylan's popularity soared in the '60s. He used poetic images and devices in his lengthy lyrics, which were patterned after the songs of Woody Guthrie and enriched by an apprenticeship with Joan Baez.

The Beatles listened to *The Freewheelin' Bob Dylan* LP upon its release in May 1963, while its second single, "Please, Please Me," dominated the British charts. Pessimism about the future characterized two songs on the Dylan album: "A Hard Rain's A Gonna Fall" and "Masters of War." Written in the years of the Vietnam War and the US involvement in that geographically distant battleground, both songs spoke of grief and impending gloom. "From the moment," Harrison once reflected, "we recognized some vital energy, a voice crying out somewhere."

The album established Dylan as a new folk singer and a figurehead of youth protest groups.

Dylan first heard a Beatles song during a 1964 cross-country drive while tuned in to the car radio. He heard "I Want to Hold Your Hand," which, at that time, swept the American airwaves. This was the song he mistook for a turn-on song, where Dylan thought the Beatles sang "*I get high, I get high*" for the actual lyrics of "*I can't hide, I can't hide.*"

Dylan commented about the Beatles: "They were doing things nobody was doing. But I just kept it to myself...Everybody else thought that they were gonna pass right away. But it was obvious to me that they had staying power. Their chords were outrageous, just outrageous, and their harmonies made it all valid...I knew they were pointing to the direction where music had to go...It seemed to me a definite line was being drawn. This was something that never happened before."

Actually, a mutual effort to listen to one another had already begun. Harrison admitted consciously listening to the contents of Dylan's lyrics and attitude and that he found both "just incredibly original and wonderful." Dylan's style influenced Harrison, as it did Lennon and McCartney who, as a result, decided to go acoustic and put more introspection into the songs they were writing.

Dylan rolled the Beatles their first marijuana joints in a room at the Hotel Del Monico in New York on August 28, 1964 during their second American tour. With them was Beat Generation figure Al Aronowitz who inducted Dylan to pot the year before. Evans offered Dylan Dirnamyl pills which he turned down, suggesting marijuana instead. In this gathering of the two major proponents of popular music, Dylan invoked Lennon, "Listen to the words, man!" Dylan obliquely commented on Beatles songs, which are typically bereft of substance and real emotion. Despite the awe, Lennon contradicted Dylan's statement by blurting, "I can't be bothered. I listen to the sound of the overall thing."

The meeting, though, substantially affected the impressionable Lennon and McCartney. Lennon started giving more emphasis to their lyrics, a la Dylan, as a natural progression for word play, and he started to imitate Dylan's persona. McCartney, on his part, said that he turned cerebral. He gushed during the time, "I'm thinking for the first time, really *thinking*."

The Beatles represented the acceptance of pop music as mainstream entertainment, while Dylan stood for the entire anti-pop impulse. The Beatles are Dylan's exact opposite, their attraction to one another proving the accuracy of the law of magnetism. Dylan reminded the Beatles of their underground past that Epstein had reinvented to make the group initially acceptable to a bigger part of the British music market.

The association with Dylan made them want to return to the pre-Epstein Beatles. Dylan inspired the Beatles to seek their roots, what Harrison termed as wanting to be "funky" again and putting "a little more balls" into the lyrics of their songs. Dylan's influence motivated them to go further in their musical explorations. It especially transformed Lennon -- he found a new father image.

The power of Dylan and marijuana melded into a dynamic combination that made Lennon cast off Presley as his father figure: a renewal process that made him the epicenter of attention. Lennon's complex personality made him vulnerable to musical personalities that closely resembled his aspiration for rebellion -- and attention. He manifested this by aspiring to clone Dylan's persona, from Dylan's emaciated appearance, stark black spectacles, Huckleberry Finn cap to the way Dylan inflected his voice in songs. Dylan influenced Lennon like Presley indirectly had in the past.

Lennon and McCartney started to write lyrics with the same attitude as Dylan. To heed the latter's unsolicited advice of giving primary importance to lyrics, Lennon began to free his repressed emotions by projecting himself in the music. Dylan indirectly made Lennon do away with the professional approach to songwriting and pursue it subjectively by expressing personal feelings. This new attitude provided a suitable solution to their predicament at songwriting -- the weak narrative that tended to be lachrymose and incongruent with the melody.

Dylan's influence resurfaced the blues in a different application. Lennon's and McCartney's absorption of the Dylan style made them realize that negativism was a perfectly acceptable means of personal expression. Although it resulted in a mockery of its application in some major songs where the theme and melody continued to be in contradiction, it was a conflict that they couldn't quite resolve consciously.

Dylan's influence changed the Beatles' theme of unresolved love to an existentialist's search for meaning. The Beatles' songs in this era began to display a higher level of musicality that some sectors took as a sign of their becoming a mature musical force. Before Dylan, the duo wrote songs devoid of real emotions. They sang of lost love to incongruously fast and happy melodies. Dylan's influence resolved this inconsistency, especially when

Lennon wrote about his personal life and feelings.

A Hard Day's Night album

With Beatlemania "filling empty heads with hysteria," the *Daily Telegraph* compared the Beatles to Adolf Hitler in this growth period of their creative cycle. It was impossible for the media not to take note of the Beatles and to snipe at them occasionally: the group shuttled back and forth from England to their global destinations. Celebrity is rewarding, but it imposes a big burden on those who bask in its glitter. Their celebrity stature made the Beatles vulnerable.

The first American tour expanded their popularity, making them relatively affluent in such a short time. But then their newfound wealth made Lennon and McCartney realize that it was not giving them the happiness they had been hankering for. They continued to lead a bohemian life of booze, pills and women. Lennon patronized prostitutes when groupies were unavailable. Beatle tours turned into *Zatyricon*-like pleasure orgies; its façade of celebration kept most of the squalid details from the media.

They returned to their home base triumphant but also physically and emotionally battered -- and only to find more pressures brought by more album and movie projects waiting to be fulfilled. This constricting situation put the Beatles at the mercy of work schedules, bringing them to the threshold of their endurance. Instead of surrendering, however, they capitalized on it and made it into art. It became clear to them that their unprecedented popularity, the kind that exceeded Presley's fame, was for them to cultivate. They lived up to its demands through perseverance and renouncement; their personal complaints became songs.

Movie idols

If Presley made movies at the height of his career, so could the Beatles at this stage, when the demand for Beatles products was extraordinarily high. United Artists signed them up for a three-picture deal. They conceptualized it with each full-length feature having an album component of the movie's soundtrack.

In 1964, the Beatles made their first full-length feature film *A Hard Day's Night*. They enhanced their status as musical icons by converting themselves into big screen stars, continuing the tradition of pop stars turning into movie idols, the way Presley did.

The movie captures four lovable musicians constantly feeling the perils of popularity, engaged in cat-and-mouse chases with hysterical fans, with cops and elders caught in the melee. The movie's thin plot centers on how the moptops outwit their fans at their game by constantly staying one step ahead. In between, the Beatles sings about labor, love, and fame. The comical approach of this documentary-cum-concert successfully captures the Beatles' magic and the mania of their followers. As to be expected, they lived up to their White Negro roots by coming up with a comedy farce straight from the Marx

Brothers.

The Beatles released its component album, *A Hard Day's Night*, their third collection, on July 10, 1964. Lennon and McCartney continued to release better songs as singles than the songs in the albums. The songs in the album were an improvement over the previous two, but were not good enough to be considered brilliant numbers. Still dependent on rehashing and on Martin to cover them up with sounds so that the imitation did not show, the Beatles were, with this album, at the crossroad of better creativity.

The first Beatles album of all self-composed songs, *A Hard Day's Night* was by Lennon and McCartney. It was a breakthrough album. The group finally realized their dream of coming up with an album entirely of Beatles-made songs, none of them a filler, a dream they had from the start. Only Dylan could come up with an album of all-original material during that time. Tracing the creative roots of the songs in the album, it would be revealed that Lennon and McCartney had become more sufficient at rehashing, having practically perfected the art, with the Bob Dylan influence.

The Beatles released "A Hard Day's Night" and "Things We Said Today" as a single simultaneously with the *A Hard Day's Night* album on July 10, 1964.

The title of **"A Hard Day's Night"** (LENNON-McCartney) most likely comes from the story of *Sad Michael,* from *In His Own Write*. The story went*: "There was no reason for Michael to be sad that morning, (the little wretch); everyone liked him (the scab). He had a hard days night (underscoring ours) that day, for Michael was a Cocky Watchtower."* But the generally acknowledged source of the title is Starr. In an interview with DJ Dave Hull in 1964, he said, "We went to do a job, and we'd worked all day and we happened to work all night. I came up still thinking it was day I suppose, and I said, 'It's been a hard day...' and I looked around and saw it was dark so I said, 'Night!' So we came to 'A Hard Day's Night'."

Lennon explained this big discrepancy in the 1980 *Playboy* interview, "I was going home in the car and Dick Lester suggested the title, 'Hard Day's Night' from something Ringo had said. I had used it in *In His Own Write,* but it was an off-the-cuff remark by Ringo. You know, one of those malapropisms. A Ringo-ism, where he said it not to be funny...just said it. So Dick Lester said, 'We are going to use that title'." But McCartney disagreed in the 1994 interview for *The Beatles Anthology*, countering that it was The Beatles and not Lester who decided to use the verbal misstep as a movie title.

The original lyrics contained the line, *"But when I get home to you, I find my tiredness is through, and I feel alright."* But *Evening Standard* journalist Maureen Cleave, Lennon's friend, opined that "tiredness" is a weak word so Lennon changed it to *"I find the things that you do, will make me feel all right."*

Lennon wrote the song, but McCartney sang the middle eight for it was too high for Lennon's vocal range.

McCartney wrote **"Things We Said Today"** (Lennon-MCCARTNEY) for

Jane Asher, the subject of most of his songs during the time. He wrote it while on a cruise in the Caribbean with Asher along with Starr and partner Maureen Cox.

Even during this growth period, Lennon and McCartney continued to write mundane and sophomoric lyrics in the last verse of **"I Should Have Known Better"** (LENNON-McCartney). It opens with a harmonica intro, the last time it was used in a Beatles song. Lennon repeated a line for the rhyming effect. But the glum tone is an early influence from Dylan.

Lennon converted **"If I Fell"** (LENNON-McCartney) from the Fourmost's close harmony style. His lead vocal double-tracked, and he also played the harmonica, one of the last Beatles songs to use the mouth instrument. This song indicated that the Beatles was moving out of this overused style. The song tells of one of Lennon's extramarital affairs, and it was his first attempt to write a ballad.

Lennon converted Cris Montez's "Let's Dance" to **"I'm Happy Just To Dance With You"** (LENNON-McCartney) with its hectic Bo Diddley rhythm structure. Sung by Harrison who had not learned to make his own material, Lennon straightforwardly stated he would have not performed the formula song himself.

McCartney composed the Latin-flavored love song **"And I Love Her"** (Lennon-MCCARTNEY). Lennon contributed the middle eight (*"A love like hers / Could never die / As long as I / Have you near me"*). There's a contradiction here. McCartney also claims having written it. He said," I wrote this on my own." It ends in the *Tierce de Picardie* technique similar to Bach.

When they were laying down the tracks, publisher Dick James and Martin opined to Lennon and McCartney that the original composition lacked a good middle-eight and was repetitive. At this stage of their career, the tandem had to be told of a song's areas of improvement. Open-minded, they proceeded to rework the number.

Thus, Lennon helped McCartney in the middle-eight when unable to expand a tune a partner created, and the other partner helped by providing the bridge, most of the time Lennon doing the part. As they had distinctively different styles, such contributions provided an effective contrast.

According to Pollack, this song has a close tonal design to Robert Schumann's "Dichterliebe (Poet's Love)."

"Tell Me Why" (LENNON-McCartney) is an adaptation of the Black-girl-group sound from New York known for its falsetto. Harrison usually sang harmony with Lennon and McCartney, but he was not included in this song because it went over his usual pitch. It tells of Lennon's belief that when parents leave or die, children are left with the feeling that they are to blame. Words used in the lyrics came from arguments from wife Cynthia. It's a work song. He knocked it off based on a request to come with an upbeat song.

The Beatles released **"Can't Buy Me Love"** (Lennon-MCCARTNEY) as a single.

Lennon adapted the chord progression of "It Won't Be Long" in **"Any Time At All"** (LENNON-McCartney). This is an unfinished song. McCartney suggested to record it without the middle-eight, using the same chords as he had not written it. On mixing time, there was still no word that is why it appears this way on the LP.

Lennon wrote **"I'll Cry Instead"** (LENNON-McCartney) after hearing the Dylan debut album, *The Freewheelin' Bob Dylan*. A French DJ gave McCartney an album copy during their 1963 visit to Paris, France. McCartney shared the copy with Lennon, who eventually came up with "I'll Cry Instead" as a version of Dylan's style. Lennon is metaphorical, as well as confessional (*"I've got a chip on my shoulder that's bigger than my feet / I can't talk to people that I meet."*). It pre-dates "Help!" which is a "cry for help," to use wife Cynthia's words. She said, "It reflects the frustration he felt at that time. He was the idols of millions, but the freedom and fun of the early days had gone."

When McCartney came up with "Can't Buy Me Love," which proved to be a better song, "I'll Cry Instead" got bumped off from the *Help!* movie soundtrack.

The Beatles released "Things We Said Today" as a single.

Influenced by The Shirelles style, **"When I Get Home"** (LENNON-McCartney) rehashes some parts of this album. It starts off with a refrain like "Tell Me Why" and contains one line from "A Hard Day's Night" (*"But when I get home to you"*).

Lennon converted the chords of Del Shannon's "Runaway," "Hey Little Girl" and others and rehashed them to come up with **"I'll Be Back"** (LENNON-McCartney). With its flamenco-style acoustic guitar, author Bill Harry wrote "… And he came up with a completely different song. As had been established by this album, Martin opened and closed Beatles album with strong materials. He placed the weaker songs towards the end but closed it what he described as "a bang." With 'I'll Be Back' as album closer, there seemed to have been a major shift."

Pollack observed the *A Hard Day's Night* songs "anticipate the folk rock style heard later on *Rubber Soul*."

"I Feel Fine" / "She's a Woman" single

The Beatles released the "I Feel Fine" and "She's a Woman" single on November 27, 1964.

While recording **"I Feel Fine"** (Lennon-McCartney), Lennon's guitar caused a feedback, for sure, an aberration. True to his developing instinct at chance art, he seized the accident and used it as the song's intro. Lennon left his guitar open too close to the amplifier, producing the feedback. McCartney's bass resonating an octave higher than Lennon's pickup produced the final version.

However, Lennon who played lead guitar for the band adapted the distinctive bouncy but bluesy guitar riff from R&B singer Bobby Parker's "Watch Your Step" and its rolling and Latin-flavored drums. The band covered the song in the Cavern from 1961 to 1962. But it was not a complete rip off altogether. Lennon added three-part harmony and a new middle-eight section. Parker could not claim copyright infringement as his song was nicked from "Manteca" of Dizzy Gillespie, a White Negro himself.

"She's a Woman" (LENNON-McCartney) adapted Little Richard's screamer "Be-Bop-A-Lula" in its use of pulsating bass chord in place of the scat chanting "Be-Bop-A-Lula," a phrase in the song. The line *"Turns me on when I get lonely"* refers to their introduction to marijuana by Dylan.

Beatles for Sale

The direct impact of Dylan on Lennon was staggering. It was so primal that it recalled Lennon modeling his image after Presley. Meeting Dylan in person changed Lennon as he initially tried to reshape himself in Dylan's image. He adopted an American twang and, more importantly, started to aspire for relevance, beginning with himself.

In *Beatles for Sale*, their fourth album released on December 4, 1963, the Beatles started to engage in social commentary. They accommodated ideas on social responsibility in their songs, thus redirecting their artistic orientations to existentialist issues expressed in realistic and surrealistic terms. The combination of the direct and indirect influences of Dylan showed the Beatles the new direction they were aspiring for, thus bringing about a new batch of songs that attempted to be meaningful. This brought the Beatles to this growth process as songwriters and musicians.

Their personal and civil responsibilities began to heavily reflect in their music that differed from their objective approach to songwriting. The taboo of expressing subjective feelings and experiences had been removed. Their characters developed from childhood and how these characters developed as the Beatles, and Lennon's rebellion, manifested in their songs as sarcasm, aggression, and bitterness. McCartney's romance manifested itself as lightheartedness, optimism, and security with a dreamer's perspective.

The first Beatles song in this growth period is **"No Reply"** (LENNON-McCartney). Lennon converted the Rays' 1957 doo-wop hit "Silhouettes," by making its happy theme a heartbreaking one. And people did notice the change in the duo's songwriting style. For instance, Dick James, their Northern Songs Ltd. partner, commented, "That's the first complete song you've written, the first song which resolves itself. It's a complete story." McCartney sang lead vocals despite being a Lennon work because the latter had shredded his voice from too much singing.

Lennon used the word "clown" in **"I'm A Loser"** (LENNON-McCartney), which he had been avoiding as a lyricist for the longest time (*"Although I laugh and I act like a clown / Beneath this mask I am wearing a frown"*). Lennon revealed: "That's me in my Dylan period, 'coz that's got the word 'clown' in it. I always objected to the word 'clown' -- or clown image that (David) Bowie was using 'coz that was artsy-fartsy -- but Dylan had used it so I thought it was all right and it rhymed with whatever I was doing."

Lennon even copied the Dylan-like blast of harmonica in the end. Definitely, Lennon failed to match the loneliness evoked by Dylan's "Boots of Spanish Leather" and "Ballad in Plain D." It was, however, a brave move to introduce candor and sincerity into a Beatle song. Until this time, Dylan's influence on the Beatles did not extend beyond copying his singing style. Although Lennon was singing about a man in a failed relationship with a female, he is referring to himself as a constant loser.

The melancholic mood of **"Baby's In Black'"** (Lennon-McCartney) suggests Dylan's early influence on Lennon, particularly his *The Freewheeling' Bob Dylan* album. The "baby" referred to is Kitchherr who had taken to wearing black to lament boyfriend Sutcliffe death by abrupt brain hemorrhage. As his way of mourning a dear friend's death, Lennon started off this song, later joined in by McCartney, making it collaborative.

Lennon sings **"Rock 'n' Roll Music"** (Berry) with the same manic fervor as Berry. Lennon recorded it "live" -- with Martin playing the piano. This song demonstrated the Beatles' charisma as a livewire act during performances.

As a tribute to Buddy Holly, who died in 1959, McCartney adapted **"I'll Follow the Sun"** (Lennon-MCCARTNEY) from Holly's style. This was a pre-fame song by the Quarry Men, which the Beatles revived for this album.

Dr. Feelgood and The Interns originally recorded an obscure song the Beatles used to do in their Cavern days, **"Mr. Moonlight"** (Roy Lee Johnson), featuring Lennon's rough lead vocals.

Part of their Cavern days repertoire, **"Kansas City" / "Hey-Hey-Hey-Hey!"** is a cover of little Richard's medley of his two big hits, "Kansas City" (Jerry Lieber / Mike Stoller / Richard Penniman) and "Hey Hey Hey Hey" (Little Richard). McCartney does a perfect copy of Little Richard's shouted vocals. This song also served as a model for Lennon and McCartney when they had two short songs which they could no longer expand and which they could combine into a full song.

"Eight Days A Week" (Lennon-McCartney) used inversion. Fade-outs usually ended songs, but the Beatles did the curious thing of beginning this song with a fade-in. This was curious since the song begins the album's B-side.

"Eight Days A Week" was also the first unfinished song that Lennon and McCartney took to the studio and there experimented in different ways of recording it. This practice allowed the Beatles to interact, expanding the song's possibilities, permitting them a greater degree of experimentation. Such a practice would become the Beatles' regular recording procedure, which explains why there are many Beatles songs with different versions.

McCartney picked the intriguing title from Starr. Starr would regularly say,

"Oh, working hard eight days a week." Lennon and McCartney were always on the lookout for such stuff, which they could use to start off new songs. Some believe though, that "Eight Days a Week" was coined by Starr to describe the Beatles' terrible work schedule. There is also the other attribution according to McCartney himself that the phrase came from Lennon's driver. Because McCartney lost his license, he had to be chauffeured by Lennon's driver. During the drive, McCartney would often ask him, "What kind of a week have you had? Have you been working hard?" The driver habitually blurted, "I've been working eight days a week, Paul!"

"Words of Love" (Holly) is the only Holly song the Beatles recorded even though he was one of their White Negro icons. Lennon admitted, "At least the first forty songs we wrote were Buddy Holly influenced." As some sort of a tribute to Holly, they never changed its arrangement. Lennon and McCartney harmonized for a faithful reproduction of Holly's style. To achieve a similar sound to Holly's "Everyday," Starr played a packing case instead of drums.

Lennon used to sing the lead vocals of Perkins' **"Honey Don't"** (Perkins) during live performances until he turned it over to Starr for the latter's token lead vocal per album. The original title of the first Perkins hit had a comma ("Honey, Don't"), but the Beatles deleted it when they covered it for this album.

"Every Little Thing" (Lennon-MCCARTNEY) is another song for Asher adapted from "Things We Said Today." But here, McCartney's lead vocal, as well as harmonies and instrumental counterpoint, provided new dimension to the song.

Lennon wrote **"I Don't Want To Spoil the Party"** (LENNON-McCartney) in country-style while he was still grappling with his guitar-playing technique. He recalled, "In the early days, I wrote less material than Paul because he was more competent on guitar than I. He taught me quite a lot of guitar really."

McCartney wrote **"What You're Doing"** (Lennon-MCCARTNEY) in the Spector style with the intro drumming adapted from The Ronettes' "Be My Baby." It is about Asher, who was giving him the runaround. Martin added piano, showing the Beatles' infinite possibilities of improving their songs inside the recording studio.

"Everybody's Trying To Be My Baby" (Perkins) completes the three Perkins songs in this album, paying him higher royalties than his post-"Blue Suede Shoes" songs combined. Martin subjected Harrison's voice to excessive STEED (single tape and echo delay) treatment, producing considerable delay in the original sound and its echo, giving prominence to the echo. This distortion begins a significant direction for the Beatles to create sounds entirely their own.

Beatles for Sale reintroduced Black music to Americans and made it respectable. During this period, the group's pervasive influence resulted in mass acceptance regardless of quality. The White Americans regarded Black music as ethnic music and disdained it as a result. When the Beatles recorded them at the peak of their fame, it was recognition Black music was the music of the times. But in reality, the Beatles used Black songs as convenient substitutes for original materials it could not produce. Very White Negro!

Like the earlier albums, the Beatles tossed in more values than what the market expected. They made a clear manifestation of moving away from their regular instrumentation, adding more percussion instruments which were highly adaptable to live performances. In a calculated way, they finally decided to get out of the last three albums' musical parameters. They began to use chance decisions in their song making and as a result of spontaneous input and incidents in the recording studio. This necessitated a change in Martin's role. Since the Beatles were working as a production unit, they no longer relied entirely on Martin when it came to technical issues because they had taken part in the process.

The majority of the album's songs remains firmly rooted on juvenile aspirations, although there were fine examples of introspection picked up from Dylan. Their somber mood was an important step towards the group moving to a higher level of creativity. Although they continued to sing with incongruity between lyrics and melody, there was an obvious attempt on the part of Lennon and McCartney to take themselves seriously.

But Martin considers *Beatles For Sale* as their weakest album. He stated, "It's not their most memorable ones."

"Ticket to Ride" / "Yes It Is" single

The group issued "Ticket to Ride" and "Yes It Is" as single on April 9, 1965.

"Ticket to Ride" (LENNON-McCartney) opens with a guitar riff from the unreleased Beatles song "That Means a Lot" turned droning. Then it proceeds to be a conversion of the Kinks' "You Really Got Me."

Lennon first sang **"Ticket to Ride"** during the filming of *Help!*'s skiing sequence in Austria. According to journalist Don Short, prostitutes in Hamburg, Germany, were required to have regular medical check-ups and were given a card to signify a clean bill of health. They carried them around like a ticket before a customer can "ride." A "ride" is British slang for sex. Music publisher Dick James recalled Lennon mentioning to him the phrase "She's got a ticket to ride" during rehearsals for the Beatles Christmas show at the Hammersmith Odeon in 1964. He encouraged Lennon to develop it into a full song. But the most plausible origin of this title was the Negro spiritual "If I've Got Ticket, Can I Ride?" to which Little Richard exposed Lennon during the second Hamburg trip.

Lennon considered this song the precursor of heavy metal music, with McCartney's driving riff and Starr's heavy drumming. This song was a defining moment for the Beatles as they were moptops turning into potheads.

With similarities in chord progression and harmonies, **"Yes It Is"** (LENNON-McCartney) is a rehash of "This Boy."

Help!, the album and the movie

Directed by Richard Lester, based on the screenplay written by Marc Behm and Christopher Wood, *Help!*, the movie, gave the Beatles the opportunity to take their fans into a virtual tour of the world. The story starts when Starr loses the ring given to him by a fan, which turns out to be the ring worn by those to be sacrificed to the god Kili. Unknown to him, he is supposed to be the next sacrifice, which is why Kili's followers are out to get him. He, in turn, tries to stay ahead of them to stay alive. The other Beatles do everything to help Starr get rid of the ring and the whole thing turns into a mad chase of the pursued with his loyal friends and the pursuers with all sorts of get-that-ring-at-all-costs schemes. When he is about to be slaughtered, Starr proves his bravery and the ring just falls off his finger.

The Beatles did the film while heavily taking drugs as a recreation. Leading double lives, the White Negroes were living the hardship of filming the full-length feature and working on the companion soundtrack. During the filming, they had bouts of continuous giggling -- no doubt a sign of their being high on drugs -- thus forgetting their lines.

The *Help!* album, on the other hand, has introspective lyrics and complicated melodies as a result of their collaboration in their extended recording sessions. The album was the first important indication the Beatles were itching to leave the growth phase, judging from the original songs in it, even as it still had cover versions, which they could not give up yet because they were useful in coming up with the required two albums annually. In true White Negro way, they used fillers, no matter how mediocre were those songs.

The Beatles had no choice but to be content with what they could produce and record because their concert tours ate up much of their time. As those global stints were appurtenances of their fame, they could not go without them. But the truth is: Lennon entered his Dylan phase without fully leaving his sophomoric songwriting techniques; McCartney had his classical rock phase even as he continued to use clichés instead of fresh expressions; Harrison started to write songs, entering the realm that was basically Lennon and McCartney's; and Starr continued to deliver great beats and a lot of charm. They still relied heavily on Martin to embellish their individual compositions, giving their songs character. They would never acquire his technical savvy so they left it to him to translate musical decisions into production terms.

"Help!" / "I'm Down" single

The Beatles released "Help!" and "I'm Down" as a single on July 23, 1965 at the same time as the *Help!* album.

"Help!" (LENNON-McCartney) has a strong similarity to "Chains," a song which they earlier covered in the *Please Please Me* LP. Despite its faster tempo, "Help" was an obvious conversion of "Chains," especially in terms of phrasing. In theme, it resembled Anka's "Lonely Boy." Cleave suggested to Lennon the use of multisyllable lyrics.

Lennon wrote "Help!" during his "fat Elvis period" as he told *Playboy* in 1980. He had been living a bacchanalian life, which caused him to be overweight. He wanted out, but could not. So he literally screamed for help in the song, expressing his stress and anxiety, because he hated and pitied himself. He was unprepared for the global fame he had achieved with the Beatles. It was depriving him of a personal life. Starting out in the downbeat style of Dylan, it was jacked up to make it an attention-grabbing song.

On another level, "Help!" could be taken as a turn on song. There's an overload of references: *"I've changed my mind," "I've opened up the doors,"* an obvious reference to Aldous Huxley's book on his experiences with the mind-altering drug Mescaline entitled *The Doors of Perception*, the same book where Jim Morrison picked The Doors' name. Of course, Huxley lifted his book's title from William Blake's quote: *"If the doors of perception were cleansed everything would appear to man as it is, infinite."*

Lennon regarded "Help!" as a "genuine song."

The Beatles wanted to replace Little Richard's "Long Tall Sally" from their repertoire, which McCartney re-wrote as **"I'm Down"** (Lennon-MCCARTNEY). Regardless of its dubious origination complete with an imitation of Richard's wild, hoarse, and screaming voice, the Fab Four had a supposedly original song in "I'm Down." But critic Richie Unterberger pointed out there is significant differences between source and rehash which is an important characteristic of Beatles' copied songs, something that gives a semblance of originality.

Help! album

The album opens with "Help!" which was released as a single.

In **"The Night Before"** (Lennon-MCCARTNEY), Lennon used an electric piano in a recorded song for the first time.

"You've Got to Hide Your Love Away" (LENNON-McCartney) is a song about Epstein's love for Lennon, which Lennon converted from Dylan's "The Lonesome Ballad of Hattie Carroll." Lennon adapted Dylan's use of the acoustic format and typical guitar-plucking style. The nasal, spoken delivery of lyrics that makes surprise vocal leaps toward the end line reveals the song's similarity to Dylan's style of singing. The use of such poetic devices as similes, metaphors, and alliteration is a manifestation of Dylan's style.

Rumor had it the song was written for Epstein, who had reportedly made some sort of pass at Lennon while they were on vacation together. Influenced by Dylan's *Another Side Of Bob Dylan*, the album features more personal and depressing tracks.

Lennon revealed his White Negro roots by stating: "That's me in my Dylan period. I am like a chameleon, influenced by whatever is going on. If Elvis can do it, I can do it. If The Everly Brothers can do it, Paul and me can. Same with Bob Dylan. When I was a teenager, I used to write poetry, but I was always trying to hide my feelings. I was in Kenwood and I would just be writing songs.

The period would be for songwriting and so, everyday, I would attempt to write a song, and it's one of those that you sort of sing a bit sadly to yourself, *'Here I stand, head in hand.'* Instead of projecting myself into a situation, I would try to express what I felt about myself, which I had done in my books. I think it was Dylan that helped me realize that..."

"You've Got to Hide Your Love Away" did not use any electronic instruments; it was primarily acoustic. Ronnie Scott played combined tenor and alto flutes in ¾ time signature. Lennon resorted to this convenient substitution to tone down the Dylan flavor. The flute substituted for the Dylan-like harmonica. This was the very first time that a Beatle song used the flute. It was also the first time a musician outside of the group played in a Beatles song.

Lennon maintained the song was "an impression of Dylan," while McCartney opined it was a "direct copy of Dylan." The lyrics' enunciation when sang is typical of Dylan's use of melisma with altered vowels. *"You've got to hide your love away"* is sung by Lennon as *"Yeeew've got to hayed...that lerv ay-wayyy."*

"I Need You" (Harrison) is Harrison's love song for then girlfriend Pattie Boyd, using a wah-wah pedal for the first time.

McCartney threatens Asher in **"Another Girl"** (Lennon-MCCARTNEY) so that she will pay attention to him because "another girl" is waiting to be his girlfriend. McCartney played lead guitar instead of Harrison, the group's designated lead guitarist.

"You're Going To Lose That Girl" (LENNON-McCartney) is an answering song, which did not make it to the final cut of the *Help!* movie. McCartney commented about this song and other tracks in the album, " It's a bit much to call them fillers because I think they were a bit more than that, and each one of them made it past the Beatles test. We all had to like it."

"Ticket to Ride" was released as a single.

Originally recorded by Buck Owens and the Buckaroos, **"Act Naturally"** (Voni Morrison / Johnny Russell) is the last non-original song to appear in a Beatles album. Starr sang it in country style.

Lennon converted **"It's Only Love"** (LENNON-McCartney) from Anka's "Lonely Boy." He inverted its chorus-verse form to verse-chorus form. Its graceful melody also originated from the song's inner rhymes. But the lyrics are sophomoric. In an attempt to be literary, Lennon jammed the first verse with 17 assonating syllables *("I get high when I see you go by / My, oh, my / When you sigh, my mind inside just Flies / Butterfly / Why am I so shy / When I'm beside you?")*. Lennon admitted in 1969 he hated this song for its terrible lyrics.

"You Like Me Too Much" (Harrison) inverted the piano duet of the 1939 hit of Larry Clinton and His Orchestra featuring Bea Wein, "Heart and Soul," music by Hoagy Carmichael and lyrics by Frank Loesser. McCartney and Martin played the tune side-by-side on a Steinway piano.

Getting a song composed by Harrison to be recorded by the Beatles had always been a problem for him. He could only squeeze in a maximum of two songs per album. Beyond that, Lennon and McCartney were against it. Besides reducing the number of Lennon-McCartney songs per album, Harrison had not mastered the art of rehashing. Lennon and McCartney found the songs Harrison presented as too derivative. Having turned pros in the art and having a wide knowledge of popular and non-mainstream songs, they found it easy to identify the origin of a Harrison composition. Until this period, Harrison could be considered not a good enough White Negro. This held him back from being more productive as a songwriter.

McCartney wrote **"Tell Me What You See"** (Lennon-MCCARTNEY) with "I'm Looking Through You" as model. The song is once more about Asher with whom he was having an on-again, off-again relationship. For not having a tune and a theme that fit the movie's narrative, Director Dick Lester rejected its inclusion in the soundtrack of the *Help!* movie.

McCartney's Auntie Gin, his father's youngest sister, loved **"I've Just Seen a Face"** (Lennon-MCCARTNEY) so much he gave it the subtitle "Auntie Gin's Theme." He wrote it during the pre-fame days and played it on the piano at family gatherings. The song represented his attempt to do a bluegrass tempo song.

That **"Yesterday"** (Lennon-MCCARTNEY) came to McCartney in a dream is an unsettled issue but it is generally accepted that Martin heard it for the first time at the posh George V hotel in Paris with the rest of the Beatles during the tour of France. When he woke up, he played it on the upright piano and called it "Scrambled Eggs" with the opening lines as *"Scrambled eggs / Oh, you've got such lovely legs."*

McCartney narrated: "I woke up with a lovely tune in my head. I thought, 'That's great, I wonder what that is?' There was an upright piano next to me, to the right of the bed by the window. I got out of bed, sat at the piano, found G, found F sharp minor 7th -- and that leads you through then to B to E minor, and finally back to E. It all leads forward logically. I liked the melody a lot, but because I'd dreamed it, I couldn't believe I'd written it. I thought, 'No, I've never written anything like this before.' But I had the tune, which was the most magic thing!"

As the melody came to him completely, McCartney was worried he might have unconsciously picked it from another artist's song. The group and Martin could not agree if it was appropriate material as it was clearly not in their style. It took 18 months for the exceptional song to be re-worked, completed, and be accepted into an album. McCartney wrote the proper lyrics. Martin suggested a one-word title.

McCartney recorded it by himself, with him playing an acoustic guitar and backed up by a string quartet. But as it would turn out, the melody was an unconscious distillation of Ray Charles' version of Hoagy Carmichael's "Georgia On My Mind," a case of cryptomnesia. Cryptomnesia is the scientific term for subconsciously plagiarizing some else's work.

"Yesterday" has similarities in the lyrics and rhyming schemes (the use of words ending in "ay") of Nat "King" Cole's "Answer Me My Love": "...*You were mine* yesterday / *I believed that love was* here to stay / *Won't you tell me where I've gone astray / Please answer me, my love...*"

McCartney slowed down the song's tempo and pared down the first stanza's lyrics to its essential, the first line from **"***You were mine yesterday***"** to *"Yesterday,"* made a specific quotation as highlighted, *"I believe that love was here to stay"* to *"Now it looks they're here to stay..."* He contemporized *"Won't you tell me where I've gone astray"* into the third stanza's *"...Something I said wrong..."*

This explains how the working title "Scrambled Eggs" changed to the final title "Yesterday."

McCartney annoyed director Richard Lester when he used the *Help!* stage to compose the lyrics, threatening to remove the piano he used. Breakthrough came while on a trip to Portugal in May 1965. McCartney recounted, "I remember mulling over the tune "Yesterday,' and suddenly getting these little one-word openings to the verse. I started to develop the idea...'*da-da da, yester-day, sudden-ly, fun-il-ly, mer-il-ly and Yes-ter-day, that's good. All my troubles seemed so far away.*' It's easy to rhyme those a's, nay, today, away, play, stay, there's a lot of rhymes and those fall in quiet places, so I gradually pieced it together from that journey. Sud-den-ly, and 'b' again, another easy rhyme; e, me, tree, fleas, we and I had the basis of it." McCartney completed the lyrics when he vacationed with Asher in the Lisbon house of Bruce Welsh using his acoustic guitar.

But there's a big difference in theme between the two songs. While "Answer Me My Love" insists for a reconciliation, "Yesterday" accepts the rejection, giving it a dramatic inflection. The lyrics construction of the latter is not repetitive, the delivery of message direct to the point and tighter. This makes the "Yesterday" more mature song-word construction, clearly an improvement of source. It was this process of editing, the process of selecting what to copy and improving on what had been copied that made the Beatles reprocessed songs have the semblance of originality and a freshness all its own.

Italian producer and songwriter Lilli Greco also hypothesized "Yesterday" to be a rehash of "Piccere' Che Vene a Dicere," a 19th century Neapolitan song. But this is an unrealistic assertion. Lennon and McCartney don't read music sheets. (Note: Could "Answer Me My Love" be based from this Neapolitan song?)

Theoretically speaking, "Yesterday" does not qualify as a Beatle song as it had zero input from the other Beatles. In fact, McCartney toyed with the idea of releasing it as a solo single. But Epstein was quick to reject it. Regardless of the song's critical merits, the recording's morbid suggestion was that other Beatle members were dispensable from the communal ownership. Although the exclusion of the other Beatles in the song's creation was unintended,

"Yesterday" was proof that a Beatle could remain sufficient by himself.

Originally recorded by R&B and rock 'n' roll singer Larry Williams, the Beatles started singing **"Dizzy Miss Lizzy"** (Williams) back in their Hamburg concerts and did so up to the time of their club gigs in Liverpool, with Lennon doing the raucous vocals.

With McCartney's "Yesterday" as the penultimate song in this album and Lennon's "Dizzy Miss Lizzy" as the last track, it started to become obvious that Lennon and McCartney were irretrievably divided and contradictory in their personal preferences for song style.

Reverse cultural osmosis

The Beatles needed to develop their songs to gain acceptance in the rarified domain of intellectuals and the art set. The label of purveyor of plebeian taste generated by their mass art piqued their egos and became an irritating designation. The youth who created Beatlemania had advance in age with them so they expected something more.

Since the Beatles themselves were aware Beatlemania would not last forever, they did as much as they could to maintain their eminence. They took efforts to improve their songs by adopting musical practices and procedures that departed from their habitual format. Gradually, they had to abandon their roots so they could grow.

The second US tour exposed them to new ways of doing things that focused on the intellect as the central point of departure. Dylan and Spector showed them the way.

The Beatles' use of drugs for recreation, inherited from their new musical godfather, Dylan, was most pronounced during this period. They started to produce mature songs.

Drug use is a gnawing problem that persists in the field of popular music because of its necessity. In the 1950s and 1960s, it was a prohibited practice that removed the impunity of rock 'n' roll musicians from exposing themselves as drug users without social and legal repercussions. The Beatles, who as White Negroes imbibed the practice as a matter of progression, were not beyond reproach. They became uncommonly vulnerable to it as their celebrity exacted above-normal requirements under conventional circumstances.

They used to take multi-colored pills to help them keep up with the rigors of live performance and the travels that went with it. To develop the energy and stamina required by extended hours of stage performance, they took uppers but had to toss in downers later to get out of the hyped physical state that prevented them from resting or sleeping. This vicious cycle of pill popping developed almost into a dependency.

When Dylan rolled them their first joints, they had developed a receptive mind for drug experimentation. The induction of the Beatles to marijuana use was painless. They were neither hesitant nor resistant initial users. Dylan introduced the quartet to a different style of drug use. The new practice was not a necessity as much as a way of life. It expanded the user's consciousness; the altered state resulted in quasi-omnipotence, a temporary shield against vulnerability.

The heightened and induced consciousness improved their artistry, which they found appealing and promising as White Negroes groping for new ways of expressing their art. It also made them insensitive to principle compromises as celebrity figures. Before accepting their Member of the British Empire investiture, the quartet smoked marijuana in the comfort room of Buckingham Palace.

Lennon and Harrison, along with their wives Cynthia and Patti, respectively, were unaware inductees to LSD use. Their London dentist-friend laced acid into their after-dinner drinks at a dinner party without their consent. The experience was a surrealistic trip, preventing the mind from functioning normally. An ordinary red light turns to a fire ready to engulf. It speeds mental processes and brings it to a manic level of creativity. Lennon called the experience both tarrying and fantastic.

Starr, Lennon, and Harrison began to take drugs regularly after a trip to California with Peter Fonda and a group of rock stars. They prodded McCartney to drop acid, but he did not budge. He became the subject of peer pressure, receiving the epithet "Mr. Clean, squeaky clean." McCartney eventually gave in a year later, by coincidence. Although he never took LSD during recording sessions, Lennon took acid by mistake instead of a pep pill. This made him go on an LSD trip, which forced McCartney to bring him home. Out of sympathy, McCartney ingested the substance as a sort of gesture, like two buddies sharing an experience, whatever it is. After many bad trips, Lennon eventually stopped popping LSD.

By this time, the individual Beatles had gained artistic confidence as they had collectively established themselves as a major musical group. Martin continued to be a collaborator. He encouraged them to experiment in their songs by expanding the self-imposed musical boundaries that existed in their minds.

Prime targets of their experimentations were traditional ideas and concepts used in their birth phase, like rehashing the rock & roll idiom and song and recording concepts. Lennon was the most responsive to this challenge. Martin introduced them to the use of classical instruments and translated their musical ideas onto tape. He manifested the abstract sounds that existed in their minds.

For the Beatles, LSD was an experiment in the spiritual search for enlightenment. They hoped the opening of various levels of consciousness would improve their mental and spiritual capacities. Lennon believed acid allowed unlimited access to creative and spiritual states as LSD send the user into the center of his mind where vivid colors explode. It was Dylan's influence on Lennon, an early manifestation of which reflected in Lennon wanting to reinvent himself after Dylan's image.

With its emphasis on sensuality and energy, stressing an eight-to-the-bar rhythm with a strong backbeat, rock and roll became rock. This year, 1964, saw the shift in terminology, suggesting continuity with, and a break from, rock and roll music. Rock became music for listening, no longer strictly for dancing. And the Beatles and other British groups were at the heart of this breakthrough change.

"We Can Work It Out" / "Day Tripper"

"We were just getting better, technically, and musically, that's all," Lennon narrated about the making of the *Rubber Soul* album. "Finally we took over the studio. In the early days, we had to take what we were given, we didn't know how you can get more bass. We were learning the technique on *Rubber Soul*. We were more precise about making the album, that's all, and (we) took over the cover and everything."

Simultaneous with the *Rubber Soul* album, the Beatles released the single "We Can Work It Out" and "Day Tripper" as a double A-side on December 3, 1965. For the Beatles, this ended the practice of releasing the superior song as A-side and a substandard song as B-side. This suggested that the Beatles had become more quality conscious.

McCartney wrote the optimistic lines (*"Try to see it my way"*), while Lennon created the pessimistic ones (*'Life is very short'*) in **"We Can Work it Out"** (Lennon-McCartney). This is another Asher song. As an actress, she joined the Bristol Old Vic Company, which meant she would no longer be available for McCartney as much as he wanted. McCartney wrote the song to ask her to see thing his way if she did not want their relationship to end. The use of slow triplet to the final refrain reflects Holly's "That'll Be the Day." According to www.beatles-discography.com, Ena Sharples used to play the song's harmonium part in the long running British soap opera *Coronation Street*.

The guitar riff of **"Day Tripper"** (LENNON-McCartney) has several attributions. The one right after the opening drum solo came from Ray Charles' "What'd I Say." In structure, it is also similar to "Twist and Shout" with the shouted ascending harmonies followed by a break in the music. Lennon might have also wanted to exceed the opening of The Rolling Stones' "(I Can't Get No) Satisfaction" in doing this signature riff.

Lennon told *Rolling Stone* in 1970 that the main idea of "Day Tripper" was his but it was McCartney who finished it off. This was corroborated by McCartney, who admitted in *Many Years From Now* that it's about drugs, probably about his reluctance to use LSD even as Lennon and Harrison had been using them since 1965. This is a double-meaning song. On the surface, it's about a female who turns the singer on (*"She's a big teaser,"* originally *"She's a prick teaser"*). The undertone is about part-time drug users or what's usually called as "weekend hippies."

Rubber Soul

Seeing the *Rubber Soul* album's front cover is an unsettling confrontation.

The Beatles' moptop had turned shaggy with Harrison, Starr, and McCartney evading the beholder's gaze. Lennon looks directly into the camera, but with an unfathomable smile. The camera's fish-eye lens captures the Beatles from the foreground, though the lens gives an altered perspective. The photo is hazy, a departure from the sharp perspective of previous album covers. The title types follow an unfamiliar font that is best described as flowery. Recognizing these unfamiliarities, the cover unsettles. To perceptive fans, they are clues that something vital had happened to the Beatles: they had become recreational drug users.

The album's title came from McCartney when he heard an old blues singer say about Mick Jagger: "Mick, Jagger, man. Well you know its plastic soul." McCartney was also recorded saying "Plastic soul, man, (it's) plastic soul" during the "I'm Down" recording sessions in 1965. For this album, he converted "plastic" to "rubber" to denote British soul.

This hysteria-free album shows the Beatles progressing technically and musically after taking over the studio and turning it into a workshop of ideas and innovations, borrowed, rehashed, and otherwise. Its somber mood reflects the Beatles' own emotional state. They added piano, harp, and the *sitar* to their conventional instruments to provide new feelings to the florid melodies and introspective lyrics.

McCartney described the *Rubber Soul* album as "a straight album" with "a lot of acoustic." But *Rubber Soul* is more than this. It is the first Beatles' album that gave a new representation to an album as more than a collection of unrelated songs.

According to McCartney, the colloquial "drive my car" is an old euphemism for sex. **"Drive My Car"** (Lennon-MCCARTNEY), the song, resembles the melody and lyrics of Berry's "No Particular Place to Go," which deals with the youth's passion for cars. Both songs end in a narrative twist. The driver's girlfriend in "No Particular Place to Go" gets stuck in her seat belt, while in "Drive My Car," her claim on car ownership is having a driver for a start. Although it was a McCartney composition, Lennon reworked the sophomoric lyrics. From *"I can give you golden rings / I can give you anything / Baby I love you,"* for instance, he wrote: *"That she wanted to be famous / Star of the screen / But that I could do something in between."*

McCartney's bass riff resembles Otis Redding's "Respect." To broaden his appeal to Whites, Redding came up with a raw and spontaneous style of "Respect" that contrasts with Motown's smooth and sophisticated music, thus making himself a White Negro.

Lennon also contributed the *"beep-beep-yeah!"* line.

Lennon sings in Dylan's droll voice in **"Norwegian Wood (This Bird Has Flown)"** (LENNON-McCartney), the narrative of which he based on his own real life extramarital affairs after he was forced to marry Cynthia after he made her pregnant (*"I once had a girl, or should I say, she once had me."*) He veiled the references, of course, as he did not want Cynthia to know. Norwegian wood, by the way, was a cheap pine paneling trendy in London at the time Lennon wrote the song while "bird" is an English slang for girl. As such, the title is an oblique reference to cheap girls.

This song shows Lennon in a new form, distilling successfully all the influences and techniques he learned in previous songs composed individually or collectively with McCartney, and coming up with a restrained and minimalist song. As a seminal work, it is a transition song that enlarged his musical jargon and later, McCartney's. The oblique use of lyrics introduced double-meaning or multi-level songs that would be important to the future direction of Beatle songs.

But Lennon achieved this accomplishment unconsciously. Wanting to hide that it is about an extra-marital affair, he came up with all sorts of devices. In his own words: "I was trying to write about an affair without letting my wife know I was having one. I was sort of writing from my experiences -- girl's flats, things like that. I was very careful and paranoid because I didn't want my wife, Cyn, to know that there really was something going on outside of the household. I'd always had some kind of affairs going on, so I was trying to be sophisticated in writing about an affair, but in such a smoke-screen way that you couldn't tell. But I can't remember any specific woman it had to do with."

McCartney contributed some lyrics.

Harrison used a *sitar* in a Beatle song for the first time. The Indian musical instrument fascinated him when he saw it during the filming of *Help!* He narrated, "We were waiting to shoot the restaurant scene...where the guy gets thrown in the soup and there were a few Indian musicians playing in the background. I remember picking up the sitar and trying to hold it and thinking, 'This is a funny sound.' It was an incidental thing, but somewhere down the line I began to hear Ravi Shankar's name... So I went and bought a Ravi record; put it on and it hit a certain spot in me that I can't explain, but it seemed very familiar to me. It just called on me...I bought a cheap sitar from a shop called India Craft in London. I hadn't really figured out what to do with it. But when we were working on 'Norwegian Wood' it just needed something. It was quite spontaneous...I just picked it up and found the notes and just played it. We miked it up and put it on and it just seemed to hit the spot."

The use of the instrument paved the way for the creation of *raga* rock, the fusion of raga into rock music. *Raga* is the Indian combination of tones similar to the diatonic scale. A *raga* (of which there are 72) usually expresses a single mood, which a *sitar* player often maintains through variations on their scale for half an hour. Donovan, the British folk singer, often referred to as "the British Bob Dylan," influenced Harrison's fascination with the exotic instrument. He pursued expertise by undergoing tutorial with *sitar* master Ravi Shankar. But it was in no way an original act. Martin used the *sitar* and the *tabla* in producing Peter Seller's "Wouldn't It Be Lovely."

Adapted in the style of the black American girl groups such as The Shirelles and Diana Ross and the Supremes, **"You Won't See Me"** (Lennon-MCCARTNEY) is another variation of Motown music, particularly its use of modulation and James Jameson bass-playing. It tells of McCartney's growing dissatisfaction with Asher. Her acting career kept her busy and didn't leave her enough time to attend to his phone calls. Combined with other rejections, McCartney told himself, "You (Asher) won't see me." Mal Evans, the former Cavern guard who became the Beatles' road manager from the summer of 1963, played Hammond Organ.

Lennon wrote **"Nowhere Man"** (LENNON-McCartney) while he was struggling to come up with a new song to complete this album's song requirement. He gave up the conscious attempt to compose and he likened himself to "a nowhere man in a nowhere land." The thought gave him the song's motive, which he expanded on. He recalled in *Playboy*, "I'd spent five hours that morning trying to write a song that was meaningful and good, and I finally gave up and lay down. Then 'Nowhere Man' came, words and music, the whole damn thing as I lay down." McCartney corroborated this when he said, "That was John after a night out, with dawn coming up. I think at that point, he was a bit...wondering where he was going."

In this lost phase, Lennon managed to find a new period in the Beatles' recording career, the philosophy-oriented songs. "Nowhere Man" is the first Beatle song that's not about romance; instead, it's a redefinition of content that takes its Existentialist approach from Dylan.

"Think for Yourself" (Harrison) is a protest song that proclaims one should not trust the government but only oneself, Harrison's warning against listening to lies. It is a fine example of the "thinking songs" that characterize this album. The word "think" in the title indicates a major shift from the romantic ideals of Beatles songs until this album, certainly a Dylan influence. The use of complex words such as "opaque" and "rectify" started the intellectualization of Beatle song lyrics. This song uses the fuzz bass.

"The Word" (LENNON-McCartney) is the product of the composers' attempt to write a one-note song like "Long Tall Sally." The word, for sure, is love. In true White Negro way, Lennon recognized the coming of the Love Generation and before anybody could declare it, he beat the rest by proclaiming "the word is love." This is a cross-over song. Lennon did not deal with personal but universal affection, preaching "Say the word and you'll be free." It's the early indication that Lennon is going into anthem-like songs.

Distilling Chet Atkins' "Trombone," McCartney made fun of a "beat" French singer in Liverpool in **"Michelle"** (Lennon-MCCARTNEY) during a party of art students. The ditty started out as a parody of French song sang by a French-looking student with groaning instead of real words to entertain the crowd. This song stayed a novelty song until Lennon encouraged McCartney to turn it into a real song. Writing parodies -- McCartney's term for his art of derivation -- was a common practice for him. His White Negro code in rehashing other artists' song was to start out playing a song's real melody, giving it different lyrics, deliberately changing them until he came up with a fairly different product. For bass lines, he usually played off notes, fifths and thirds, to add tension to the song's mood.

Generally credited as a McCartney song, several persons helped finish it off.

For the lyrics' French part, he got a lot of help from Jan Vaughan, the wife of his old friend Ian Vaughan who spoke French. He asked for a French name and a two-syllable phrase that rhymed with it. She came up with the name Michelle and changed trite lyrics like *"goodnight sweetheart"* and *"hello my dear"* to *"Michelle ma belle."* Later, Vaughn translated *"these are words that go together well"* into "*sont des mots qui von tres bien ensemble.*" During the recording, McCartney pronounced the French lines with imperfect accent.

Lennon contributed the song's middle eight based on blues singer Nina Simone's "*I love you*" from the song "I Put a Spell on You" which he heard her sing in a cabaret show the night before they recorded "Michelle." He copied *"I love you, I love you, I love you"* with the emphasis on "you.' McCartney wrote the bridge.

Of course, this was not the first time a foreign language was used in rock music. Berry had done it in "You Never Can Tell" (" '*Ces't la vie,*" the old folks say...").

Martin wrote the lead guitar melody which is played in the middle and coda.

McCartney converted the bass line from French composer Georges Bizet, experimenting on it. He recounted to Tom Mulhern of *Guitar Player,* "There's that descending chord thing that goes *[sings bass notes]* '*do do do do words I know do do do do do my Michelle'* -- you know, the little descending minor thing. And I found that if I played a C, and then went to a G, and then to C, it really turned that phrase around. It gave it a musicality that the descending chords just hadn't got. It was lovely. And it was one of my first sort of awakenings: 'Ooh, ooh, bass can really change a track!' you know, if you put the bass on the root note, you've got a kind of straight track."

Such White Negro experimentations would evolve the bass sound into something more than itself.

Lennon wrote **"What Goes On"** (LENNON-McCartney) in the style of Perkins. It used to be an instrumental until it was revived for Starr's customary vocal solo per Beatles album. When they were asked by Martin to submit compositions for a followup single to "Please Please Me," Lennon and McCartney presented "What Goes On" along with "From Me To You," "Thank You Girl," and "The One After 909." The *Rubber Soul* album was about to wrap up, but Starr did not have his standard one song per album yet. The Beatles thought of reviving "What Goes On" from the *Help!* album recording sessions. Starr contributed five words to the lyrics. According to author/journalist Ritchie Unterberger in *All Music Guide*, Harrison's guitar work was patterned after Perkin's "Everybody's Trying To Be My Baby."

Lennon adapted the idea for **"Girl"** (LENNON-McCartney) from the book entitled *Pain and Pleasure,* which tackles discourses on the Christian theme that to have pleasure, pain must be experienced first. Lennon disagreed with this point of view, believing that one can have pleasure without pain. Thus he wrote this negation.

According to McCartney, he contributed the lines *"Was she told when she was young that pain would lead to pleasure"* and *"A man must break his back to earn his day of leisure."*

Lennon delivers *"Ah, gir-ir-irl"* with the unmistakable sound of a marijuana user inhaling smoke. It's as if he is trying to seduce the listener to smoke pot. McCartney and Harrison sing the naughty *"tit-tit-tit-tit"* harmony. The final solo resembles the texture of Greek music.

By this time, McCartney wrote mostly about his love for Asher, but his chauvinism stayed. He never changed his selfish attitude towards women. In **"I'm Looking Through You"** (Lennon-MCCARTNEY), his resentment when their relationship came to an end with her decision to move to Bristol, living away from him, shows. Of course, this is McCartney's version of the Dylan style -- introspective on a superficial level.

Lennon wrote **"In My Life"** (LENNON-McCartney) as a response to Kenneth Alsop John, an English journalist and writer, who suggested that he put his introspective style of writing in *In His Own Write* in his song compositions. Lennon told *Playboy* in 1970: "It was the first song I wrote that was consciously about my life. [Sings] *'There are places I'll remember / all my life though some have changed....'* Before, we were just writing songs a la Everly Brothers, Buddy Holly -- pop songs with no more thought to them than that. The words were almost irrelevant."

He started composing the song by reflecting on his boyhood, naming all the places that he saw during a bus ride (*"Penny Lane is one I'm missing / Up Church Rd to the clocktower / In the circle of the abbey / I have seen some happy hours"*). It then proceeded from Menlove Ave. to the docks, mentioning such places as Penny Lane and Strawberry Field. But the lyrics turned tedious, so he dropped the idea and changed it into a general recollection of places of special significance to him, as well as of living and dead friends and lovers he had left behind when he became famous. According to Shotton in his book *John Lennon In My Life,* the friends Lennon referred to were Sutcliffe and him. In this rewrite, "very few lines" remained from Lennon's original.

Martin wrote the middle eight's Elizabethan piano background based on Bach.

There was a disagreement between Lennon and McCartney regarding the song's authorship. In 1980, Lennon claimed McCartney's contribution was limited to helping out with the middle eight. This was an odd claim -- most likely a wrong one -- as it is without a bridge section. McCartney, on the other hand, claims song authorship, revealing he rewrote all of Lennon's opening lines and adapted the minors and harmonies from Smokey Robinson and the Miracles' "You Really Got a Hold on Me" and "Tears of a Clown." They never reached an agreement. McCartney commented, "I find it very gratifying that out of everything we wrote, we only appear to disagree over two songs." (The other song is "Eleanor Rigby.")

The issue remains unresolved until now -- and most likely will stay that way forever!

But whoever wrote the lyrics used White Negro technique. The lyrics might have been loosely based on Charles Lamb's 18th century poem "Old Familiar Faces" (*"How some they have died, and some they have left me, And some have taken from me; all are departed -- All, all are gone, the old familiar faces"*).

The transposition of poem words to song lyrics was a sophisticated one as it tried to avoid a direct quotation similar to the lazy creative ways of the White Negroes. He dropped the figures of speech and opted for colloquial lyrics. He converted *"the old familiar faces"* to *"there are places I remember,"* then switched it as the verse opener instead of the closer. The similarity could be gleaned in the same sound of "faces" with "places," approximating at the same time the phrases seven-syllable count. Words have been updated like "friends" for "cronies" or "dead" for "departed."

The Beatles originally recorded **"Wait"** (Lennon-McCartney) for the *Help!* album, but they rejected it because it did not meet their quality standard. But they improved its instrumentation and thus included it in this new album to complete its song requirement. It was simply a filler, ditching the old idea that the quartet, by this growth period, had turned quality conscious.

"If I Needed Someone" (Harrison) is about Harrison's then girlfriend Pattie. Written around the D chord, Harrison adapted its introduction and coda from the introduction and coda of The Byrds' "The Bells of Rhymney" and "She Don't (sic) Care About Time." The Byrds, the California group specializing in electrified and harmonized covers of Dylan songs, clipped the length of "Mr. Tambourine Man" and turned it into a big hit.

Lennon adapted **"Run for Your Life"** (LENNON-McCartney) from two lines of Presley's "Baby Let's Play House." Those lines are: *"I'd rather see you dead, little girl / Than to be with another man."* On the other hand, Presley's song was based on Eddy Arnold's 1951 country hit "I Want to Play House With You" as composed by a preacher's son from Nashville named Arthur Gunter. This shows Presley's White Negro roots and how he linked with the Beatles. Because of its chauvinistic treatment of females, Lennon said in a 1973 interview that this song was his "least favorite" and the one he most regretted writing. On the other hand, Harrison rated it as his most favorite in this album.

In *Rubber Soul*, the Beatles songs that one expects to hear never came. In their place, the Beatles sing about escape, extra-marital relationships, false aspirations, French lyrics, attempts to understand human behavior, and serious words. The sounds are unfamiliar as the Beatles had shifted from an electronic to an acoustic sound with exotic Indian instruments completing the aspiration. The Beatles kept the track list intact, extracting no single release that made the mystery even more obvious. The entire album brings the listener to the realization of the absence of formula and forces listening -- active listening.

NME opined about *Rubber Soul*: "Cynicism, melody and jangly guitars.

Rubber Soul has it all. Every Paul McCartney tune a potential hit single, every Lennon song a bitter and twisted pop epic, the first great studio pop LP." *Newsweek* stated: "The Beatles blend gospel, country music, baroque counterpoint, and even French popular ballads into a style that is wholly their own." Author Ron Schaumburg rated it as "a masterpiece" in *Growing Up With The Beatles.*

Richard Goldstein in a 1973 review of Beatles song in *Stereo Review* stated that *Rubber Soul* is "the most important rock LP of the Sixties. It did for rock what Benny Goodman did for the swing: it created an authentic melodiousness that took the music off the killing floor of race. So, the achievement of the middle Beatles was that they made rock respectable, and they also made it white."

This statement is important because it is one of the first references to the Beatles having made Black music White, meaning they made music that originated from the Blacks acceptable to the White market. This is an indirect recognition of the quartet's White Negro character, that is, without using the terminology. *NME* was, however, less enthusiastic about *Rubber Soul*. The album, it said, was "not their best" and "monotonous."

But despite these contradictory reviews of its quality, *Rubber Soul* did accomplish one thing. If Spector made art out of the 45-rpm disc, with *Rubber Soul* the Beatles and Martin transformed the album as an art form.

This album narrowly misses being classified in the maturity phase of the Beatles' creative cycle because of the inclusion of "Wait," a song rejected from the *Help!* album.

"Paperback Writer" / "Rain" single

The Beatles released "Paperback Writer" and "Rain" as a single on June 10, 1966.

With bass and harmonies converted from the Beach Boys' *Pet Sounds* album, McCartney wrote **"Paperback Writer"** (Lennon-MCCARTNEY), his first song which is not about love. The song's motive came when McCartney saw Starr reading a book. British disc jockey Jimmy Savile retold, "He took one look and announced that he would write a song about a book." Lennon contributed the line "a man named Lear" in reference to the Victorian painter Edward Lear whose nonsense poems he loved dearly. *The Daily Mail* was the broadsheet he subscribed to. Otis Redding and Wilson Pickett had used boosted bass sound and the Beatles caught up in this song, The hooks included a riff from The Who's "Substitute," a "mod" rock number with its distorted, circular guitar hook, high-pitch harmonies and pounding drums. It contains tambourine passages similar to another Who song, "I Can't Explain." The backing harmonies in the final verse were patterned after the French nursery rhyme, "Frere Jacques" (English translation, "Are You Sleeping"). Lennon and McCartney failed to come up with one-chord song which they aimed to do.

Experimenting heavily with backward tapes, backward singing, and slowed down backing track, Lennon used them for the first time in a Beatle song in **"Rain"** (LENNON-McCartney). Tinkering with backward tape loops, he produced a distorted sound, which he decided to use as chance art, giving its sound a rare hypnotic quality. The lyrics *"When it rains and shines / Just a state of mind"* announces the arrival of psychedelic elements in Beatles songs.

No question of originality

With all of the extraneous sources that went into the creation of Beatles songs thus far, did Lennon and McCartney -- or for that matter, Harrison -- do the imitation consciously or unconsciously? The assimilation of songs in the various levels of consciousness being normal, is it not possible that the composers within the group were merely expressing what they remembered in an unconscious way? Having retained the information, they culled from their extensive data bank of extraneous information which they would draw from at the right time, whether planned or unintended.

While the unconscious application was certainly possible, as the case of "Yesterday" showed, most of the time it was a deliberate attempt to rehash. They did this consciously, aware of what they were doing and in several instances, not even denying such extraneous sources. A clarification at this point is crucial because it would explain the originality aspect of Beatles songs. Although they had displayed some pure genius in their White Negro style of songmaking, it remained opportunistic and derivative at best.

If the Beatles were such copycats, what brought about their artistic peak?

Chapter 4
The maturity phase
Beyond recognition

"Works of art are indeed always products of having been in danger, of having gone to the very end in an experience, to which man can go no further."

- Rainier Maria Rilke

Refining and editing mark the maturity period when the artist can step back from the work and look at it with a critical eye without interrupting the creative flow. This creative fire reaches a peak of intensity, a period for best work. There's no panic or doubt of developing a new born idea while absorbed in work and experiencing extra creative energy.

When realized, the best conceived works offer opportunities to transcend the barriers of the work of art's own realities and conventions. The transcendence must "go further identification," which author Craig Owens called in *Beyond recognition: Representation, Power and Culture* as "transforming the object, the work of art, beyond recognition."

Refined art, therefore, refers to the success of the artist in assimilating influences "beyond recognition."

Refinement is usually determined by the artist's experience and commitment that have a congruent relationship with the output: the greater the degree of experience and commitment, the greater the refinement. This relationship determines the novelty of the output, the freshness of the concept embodied in the output, from which freshness creates the appeal of the output, and -- in the long run -- the output's value.

Refinement necessarily affects and reflects the quality of the artist's body of work. Refinement imparts an uneven characteristic to it as a result. It tends to vary in terms of importance and beauty as an artist goes through the phases of his creative cycle.

The measure of a good artist is, therefore, his ability to determine the intrinsic value of output, exercise self-editing, and create only the acceptable kind available for public consumption.

According to art critic Clement Greenberg and art critic/art historian Michael Fried, change matters if it counts as progress. Derived art becomes important when the artist succeeds in transforming input into a progressive output, the product being an improvement of its sources. Derivation must improve the original sources if it must transcend the identity of the original sources.

Or as Angelican priest, English author, and professor of divinity at Cambridge William Ralph Inge gloomily defined, originality is the "undetected plagiarism."

Tutorial with Dylan

Before the next album release, Lennon and McCartney had a tutorial with Dylan on how to write lyrics. Dylan invited them to his London Hotel suite after a concert which ended up at what they did best -- sharing joints and songwriting. He thanked them for taking him out of the acoustic guitar format and introducing him to electric guitar. But the reverse osmosis continued. Dylan showed them that by calling out words and phrases that came into their minds and stringing them together, they could actually write sophisticated lyrics like him. Lennon or McCartney would blurt words and phrases out, finish the couplet with a rhyming line with Dylan taking care of typing them out.

The product of that exercise which is entitled "Pneumonia Ceilings," the unfinished and unreleased Lennon-McCartney-Dylan collaboration as Dylan had typewritten it, typos included, as author Mark Shipper wrote in the book *Paperback Writer*: "Words and phrases right / Cigarette ash keeps me up all nite // How comes mama type so fast? / Is daddy's flag flying at half mast? // Pneumonia celings, pneumonia floors / Daddy ain't gonna take it no more // Elephant guns blazing in my ears / I'm sick & tired of your applesauce tears! // Thermometers don't tell time no more / Since aunt mimi pushed them off the 20th floor // So say goodbye to skyscrapers / You'll read about it in the evening paper // I picked my nose & I'm glad I did."

This tutorial did not only make it easy for Lennon and McCartney easy to write lyrics but gave their new songs depth like they did not know it was easy to do. This new skill, some sort of fast track "art of selection," would surface in their new compositions. As you would see later, the quality of output depended on the refinement of they put into those lyrics. Their next single release would be the initial sample.

"Eleanor Rigby"/"Yellow Submarine"

Simultaneously with the *Revolver* album, the quartet issued "Eleanor Rigby" and "Yellow Submarine" as a single on August 5, 1966.

"Eleanor Rigby" (Lennon-MCCARTNEY) took its form and content from Dylan's "The Ballad of a Thin Man," and it is a superb distillation. Both songs moan about desolation and the futility of human action. That of the Beatles dwell on the physical (*"Picks up the rice in the church where a wedding has been"*), while the latter deals with the psychological (*"You try so hard but you don't understand!"*).

The two songs have the same verse construction: beginning with a narrative and ending with a question. Dylan ends the verse *"But you don't know what it is / Do you Mr. Jones?"* while The Beatles with *"Wearing the face that she keeps in a jar by the door / Who is it for?"*

The line *"Wearing the face that she keeps in a jar by the door,"* refers to makeup and is a modification of the Dylan metaphor, *"You put your eyes in your pocket..."* which refers to a pair of eyeglasses.

The Beatles translated "The Ballad of a Thin Man"'s catchy ending verse construction into the refrain (*"All the lonely people / Where do they all belong?"*).

The fourth verse of Dylan's song starts with *"Aaah, you've been with the professors and they've all liked your looks."* The chorus of The Beatles song is *"Aaah, look at all the lonely people"* repeated twice.

While Dylan's song remains an exposition of Mr. Jones' pathetic situation, the Beatles' song expands it into a narrative of two characters, Eleanor Rigby and Father McKenzie, and how their respective desolation intertwines their fates and seals it to make the Beatles song more poignant.

McCartney originally named the song's main character as Miss Daisy Hawkins, similar to Edgar Allan Poe's plain young heroine, Annabel Lee. But he was not happy with the name so he came up with another.

The name "Eleanor Rigby" has several identified sources. One source says it was McCartney's subconscious recollection of a tombstone he saw as a child during a function at St. Peter's Church in Woolton. Another says he got the first name "Eleanor" from Eleanor Bron, a co-star in the Help! movie, while the surname "Rigby" came from the company name "Rigby & Company," which he saw while walking to the theater in Bristol where Asher acted.

McCartney originally named Father McKenzie as Father McCartney, but decided against it because he did not want his father's surname to be associated with a sad song. He picked up the telephone directory and randomly pointed to "McKenzie." McCartney thought this surname fit the character perfectly.

Beatles members and friends helped finalize the lyrics. Harrison made up the line *"Ah, look at all the lonely people."* Shotton suggested that Father McCartney be changed to avoid being mistaken for McCartney's father. Starr contributed the lines *"writing the words of a sermon that no one will hear"* and *"darning his socks in the night..."* Shotton came up with the idea of making the two lonely people come together at song's ending which Lennon rejected but implicitly accepted by McCartney by not commenting.

Besides McCartney's lead vocals and Lennon & Harrison's backing harmonies, the Beatles did not play their regular instruments. Instead, four violins, two cellos and two violas played by professional musicians did the understated string score composed by Martin based on Bernard Heman's score of Alfred Hitchcock's *Psycho*.

"Eleanor Rigby" is not the first rock song to deal with death and desolation. The Shangri-las released "Leader of the Pack" in 1964 about a star-crossed lover's death.

Some books on classical music refer to "Eleanor Rigby" as comparable to the *lieder* (art songs) of the great composers.

The Beatles distilled **"Yellow Submarine"** (Lennon-MCCARTNEY) from two sources: Dylan's riotous song "Rainy Day Woman #12 and #35" and Paul Anka's "The Longest Day," the theme song of the war epic of the same title released in 1962. By combining the two songs, McCartney largely diffused their essence. While it resembled specific passages of the model songs, "Yellow Submarine" refined the treatment of the intro's march song features, the brass accompaniment, and the jocular ribbing that refined the influence of Anka's song. Its mid-to-end sections were given the boisterous treatment of a Dylan song. It re-created the ambiance that gave Dylan's song its uniqueness and appeal. It even imitated the *"who-aah!"* scream. This first instance in ambiance creation through the use of sound effects would later develop into the Beatles song concept known as the "sound picture."

The title of this children's song refers indirectly to the Nembutal capsule, a barbiturate, yellow in color and submarine-shaped. Contrary to this association with drugs, McCartney revealed that the title alludes to a sweet called a "submarine," which he ate in a holiday in Greece. Made of icing, the candy is dropped in water, which dissolves and becomes a saccharine drink.

Lennon and McCartney collaborated on the verses while McCartney wrote the catchy chorus. As the musical arrangement relies mainly on guitars and drum, the sound effects create the music. These sound effects play a pivotal role in creating the matchless innocent excitement, capturing the simplicity that defines children's songs. In fact, the lyrics do not contain any complex word.

Donovan contributed the lines *"Sky of blue and sea of green in our Yellow Submarine."*

The Beach Boys' threat

At this point in their career, The Beatles -- particularly McCartney -- considered the Beach Boys a threat to their popularity and stature. Copying the vocal harmony of the Five Satins, the Beach Boys sang about the diversions of West Coast youth and largely succeeded. With Mike Love as lead singer and the Wilson Brothers (Brian as bassist, Dennis as drummer, and Carl as guitarist) and Al Jardine as guitarist, the Beach Boys claimed musical heritage from Spector, pointing the group towards the direction of "Wall of Sound" by adopting its production methods.

As its chief songwriter, who was also the group's bassist like McCartney with the Beatles, Brian Wilson served as a formidable competitor for McCartney. Brian became evidently jealous of the Beatles' accomplishment with *Revolver*. Imitating the Beatles' marijuana habit, which brought him to a higher level of consciousness, Brian reclaimed lost glory by coming up with the seminal album *Pet Sounds*, a richly textured work blending the group's choir-voice sound and Spector's lavish combination of sound elements.

For McCartney, the *Pet Sounds* influence came in the form of the idea that he could make bass as a major sound. He told editor Tom Mulhern: "The Beach Boys' *Pet Sounds,* a big influential album for me. If you're in C, and you put it on something that's not the root note -- it creates a little tension. It's great. It just holds the track, and so by the time you go to C, it's like 'Oh, thank God he went to C!' And you can create tension with it. I didn't know that's what I was doing; it just sounded nice. And that started to get me much more interested in bass. It was no longer a matter of just being this low note in the back of it."

Every track of *Pet Sounds* is a masterwork for the Beach Boys, the whole album rich and diverse. Brian sings solo in "Don't Talk" and "Caroline No," but the harmonies of "You Still Believe In Me," "Sloop John B," and "God Only Knows" are brilliant as group work. There are amazingly imaginative touches everywhere, from highly complex orchestral arrangements to astoundingly simple *a capella* harmony. If *Pet Sounds* were to be assigned an importance in rock history, it would be as the first "concept album" with its introspective lyrics, unified tone, and high-quality recording.

In fact, even McCartney, Lennon, and Harrison considered *Pet Sounds* as having elevated rock's standards. It became a reference point for the Beatles, most especially McCartney, in creating their next album.

By taking Berry's partiality for contemporary youth culture and adding a distinctive, West Coast twist, blending in vocal harmonies from '50s pop, rock, and rhythm 'n blues groups and singing songs about sun and surfing, Brian almost single-handedly created an image of Southern California as a modern utopia. As the Beach Boys evolved, Brian began to play the role of Spector while the band toured. He stayed home, wrote new songs and recorded backing tracks in the studio, using Spector's "Wall of Sound."

Spector influenced the Beatles by powering up the Beach Boys.

Spector's "Wall of Sound"

Spector created the "Wall of Sound" in the early '60s as a boy wonder in the fiercely competitive American music industry. Starting as a composer-singer in 1958 with the Teddy Bears' "To Know Him Is To Love Him," he proceeded to produce the famous classics of the rock era -- ambitious single records, among them Ike and Tina Turner's "River Deep Mountain High," the Righteous Brothers' "You've Got That Lovin' Feeling," the Crystals' "He's a Rebel" and "Da Doo Ron Ron," and Ronettes' "Be My Baby." His genius earned him the sobriquet as the most revered rock record producer of the last century.

Spector conceived the 45-rpm record as an art form and executed it in a Wagnerian scale, combining classical and popular music traditions with a flair for drama. He operated on the belief that the producer is the most important person in record production and central to this authority is strict technical and artistic control. His innovative methods created an encompassing revolution in the entire record industry, which certainly boosted the careers of the Beatles and the Beach Boys.

How did Spector discover the "Wall of Sound?" By chance. And this, in turn, led to the prevalent use of chance art in rock.

When Spector and Jimmy Lovine were recording the Walt Disney song, "Zip-A-Dee-Doo-Dah," Spector demanded that Levine increase the loudness. When Lovine complied, the needles of the soundboard meters jumped into the red zone. In frustration, Levine turned everything off and resorted to another approach. By bringing up the volume of each instrument one at a time, Levine attained the volume required by Spector without distortion, making loudness integral in his idiosyncratic recording style.

The "Wall of Sound" works on the following principles: echo, blending, chance music, and baffling. Spector wanted natural reverberation on all sound elements through the use of echo chambers that gave texture and depth to the recorded music. All elements of the record must combine until the required sounds blend. The principle of blending relies on the combination of the song elements into a harmonious whole.

Spector relied on chance input to add to the beauty of the song. He picked impromptu riffs during recording sessions that provide a spontaneous addition to the sound's unrestrained richness. The unintended input adds interesting texture no matter how inconsequential a sound element happens to be.

The "Wall of Sound" also relied on a multi-tracking recording system. Its techniques of multi-tracking, massed instrumentation, and overdubbing apply only to multitrack recording machines. The advancement of this system, from four to eight tracks during the time of the Beatles, allowed the infusion of a greater number of sound elements into a song.

By this period, the Beatles were heavily into experimentation. As echo is a major component of Spector's recording technique, the Beatles adopted it as a prime component of sound distortion. The Beatles relied on the echo to give a fuller sound to a song element. This is an undesirable sound element but the Beatles, through Spector's initiation, explored it as an integral sound characteristic.

Another invention developed at Abbey Road, which the Beatles also used extensively in recording their forthcoming songs was Single Tape Echo and

Echo Delay (STEED). It creates the effect of double-tracking a sound to give it a richer texture and fuller presence. As such, it is an artificial method of double-tracking known to simulate manual double-tracking, backward tape loops and fuzz bass, which is a bass guitar attached to a fuzz box.

Revolver

Revolver (original title: *Abracadabra*) is the first major rock album by the Beatles. It is made up of all-original songs recorded when the Beatles entered the maturity period of their creative cycle. With each member at the peak of their creativity, and with common objectives in mind, the Beatles took their art of derivation seriously, therefore managing to come up with songs with relatively new sounds and multilevel meanings.

The Beatles released *Revolver* on August 5, 1966.

"Taxman" (Harrison) opens the album. With some help from Lennon, Harrison converted it from a riff on Neal Hefti's "Batman Theme," which was the theme song of the popular superhero series in the '60s. He knocked off the chorus "*Batmaaan*" into "*Taxmaaan*." It foretells the changing nature of Beatles songs, from materials suitable for live performances to studio sound. It opens with a fake count in, followed by a cough, to approximate a live performance. McCartney played the opening lead guitar, not Harrison, as generally believed, being the group's lead guitarist. Harrison plays the taxman who maliciously finds every way to confiscate money from people (*"If you try to sit, I'll tax your seat."*)

After Harrison was placed in the "super tax bracket," he composed "Taxman," a song mocking the much-feared British taxation system. Lennon admitted he reluctantly helped Harrison with the lyrics and later expressed bitterness for not receiving credit.

"Taxman" is a protest song about the confiscatory nature of said tax system, which was hurting badly the Beatles' newfound affluence. With a large part of their income from three and a half years as a group having been paid to the government, Harrison wanted to protest. Lennon recounted in the *Playboy* interview, "I remember the day he called to ask for help on 'Taxman,' one of his bigger songs. I threw in a few one-liners to help the song along, because that's what he asked for. He came to me because he couldn't go to Paul, because Paul wouldn't have helped him at that period. I didn't want to do it. I thought, oh, no; don't tell me I have to work on George's stuff. It's enough doing my own and Paul's. But because I loved him and I didn't want to hurt him when he called me that afternoon and said, 'Will you help me with this song?' I just sort of bit my tongue and said OK."

Despite the clear derivation, Harrison got away with it because it did not reach the required two bars to constitute plagiarism.

In the song's end, Harrison mentions "Mr. Wilson" and "Mr. Heath," referring to Prime Minister Harold Wilson and Edward Heath, leaders of the opposition during that time, to make direct catcalls.

McCartney told Mulhern he patterned the bass line of "Taxman" from Jimi Hendrix. He explained, thus revealing how he distilled other artists' ideas: "It was really my first voyage into feedback. I had this friend in London, John Mayall of the Bluesbreakers, who used to play me a lot of records late at night -- he was a kind of DJ-type guy. You'd go back to his place, and he'd sit you down, give you a drink, and say, 'Just check this out.' He'd go over to his deck, and for hours he'd blast you with B.B. King, Eric Clapton -- he was sort of showing me where all of Eric's stuff was from, you know. He gave me a little evening's education in that. I was turned on after that, and I went and bought an Epiphone. So then I could wind up with the Vox amp and get some nice feedback. It was just before George was into that. In fact, I don't really think George did get too heavily into that kind of thing. George was generally a little more restrained in his guitar playing. He wasn't into heavy feedback."

The Beatles released "Eleanor Rigby" as a single.

"I'm Only Sleeping" (LENNON-McCartney), featuring a double guitar solo by Harrison, is Lennon's tribute to his favorite furniture, the bed. He would compose a song on it, read his favorite book there, and, of course, sleep on it. Later, he would use the use a bed to propagate his peace campaign.

Harrison's contribution showed he had turned into the consummate lead guitarist. For his guitar solo, he wrote the line, rewrote it in reverse, and overdubbed it onto the song's recording running backwards. And he was not done. He recorded two versions, one clean and the other with the guitar distorted. For this brief dreamy blast, it took him six hours to record according to *New York Times* music critic Allan Kozinn. This was the kind of attention to details each Beatle gave to songs in this album, maybe superfluous but showing each member was pushing their creativity to the limit, of course, still within the context of being White Negroes.

Harrison based the lyrics of **"Love You To"** (Harrison) on his reflections on the Eastern philosophy he learned from Maharashi Mahesh Yogi. He wrote the tune using the sitar for the first time. With the working title "Granny Smith," after the apple variety he loved to munch, Lennon started the practice of not helping Harrison out in composing a song. It worked. Harrison started to be self-dependent, managing to complete this song by himself.

"Here There And Everywhere" (Lennon-MCCARTNEY) is McCartney's reply to the Beach Boy's breakthrough song "God Only Knows" from the *Pet Sounds* album. After listening to the LP, he converted "Don't Let the Sun Catch You Crying" to this song. It opens with the spoken verse *"To lead a better life / I need my love to be here...,"* a '30s style song beginning as such device had not been used in a Beatles song. From here, McCartney's willingness copied anything to give his songs a new form. Evans contributed the lines *"Watching your eyes / Hoping I'm always there"* when McCartney asked for help in a problematic passage. McCartney's high vocals copied Marianne Faithful's style of singing.

This song made McCartney realize the possibilities of poetic lyrics, complex orchestration, and wonderful vocals. As a White Negro, he was ready to do the same and he started it in this song by rehashing "God Only Knows." He liked what he produced so it set him off to the Beach Boys-style, which he would perfect to the extent of beating them eventually at their own turf.

The Beatles released "Yellow Submarine" as a single.

"She Said She Said" (LENNON-McCartney) summarizes what the then relatively unknown actor Peter Fonda said about death. His heart stopped beating when he was shot in the stomach as a child. Fonda is the brother of Jane Fonda of *Barbarella* fame and the future star of the cult movie *Easy Rider*.

During their second U.S. tour in 1965, the Beatles lived in a posh Los Angeles house where Fonda supplied Lennon and Harrison with LSD for the first time. At one occasion, Fonda hovered around Lennon, repeatedly declaring, "I know what it's like to be dead." Pissed off, Lennon asked him, "You know what it's like to be dead? Who put all that f----ing s--- in your head? You're making me feel like I've never been born." A slightly different variation of these lines ended up as the song's lyrics.

Lennon recounted how he composed the song, "Yeah, right. That was pure. That was what I meant, all right. You see, when I wrote that I had the 'She said she said,' but it was just meaning nothing. It was just vaguely to do with someone who had said something like he knew what it was like to be dead, and then it was just a sound. And then I wanted a middle-eight. The beginning had been around for days and days and so I wrote the first thing that came into my head and it was *'When I was a boy,'* in a different beat, but it was real because it just happened. It's funny, because while we're recording we're all aware and listening to our old records and we say, we'll do one like 'The Word'...make it like that. It never does turn out like that, but we're always comparing and talking about the old albums -- just checking up. What is it...like swotting up for the exam -- just listening to everything."

To soften the hard edge, Lennon converted it to feminine perspective.

Due to a disagreement on how to record the song, McCartney absented himself from the recording sessions. Starr contributed his most inventive drumming in this piece.

McCartney converted **"Good Day Sunshine"** (Lennon-MCCARTNEY) from The Lovin' Spoonful's feel-good song, "Daydream." Lovin' Spoonful's leader John Sebastian commented that the wonderful thing about the Beatles was that they could copy ideas without giving a hint in the final product that they did so.

While **"And Your Bird Can Sing"** (LENNON-McCartney) has a great guitar riff and an impressive vocal by Lennon, it has pretentious lyrics, showing Lennon was not all the time the great lyricist that people knew him to be. Without a background on how the song came to be, the title offers little sense; one has to wring gray matters to make sense out of the song's impenetrable lyrics, becoming a string of words with no message to convey.

But placed in the correct perspective, Cynthia giving a mechanical caged bird to Lennon as a metaphor for herself, the song turns into a wry commentary of what she had done. Lennon was harsh in his judgment. He invariably described it as "a horror" and "a throwaway." He described it as "full of fake wisdom, of those philosophically lightweight days when it seemed as if the world could be turned on its axis by a tab of acid and a few seconds' thought." He also considered it as "fancy paper around an empty box." Perhaps he was being overly critical as the song is an excellent example of the psychedelic mindset operating him during the period.

Clearly, this happened because he mishmashed Dylan's style of confounding dissector of his "message" with cryptic lyrics that made no sense (*"You say you've seen seven wonders / And your bird is green / But you don't see me..."*).

But there was more to these negative comments than what Lennon was ready to own up. He was jealous of McCartney and Harrison who collaborated on an intricate harmony guitar work that showcased they were accomplished musicians. This led Lennon to state in the 1970 *Playboy* interview that he disliked this song.

"For No One" (Lennon-MCCARTNEY) showed that while recording the new album, the Beatles had started to splinter. Only McCartney and Starr plus London Philharmonic Orchestra French horn player Alan Civil recorded this song. He forced Civil to play a note over the instrument's range (a Super-D sharp, an octave above the standard "high D#.") Going over the normal earned for him the high praise of "performance of his life." Originally entitled "Why Did It Die," it's about McCartney's failing relationship with Asher, ending abruptly to indicate the sudden end of their relationship. Lennon rated is as "one of my favourites of his -- a nice piece of work."

"Doctor Robert" (LENNON-McCartney) is about Dr. Robert Freymann, a 60- year-old, German-born physician, who practiced on East 78th Street in New York. He was known as a "Speed Doctor" who supplied rock stars like Charles Parker and Theolonius Monk with amphetamines and all sorts of exotic drugs on demand. But Lennon once claimed that "Doctor Robert" is a metaphor for himself as he was the one who carried the pills in their early tours.

As usual, Harrison had trouble naming his song **"I Want To Tell You"** (Harrison). So Lennon suggested "Granny Smith Part Friggin' Two," in reference to the working title of "Love You To." Geoff Emerick was more original. He suggested "Laxton Superb," another variety of apple. McCartney modified the original song by giving it a discordant two-note piano to indicate frustration. Harrison wrote this for "the avalanche of thoughts that are so hard to write down or say or transmit." In theme, it's very similar to The Who's "I Can't Explain" which is about being able to express one's feelings. McCartney repeated the fade-in of "Eight Days a Week" to open the song. In melody, it's built around a drone that rarely strays from the A major key including the bridge.

McCartney adapted the soul sound of Tamla-Motown music dominating the British charts in **"Got to Get You Into My Life"** (Lennon-MCCARTNEY), particularly the revue-style horns of Stax label artists. He wrote it after being introduced to pot -- his tribute to marijuana, which gives "another kind of mind," as the lyrics states. Like true White Negroes, Lennon recalled, "We were influenced by our Tamla Motown bit on this. You see, we're influenced by whatever is going on. I think this was one of his best songs because the lyrics are good and I didn't write them." Lennon rated this song as "Paul at his best" in the 1980 *Playboy* interview.

Lennon lifted the lyrics of **"Tomorrow Never Knows"** (LENNON-McCartney) almost entirely from Dr. Timothy Leary, Richard Alpert, and Ralph Metzner's guidebook, *The Psychedelic Experience*, which he read while tripping on LSD. The guidebook was an adaptation of *The Tibetan Book of the Dead*, which he bought from Indica Gallery. He pored over it overnight and the following day, Lennon feverishly worked on his musical interpretation of the book's ideas in Abbey Road. The "Ego Death" experienced during the use of psychedelic drugs is the same as the dying process and requires similar guidance. He nicked the opening lines *"Turn off your mind, relax, float downstream"* by deleting "Whenever in doubt" at the beginning of the same line.

Derived from Indian music, the song's harmonic structure was based upon a C drone.

The title came from Starr, who used to say, "Well, tomorrow never knows."

But "Tomorrow Never Knows" is an aural experience distilled by Lennon after Karlheinz Stockhausen. Stockhausen was an avant-garde German composer and theoretician of electronic music who influenced a whole generation of European composers such as Pierre Boulez and Luciano Berio.

Before Lennon delivers his lead vocals, Starr introduces it with overpowering drumbeats that Martin achieved by placing the microphone much closer to the bass drum stuffed with a woolen sweater. Martin got the sound of the "Dalai Lama from the highest mountain top," as Lennon specified, by making him sing in a microphone but routed through an organ before reaching the tape machine, inside of which was a revolving loudspeaker.

"Tomorrow Never Knows" signals the Beatles' crossover to their actualization period -- psychedelia -- their creative cycle's peak. This sophisticated orchestration of Beatles' songs was taking place due to the adoption of Spector's "Wall of Sound" as an integral component of the group's song formula.

Revolver is the best Beatle album in the opinion of conductor Leonard Bernstein. *NME* described the album as "blindingly inventive" where Lennon wrote the "best music of his career."

The critical concurrence was that *Revolver* is an exceptional album. Analyzing it, however, reveals a strong Beach Boys influence in the McCartney songs. While an altered sensibility characterized Lennon's songs, Brian Wilson's musical devices drenched McCartney's songs. By tampering with Beach Boys production methods and choirboy harmonies, and reducing them to their essentials, McCartney imparted a fluid quality that immensely enhanced the Beatles' melody. The unadorned bass sound, usually a background song element, took a prominence as dominant as the lead vocals. McCartney adapted another distinct Beach Boys trademark, the abrupt change of tempo in contradictory terms, from high to low, from fast to slow, etc.

Brian Wilson admitted *Revolver* exceeded *Pet Sounds*. The score settled between the Beatles and the Beach Boys, they would face another challenge: Which group would come up with the next breakthrough album?

A Collection of Oldies But Goldies

Unable to come up with an album with new materials to fulfill their twice-a-year quota with Parlophone Records, the Beatles decided to come up with greatest hits album on December 9, 1966, called *A Collection of Beatles Oldies But Goldies*. The track list includes **"She Loves You," "From Me To You," "We Can Work It Out," "Michelle," "Yesterday," "I Feel Fine," "Yellow Submarine," "Can't Buy Me Love,"** "Bad Boy," **"Day Tripper,' "A Hard Day's Night," "Ticket To Ride," "Paperback Writer," "Eleanor Rigby,"** and **"I Want To Hold Your Hand."**

Lennon sings **"Bad Boy"** (Williams), the third cover version by the Beatles of a Larry Williams song.

I'd love to turn you on...

Seduced by the potency of mind-altering substances, the Beatles began associating with fellow believers in drugs' powers to provide recreation and genius. As veritable drug orgies, their concert tours allowed access to the American counterculture that established their cultural affiliation with the underground. As the hippie movement began to emerge in the mid-'60s as Lennon, McCartney, and Harrison's encounter with the esoteric set became unavoidable.

Lennon gravitated to the curious types entrenched in mind alteration. Harrison sought tutelage in Indian music and became a devoted adherent of Eastern philosophical tenets. While Starr cultivated domestic bliss, McCartney's bachelorhood and London residency allowed him to circulate the sprouting London avant-garde art scene. Aligning with the London set, he organized Indica Gallery with Robert Fraser, attended far-out music performances, and helped finance the seminal underground newspaper *IT* (*International Times*). McCartney became a well-entrenched member of the glitterati, but maintained a laid-back position, thus keeping his name out of the headlines.

As Lennon continued artistic dominance of the Beatles, McCartney turned more aggressive in staging his claim for the position. After Lennon's use of the flute in "You've Got To Hide Your Love Away" that gave impetus to classical rock, McCartney staged an artistic coup with the string-led "Yesterday" that not only dispensed with the Beatles song format, but excluded from it the other Beatles altogether. Although McCartney recorded the song solo with the concurrence of Lennon, it showed an altered frame of creative thinking for McCartney that eventually overshadowed Lennon's musical accomplishments and the need for the rest of the Beatles to be present in a recording session.

The competition between Lennon and McCartney had become pronounced by this time. Both were exposed to the creative ferment of underground and mainstream artists at both sides of the western world, such as those brought up by the Beach Boys, Frank Zappa, and San Francisco bands like Grateful Dead, Jefferson Airplane, Quicksilver Messenger Service, and Country Joe and the Fish. What started as a musical predilection for Lennon and McCartney became the departure point for a latently fierce affirmation of who had better abilities as a composer. McCartney expressed aggressiveness towards Lennon and towards musical groups that attempted to supersede his musical accomplishments. While this competition translated into creative ferment that tended to produce superior songs, it was only effective in a constructive context and positive environment. It imposed negativity when it turned obsessive or defeatist.

The studio years

The Beatles decided to stop touring as it had turned routinary. Two events involving their security also made it dangerous. They largely brought out the worst excesses of late Beatlemania, exposing its negative capabilities.

The Beatles and their entourage suffered lynching after the July 4, 1966 concert in Manila, Philippines over a controversial misunderstanding arising from not being able to appear at the presidential palace upon the invitation of First Lady Imelda Marcos. For the first time, they were physically hurt and held hostage. [This author's next book entitled *The Beatles In Manila: Run For Your Life* details the circumstances of their three-day stay in Manila. It clarifies details and bares unknown information. Cover photo (copyright by the author) was taken from said concert.]

When the Beatles returned to London after this terror, Lennon had to face another controversy that broke out five months before. On March 4, 1966, London *Evening Standard* reporter/friend Maureen Cleave interviewed Lennon who frankly talked about a subject banned by Epstein for the group to talk about publicly -- religion. The irrepressible Lennon broke sacred ground. He told Cleave:"Christianity will go. It will vanish and shrink. I do not know what will go first, rock 'n' roll or Christianity... We're more popular than Jesus now."

Nobody paid attention to the thought-provoking claim when it appeared in staid Britain as it seemed an insignificant sentence in a long-winding article. It was hardly noticed as Lennon was being true and glib as possible. When American teen magazine *Datebook* reprinted the inaccurate quote as "We're more popular than Jesus" on its July 29 issue front cover, three weeks after horrible experience in the Manila, the backlash on Lennon and the Beatles started to happen.

The article singled out the sentence and deleted the word "now," giving it an entirely a controversial color if malicious tone. The statement was perceived as anti-Christianity which angered fundamentalists in the American Bible Belt. Boys and girls held spur-of-the moment rallies, stomping on Beatles records and Beatlemania memorabilia in some kind of late-occurring remorse, before burning them. Radio stations banned Beatles songs and concert venues cancelled scheduled performances. Lennon received death threats, and the KKK protested a Beatle concert in Alabama. Even the conservative Vatican dipped its fingers into the unholy statement by denouncing Lennon publicly.

Epstein quickly flew to the US to try to quell the public relations debacle. On August 11, Lennon told a news conference in Chicago, Illinois, he still thought the statement as true, wryly adding, "I apologize if that will make you happy."

As a direct reaction, the Beatles collectively decided to stop touring. Used to hectic touring foreign countries, the next destination was no longer coming. Each Beatle had so much free time and creative energy to spare they were clueless how to get by. Lennon, for his part, accepted the role of Private Gripweed in *How I Won the War* which took him to Almeria, Spain for the principal photography. Quite naturally, they sought a little help from their co-Beatles, using the excess at what Lennon, McCartney, Harrison, and Starr did best, music-making, expressing them mostly at Abbey Road studio that eventually led to their artistic peak as White Negroes.

The ambition for continued dominance of popular music made them receptive to Martin's solicitations for experimentation. The Beatles needed to expand their music as the compelling musical trends they popularized became starting points for emerging musical groups that showed potential to overtake the success of the Beatles themselves. The group had an advantage though: Martin's background as classical musician and record producer prepared him to tackle whatever the Beatles required to concretize their ideas. They were gearing for greater artistic challenges.

Music critic Nat Hentoff observed the "continuing eclecticism" of the Beatles that fused various parts into a whole during this period. As the Beatles borrowed from more sources, as they made their art of derivation more sophisticated, their songs became profound and multidimensional. Narration did not prevail as they relied on the exposition technique to reflect situations and conditions as involved participants and detached observers.

The songs became more experiential; this time learned devices cloaked direct references to self and popular subjects with new literary clothing. As Lennon and McCartney relinquished the juvenile relationship songs of the birth period and first-person accounts of the growth period, they diversified their approaches to include unabashed baring of the soul and a masked search for intellectual ruminations and psychological reflections.

"Strawberry Fields Forever" / "Penny Lane" single

The quartet released "Strawberry Fields Forever" and "Penny Lane" as A-sides on February 17, 1967. Both were about Lennon's and McCartney's childhood. Although both breakthrough songs, the single surprisingly failed to reach the music chart's number one spot, which at that time was occupied by Engelbert Humperdinck's "Release Me." As such, Martin decided to pull them off from the yet-to-be-released next album.

Lennon composed **"Strawberry Fields Forever"** (LENNON-McCartney) at the time he accepted a small role as a foot soldier in *How I Won the War*. This happened at the point when he was in a creative limbo as the Beatles had stopped touring and he did not know how to use his free time.

The song was adapted from a real place in Liverpool called Strawberry Field, a Salvation Army facility near the house of Lennon's Aunt Mimi in Woolton. It is a memorable place in Lennon's childhood because it was where he attended garden parties and licked ice cream cornets. He wrote this song on the beach of Almeria, Spain while filming *How I Won the War* in the fall of 1966. In this masterpiece, he distilled the best features of earlier songs "Tomorrow Never Knows" and "She Said She Said" from the *Revolver* album to come up with one of his best works.

He started wearing the free spectacle from the British National Health Service while shooting *How I Won the War*. Having met Dylan and impressed by the black shades he wore all the time by this period, he thought to wear one to make himself as hip true to being a White Negro.

The theme of loss is similar to the "going down" device used by Caroll in *Alice in Wonderland* when Alice enters the rabbit hole in pursuit of the White Rabbit. This children's book published in 1865 is central to the imagery of some of Lennon's songs. The book neither educates nor moralizes; its only end is pleasure. Released from conventional reality, the book's approach allows the narration of a broad range of plots and possibilities of fantasy, a central theme Lennon would pursue starting with this song onwards.

"Strawberry Fields Forever" attempts to do in a song what film director Michelangelo Antonioni did in the 1966 film *Blow-up*. This pertains to the scene in which the photographer tells his friend in a full-blown psychedelic party that he believes he saw a murdered man lying behind a tree in a park. He asks the friend to help him investigate, but he does not get any cooperation.

Alice in Wonderland has a chapter entitled "Alice Goes Down in the Rabbithole," which narrates the story of the shrunk Alice getting sleepy. It has a line which goes *"...it didn't much matter which way she put it..."* which reminds of "Strawberry Fields Forever's" *"It doesn't matter much to me,"* right? The phrase "it doesn't matter" is a Ringoism.

The refrain becomes the bridge between reality and fantasy. "Hung about" refers to the corruption of the '60s phrase "hung up about" that means sexual inhibitions or difficulties are non-existent.

This song had two different versions in entirely different tempos and keys. The first version was a rehash of Jefferson Airplane's acid rock sound using the Mellotron, the technological innovation in this song. The Mellotron is a box with 70 tape recorders which Lennon had acquired for 1,000 pounds. Martin created an elaborate score for the second version that featured backward cymbals in the verses. Martin edited them together by varying tape speeds to come up with the final version.

Hearing "Strawberry Fields Forever" on the car's radio disturbed Brian Wilson so much that he pulled over until the song finished. He was working on the *Smile* album, what he hoped would break his accomplishment in *Pet Sounds*. When he realized the Beatles had done the kind of sounds he was developing for the new album, he abandoned the *Smile* project.

McCartney modified the high opening notes of **"Penny Lane"** (Lennon-MCCARTNEY) from the Beach Boys' "God Only Knows." McCartney used the B-flat piccolo after he watched a performance of Johann Sebastian Bach's "Brandenburg Concerto Number 2" by The New Philharmonia at a BBC television program that featured the distinctive high sound. David Mason, the trumpeter responsible for this sound, was hired to play it in "Penny Lane." He brought six trumpets and selected the B-flat piccolo trumpet. He also nicked the four-in-the-bar block piano chords and the bass' loping rhythm from "Caroline No," another Beach Boys song off the *Pet Sounds* album.

McCartney pinched the narrative theme and style from Dylan Thomas' "Fern Hill" poem. According to author Nicolas Schaffner, he had been reading the poem around the time he worked on the lyrics. The poem's narrator, a man, recalls the Welsh countryside where he frolicked as a young boy. Made up of five verses, he depicted the scenes various aspect in colorful and dramatic language. McCartney, on the other hand, moved the location to Penny Lane and proceeded to describe characters that people the busy Liverpool street in charming terms in the Thomas style. Good thing about it, he did not quote any of his line, hiding the source so expertly, for sure, a non-White Negro tradition. Penny Lane is an actual street in Liverpool, also the name of the area surrounding its junction. Although only a nondescript shopping area, Lennon and McCartney grew up there and spent many years in the neighborhood. Lennon first referred to Penny Lane in his song, "In My Life." But it was McCartney who thought of using the place in a full song.

McCartney based the narrative on his remembrances of real people in Liverpool during his growing-up years, as such achieving an intense sense of local color made more colorful by sexual slangs popular among Liverpool boys, jokes such as "four of fish and finger pies" and "keeps his fire engine clean."

According to *Beatles for Sale* author David Rowley, the end fade-out and fade back is a direct copy of the ending of the Beach Boys' "Caroline No" from the *Pet Sounds* album.

Martin decided to release this single as a double-A-sided disc. In the U.K., Humperdinck's "Release Me" reached #1 while the Beatles' single charted at #2. Although his record sold less, the two Beatles songs got credit for only half. Realizing his wrong decision, Martin self-admitted, "The biggest mistake of my life!"

These songs had promotional films each. Directed by Peter Goldman, they feature special effects, stop motion animation, disconcerting cuts and jumps, jarring juxtaposition, fairly establishing the music videos' visual language.

Sgt. Pepper's Lonely Hearts Club Band album

Alvin Sanoff, author of *The Saturated Self, Dilemmas of Identity in Contemporary Life*, referred to The Beatles as "perhaps the first important indicator of modernism's demise." This death ushered in what became known as the age of postmodernism in the '80s, which was tagged in the '90s as cross-culturalism or multiculturalism in the New Millennium.

No longer a close-knit group, the Beatles became creative vagabonds. McCartney, who had taken it upon himself to be the group's creative leader, thought of creating an alter ego group since they were tired of being the Beatles. He found the solution in the funky Sgt. Pepper's Lonely Hearts Club Band. At a time when they felt capable of doing anything and being distinguished for it, they entered the Abbey Road recording studios and came out with a masterpiece, *Sgt. Pepper's Lonely Hearts Club Band*, attributed as an artistic triumph, of course, for McCartney.

With *Sgt. Pepper's Lonely Hearts Club Band* released on June 1, 1967, the Beatles reached their artistic peak by refining their influences and coming up with a relatively superior album. It became the ultimate example of the possibilities of rock. Its acoustic, percussion, and vocal components drastically redefined it. The electronic texture, the use of classical music instruments and the exuberant production broke rock traditions. The album as art was born.

The album's revolutionary cover says it all: life-sized, colored cutouts of The Beatles with their favorite people -- from Mahatma Gandhi to Adolf Hitler, from Joan Baez to Mae West, from Dylan Thomas to Bob Dylan -- were taken by graphic artist Peter Blake and arranged to look like an after-concert souvenir photo. The suggestion is clear: the Beatles were the totality of their influences and whatever philosophies and pretensions they represented, formalizing their declaration as White Negroes.

McCartney developed the Sgt. Pepper name in **"Sgt. Pepper's Lonely Hearts Club Band"** (Lennon-MCCARTNEY) on the flight back to London when he and Evans went on an African safari. During a meal, as reports go, they were served sachets marked "S" and "P." Figuring out that it meant "salt" and "pepper," respectively, McCartney quipped, "Sgt. Pepper!" Much later, McCartney asked Evans to drop composer credit on the album title song for himself, to which Evans agreed. And he copied the U.S. trend of giving bands with western-sounding names like Laughing Joe and His Medicine Band or Col. Tucker's Medicinal Brew and Compound. He decided to adapt it in the Beatles' case by assuming a different persona and acting it out in the new album.

But a more probable origin of the album and song title came from Tony Barrow. He recounted that during the Beatles' drop-in on Elvis Presley in Memphis in early 1966, Presley handed Lennon, McCartney and Harrison a guitar so they could jam. Writer Chris Hutchins who was present during the visit jokingly called the grouping as "Sergeant Presley's Lonesome Heartbreak Band." This mock title played on the words "Sgt.," a punning of manager Col. Tom Parker's military designation; "Lonesome" from Presley's hit "Are You Lonesome Tonight," "Heartbreak" from the other Presley hit "Heartbreak Hotel' and appended "band" as they were playing as a musical group. McCartney approximated the whole title, refining it to its final form, snatching "Pepper" from the sachet and "lonely hearts club" from the organizations of single persons popular during that era.

McCartney's shouted introduction of the band was a rehash of the *Jimi Hendrix Experience,* which he watched five times between late 1966 and 1967. Hendrix played his guitar wizardry with its thundering, distorted guitar chords closely followed by lead "fills" in such numbers as "Foxy Lady" which McCartney copied in this song. Its husky, shouted vocals were nicked from the Cream's Jack Bruce.

The Abbey Road engineers plugged the electric guitars directly into the recording console, creating the technique known as Direct Injection (DI). The old practice was to record with a mike from the amplifier.

The start-up sound of musicians tuning up came from the "A Day in the Life" recording, while the audience sound came from the Abbey Road collection of sound effects. Four musicians played the brass section using French horns.

A rehash of "Yellow Submarine" with its simple melody and lyrics, **"With A Little Help From My Friends"** (Lennon-MCCARTNEY) is definitely Starr's best vocal work in a Beatles song. Originally entitled "Bad Finger Boogie," this working title inspired the Apple band Badfinger. But before recording the song, he objected to the original line as written by McCartney, *"Would you stand up and throw ripe tomatoes at me?"* Afraid fans would resort to it during live performances, he asked for a rewrite. Lennon changed it to *"Would you stand up and walk out on me?"* This shows that despite having reached their maturity period, McCartney had not turned into an astute lyrics-writer regardless of how he had progressed as a melody-maker.

By this time, Lennon and McCartney had perfected writing double-meaning lyrics. While the song is very much about pot, it remains on the level of innocence. McCartney explained, "I remember giggling with John as we wrote the lines *'What do you see when you turn out the light? I can't tell you but I know it's mine.'* It could have been him playing with his willie under the covers, or it could have been taken on a deeper level; this was what it meant but it was a nice way to say it, a very non-specific way to say it. I always liked that."

McCartney played bass as a main instrument.

Lennon got the **"Lucy in the Sky with Diamonds"** (LENNON-McCartney) title phrase from the drawing of his four-year-old son Julian Lennon. The young Lennon came from school and brought home a drawing of his classmate Lucy O'Donnell, the girl seating next to him at Heath House School, floating in the sky with what looked like sparkling diamonds. When asked by his father what it was about, the boy answered, "Lucy in the sky with diamonds!" How he came up with the metaphor at such a young age? The English nursery rhyme "Twinkle Twinkle Little Star" contains the line "like a diamond in the sky." It seemed he had the knack for his father's talent for wordplay. The Mad Hatter has a parody of this nursery rhyme in *Alice in Wonderland*.

The opening's distinctive pulsating notes is a distillation of the Beach Boys' instrumental opening used in "Good Vibrations," "Wouldn't It Be Nice" and "God Only Knows." McCartney used a Hammond organ taped with a special organ-stop to give it a celeste-type sound.

But the song's style was a knocked off from Dylan's "Desolation Row" from the *Highway 61 Revisited* album. Rock's poet laureate used abstract imagery to whip up moods and tones to tell fragments of a storyline instead of a complete narrative. If Dylan's imagery is bleak, Lennon's images are colorful, a clear attempt at conversion to establish the difference.

Lennon continued the unabated borrowings from extraneous sources like a true White Negro, and claimed them as his own by interpreting them in his idiosyncratic style. He lifted the chase concept from the *Wool and Water* chapter of Caroll's *Through the Looking-Glass* where Alice is taken down a river in a row boat by the Queen, who had suddenly changed into a sheep. "Plasticine ties" came from Lennon's favorite *The Goon Show* translated as *"Plasticine porters with looking glass ties."*

But this idea was in no way original. A year before, Jefferson Airplane's lead singer Grace Slick wrote and released "White Rabbit" whose lyrics are a mix of *Alice in Wonderland* and LSD imagery. By this time, Lennon and McCartney were aware of the West Coast psychedelic scene.

The song got its drug association from the title's initials (LSD) and its drug-induced imagery. From its release, Lennon and McCartney refused to acknowledge that the song was about an acid trip. (Note: McCartney admitted in the June 2004 issue of *Uncut Magazine*, "It's pretty obvious.")

"Lucy in the Sky with Diamonds" is an extraordinary distillation of Lennon's influences and creative ideas of the time.

"It's getting better all the time," the catchphrase where McCartney based **"Getting Better"** (Lennon-MCCARTNEY), came from Jimmy Nichols. Nichols used to say it frequently whenever the rest of the Beatles asked him to relieve Starr for his tonsil problem. He had a tonsil operation during the recording sessions. The other supposed source of the title was when McCartney took a walk with Beatles biographer Hunter Davis and told the latter what a nice spring day it was, commenting the weather's "getting better all the time."

Lennon contributed the lines: *"I used to be cruel to my woman / I beat her and kept her apart from the things that she loved. / Man I was mean but I'm changing my scene...,"* indicating that he regretted his chauvinistic attitude towards women. "Women's liberation" having taken root in western societies at the time, this song suggests Lennon's own liberation.

He also contributed the sardonic line *"It couldn't get much worse"* during the recording session.

Martin created the pulsating notes by hitting the piano strings with a mallet, a Beach Boys technique, instead of playing the keyboard in the normal way.

"Fixing A Hole" (Lennon-MCCARTNEY), believed to be about drugs, was actually about a house that McCartney bought in Scotland called High Park. The house, built in a 400-acre property, was in very poor condition. It had a hole on the roof where the rain came in, thus the song's lyrics.

"This song is just about the hole in the road where the rain gets in," McCartney explained to deny it is about shooting up heroin. "It's a good old analogy -- the hole in your makeup which lets the rain in and stops your mind from going where it will. t's you inferring with things...If you're a junkie sitting in a room fixing a hole then that's what it will mean to you, but when I wrote it, it meant if there's a crack or the room is uncolorful, then I'll paint it."

The *"See the people standing there"* verse is about fans who hung around his house the whole days which irritated him.

Evans helped compose the song, but settled for a straight payment instead of a composer credit. He agreed to this arrangement to preserve the Lennon-McCartney writing tandem which the partners had maintained as their only professional name until this time. But according to *The Beatles: Off the Record* author Keith Badman, he never received royalties.

When he was virtually free of negative impact, McCartney did admit in 1997 interview with *Q* magazine during the launch of his *Flaming Pie* CD that "Fixing a Hole" was inspired by marijuana which he was smoking a lot during its creation.

McCartney distilled **"She's Leaving Home"** (Lennon-MCCARTNEY) from the Beach Boys sappy songs "You Still Believe in Me," "The Little Girl I Once Knew," and "Caroline No." The narrative was from a news item he read in the *London Daily Mail* entitled "A-level girl dumps car and vanishes" about 17-year-old Melanie Coe who had been missing for two weeks. Her father could not understand why she left home despite the material comforts she enjoyed. McCartney knew Coe. Three years before, he had presented her an award in the teen-oriented music and dance show *Ready Steady Go!*

The melody recalls Edvard Greig who composed the incidental music of "Peer Gynt," the Henrik Ibsen's play, and Antonin Dvorak, the Czech composer of romantic music and his "New World Symphony." For sure, White Negro McCartney had turned into classical music for riffs he must nick to start up songs.

Lennon added the counterpoint Greek chorus lines, expressing the parental views of disappointment which Lennon and McCartney sang its long sustained notes in falsetto style. They were actually admonitions that Aunt Mimi used to say to Lennon in his younger days. Mimi took care of Lennon when his mother remarried and later died in a car accident.

A misunderstanding cropped up between McCartney and Martin during the recording of this song. McCartney was fired up about completing "She's Leaving Home," but Martin failed to show up due to a previous commitment to produce British singer Cilla Black record. He decided to ask Mike Leander to write the musical score so the Beatles could proceed with the recording. Martin did not like it, but had the good sense to correct two notes he did not like in the score.

Lennon copied and created the lyrics of **"Being for The Benefit of Mr. Kite"** (LENNON-McCartney) from an original poster advertising a circus near Rochdale, Lancashire in Feb. 1843. Lennon bought it from an antique shop while in Sevenoaks, Kent on January 31 for the filming of the "Strawberry Fields Forever" promo clip. The poster quoted verbatim reads: *"Being for the benefit of Mr. Kite / Over Men & Horses, through Hoops, over Garters / And lastly through a Hogshead of REAL FIRE / In this branch of the Profession MR H. challenges the world / Mr. HENDERSON will undertake the arduous / Task of THROWING TWENTY-ONE SOMERSETS, ON THE SOLID GROUND."*

Using the evocative character of Pablo Fanques and old-English-style direct (as highlighted) or adapted quotations from the poster, here's how Lennon transposed them: "For the benefit of Mr. Kite / *There will be a show tonight on trampoline* / The Hendersons will all be there / Late of Pablo Fanques Fair-*what a scene* / Over men and horses hoops and garters / Lastly through a hogshead of real fire! / *In this way* Mr. K. will challenge the world! / *The celebrated* Mr. K. / *Performs his feat on Saturday at Bishopsgate* / The Hendersons will *dance and sing* / *As Mr. Kite flies through the ring don't be late* / Messrs. K and H. assure the public / *Their production will be second to none* / And of course *Henry The Horse dances the waltz!* / *The band begins at ten to six* / *When Mr. K. performs his tricks without a sound* / And Mr. H. will demonstrate / (Ten) summersets he'll undertake on solid ground / *Having been some days in preparation* / *A splendid time is guaranteed for all* / And tonight Mr. Kite is topping the bill."

Lennon's streak of genius in this lyrics is *"A splendid time is guaranteed for all"* which was used for the album jacket's blurb.

Lennon specified to Martin: "I want to smell the sawdust on the floor." To get the circus atmosphere that he wanted, he took a tape of calliope, a steam organ, cut it into fragments, threw them in the air, and had them reassembled at random. Providing the calliope background for the song was chance art at its best.

In 1869, Carroll published a collection of poems called *Phantasmagoria* which turned out similar to the process of creating the crescendo. It states: *First you write a sentence, / And then you chop it small; / Then mix the bits, and sort them out / Just as they chance to fall: / The order of the phrases makes / No difference at all"*.

Lennon recorded a series of individual organ notes, then marking the tape where each note began and ended. He took a scissors in hand and cut the string of notes into individual pieces. Each piece contained one note. He took the pile of individual notes and threw them up in the air. Then retrieving the pieces, Lennon spliced back together the notes in the order that they had chanced to fall. The end result was used as a crescendo to the song.

Lennon had an extreme assessment. He once stated he "wasn't proud" and "was just going through the motions" while in the 1980 *Playboy* interview, he described it as "pure, like a painting, a pure watercolour."

BBC banned this song for the phrase "Henry the Horse," the two words being street words for heroin. As to be expected, Lennon denied the association when it happened.

During dinner at the house of artist Klaus Voormann in Hamstead, London, talk among Harrison and close friends centered on theories about LSD experimentation and the death of ego with Hindu mysticism while everybody was high on marijuana. It floated around cosmic issues like "wall of illusion" and "the love that flowed between us all." After dinner, Harrison doodled with the harmonium, a reed organ with hand-pumped bellows. He came up with the tune of **"Within You Without You"** (Harrison), its lyrics turning out a verbatim report of the dinner conversation, starting with the first line, "*We were talking about the space between us all,*" which opens each of the three verses.

This turned out a repetition of the way Lennon created "She Said, She Said."

Harrison modified the song's music from the three-part recording of Ravi Shankar for All-India Radio. Shankar's piece runs for 30 minutes so Harrison decided to abbreviate drastically into six minutes which was further abbreviated into five minutes by edit.

Only Harrison was the Beatle present during the recording sessions, with Indian musicians and a string section doing the score as composed by Martin. This makes it the second Beatles song with only a Beatle involved in the entire creation after McCartney's "Yesterday." The composer's idea, the canned laughter at the end was placed there to lighten the mood and to follow the album's theme. This technique set a precedent in Beatles' songs as its use would be repeated in future songs.

McCartney claimed he wrote the melody of **"When I'm Sixty-Four"** (Lennon-McCartney) when he was 16 years old. He supposedly revived the composition in the new album as a tribute to his father who turned 64 in 1966 when recording the album started. Lennon recalled, "Paul wrote it in the Cavern days. We just stuck a few more words on it like 'grandchildren on your knee' and "Vera, Chuck and Dave'." But close scrutiny reveals the song is a rewrite of the downbeat The Shirelles hit song "Will You Still Love Me Tomorrow," the B-side of the hit single "Boys," which was interpreted by McCartney as a swing number.

If one takes note of the similarity in the theme of insecurity about the future and how McCartney changed its melodic approach, the theme of "When I'm Sixty-Four" is basically what "Will You Still Love Me Tomorrow" asks: Will you still love me tomorrow? "When I'm Sixty-Four" asks: *"Will you still love me when I'm sixty-four?"* -- with "*tomorrow*" simply converted into "*sixty-four.*"

McCartney constructed his song using the exposition technique and by ending each question like the Goffin-King song. The difference lies in McCartney's expansion of Goffin-King's two lines into five lines, retaining the phrasing while diffusing much of the source.

"Will You Still Love Me Tomorrow" reads *"Tonight you're mine completely / You give your love so sweetly / Tonight the light of love is in your eyes / Will you still love me tomorrow,"* which was distilled by McCartney as "*When I get older losing my hair / Will you still be sending me a Valentine / Birthday greetings, bottle of wine / If I'd been out till quarter to three / Would you lock the door? / Will you still need me? / Willl you still feed me? / When I'm sixty-four.*"

The similarity in the question device is more evident in the second verse that asks three questions: "*Is this a lasting treasure / Or just a moment of pleasure / Can I believe the magic in your sighs? / Will you still love me tomorrow.*"

The distinct phrasing used by Goffin-King in the last line of the refrain (*"When the night (caesura) meets the mor---ing sun?"*) with a melisma between the syllables of "morning" was converted by McCartney as "*I (caesura) could stay with (caesura) you."*) McCartney used the refrain twice and even quoted the repetition of the same line with vocal harmony in his second refrain: "*Tonight with words unspoken / You say that I'm the only one / But will my heart be broken / When the sun meets the morning sun"* to (Oooh-) */ You'll be older too. (aah-) / And if you say the word / I could stay with you.*"

Not contented with the above derivations, he copied from Goffin-King in the last refrain, a demand for an answer for the questions asked: *"I'd like to know that your love Is love I can be sure of So tell me now, and I won't ask again / Will you still love me tomorrow me?"* to "*Send me a postcard, drop me a line / Stating point of view / Yours sincerely, wasting away / Give me an answer / Fill in a form / Mine forever more / Will you still need / Will you still feed me / When I'm sixty-four?*"

Lennon commented in the 1980 *Playboy* interview, "I would never even dream of writing a song like that."

McCartney based **"Lovely Rita"** (Lennon-MCCARTNEY) on a real policewoman named Rita who apprehended him for wrong parking. A parking meter attendant is known as a "meter maid" in the U.S. But more than this background information, the song's accomplishment is the strong-woman character that McCartney gave to Rita.

True to Spector's "Wall of Sound" techniques, the song used combs and paper to create it.

Lennon adapted the title of **"Good Morning Good Morning"** (LENNON-

McCartney) from a Kellog's Cornflakes TV commercial. While sitting on the piano, unable to compose a song, he heard from the TV set, "Good morning, good morning. The best to you each morning. Sunshine Breakfast, Kellogg's Corn Flakes, crisp and full of fun" line from the Kellog commercial, and it gave him the motive for a song about having nothing to say, adding Sounds Incorporated-like saxophone as Lennon requested to Martin.

But it is not correct to claim that Lennon got the song's motive from the Kellogg TVC. Even before he could mishmash the *"Good morning, good morning"* line, he already have the lines, *"People running round / It's time for tea and Meet The Wife."* He had been avidly following this BBC comedy series, a Freddie Frinton and Thora Hird starrer.

"Good Morning Good Morning" turned out to be a mediocre output, which Martin spiced up by adding backing vocals and adding the animal sounds. No doubt the idea behind these cries was picked from the Beach Boys' "Caroline No" which has Brian Wilson's dogs Banana and Louise barking in the closing. The song's sound effects were taken from the EMI sound effects tapes "Volume 35: Animals and Bees" and "Volume 57: Fox- hunt," with Lennon specifying that they be ordered based on the ability to eat its predecessor. The sound of a chicken clucking at the song's end had the same key as the initial guitar note at the beginning of the penultimate line linking these two tracks almost seamlessly. Martin described this as one of "the luckiest edits one could ever get."

The chicken clucking changes the guitar on the following track, one reason this album is considered as the first concept album.

This case explains the richness of the Beatles' songs. Besides the song's main body, the Beatles' creative team embellished its sound with all sorts of gimmicky, giving it a rich, diverse, and even intelligent feel. They did this by having an uninhibited attitude towards borrowing. Like true White Negroes, they added what they thought would give the song a fuller, therefore, more prominent sound. But rather than chance input, these were studied, with members spending long hours to perfect it. This was what differentiated the early Beatles from the mid-Beatles. They had the luxury of time and the ambition to break barrier.

To end the album, road manager Neil Aspinall suggested a short version of the title song, which turned out to be **"Sgt. Pepper's Lonely Hearts Club Band (Reprise)"** (Lennon-MCCARTNEY), this time, done as a farewell song. Before they stopped touring, McCartney announced the set's end before the closing song, so the role fell to him in this penultimate number. Again imitating *The Jimi Hendrix Experience* by doing straightforward heavy rock, it opens with an augmented ninth, a Hendrix chord with distorted guitar strumming. The Beatles did this song in faster and at a higher key, with the same melody but different lyrics. Applause simulates a live performance at the track's ending to segue into the album's final track.

"A Day in the Life" (Lennon-McCartney), with its T.S. Elliot-type lyrics, distilled the best songwriting style of Lennon and McCartney, bringing the tandem to an artistic peak. Lennon had the main body with he mixed with McCartney's middle eight.

It begins with the *"I read the news today oh boy"* first version with a copy of the *Daily Mail* in front of the piano, opened in the news brief section. The day's news was about an heiress who got killed in a car mishap as basis for the opening verse.

Lennon's inspiration for the second verse, the *"He blew his mind out in a car"* section, came from the death of their Irish friend, Tara Browne, Lennon revealed. In truth, a car accident killed Browne on December 18, 1966. He had been driving a Lotus Elan on Redcliffe Gardens when a Volkswagen pulled out in front, causing him to swerve the car which hit a parked van. Browne died on the way to the hospital.

Lennon did not resort to a straight reporting on the incident. He fictionalized it. He explained, "I didn't copy the accident. Tara didn't blow his mind out. But it was in my mind when I was writing that verse. The details of the accident in the song -- not noticing traffic lights and a crowd forming at the scene -- were similarly part of the fiction."

The next section refers next to Lennon's solo movie *How I Won the War*.

To connect the two parts, Lennon seduces the listener with *"I'd love to turn you on...,"* followed by the crescendo. McCartney had a lick floating in his head for some time, which he was able to use for this song in the form of this crescendo performed by a 40-piece orchestra. This abrupt shift after the 24-beat crescendo is reminiscent of Donovan's "Bert's Blues," and it is a device with an intended meaning of its own. McCartney arranged the crescendo using ideas from the avant-garde composer Stockhausen.

To mark the next section, the sound of a ringing alarm clock ends the bridge. The intention was to edit it out once the missing section had been finalized and recorded. But it was decided to keep it as it complemented the beginning of the next section (*"Woke up, fell out of bed / Dragged a comb across my head"*), rushing to another daily routine which would been time marked. Even if members wanted to delete, it was technically impossible as assessed by Martin.

McCartney explained how he came up with the mid-portion,"It was another song altogether, but it happened to fit. It was just me remembering what it was like to run up the road to catch a bus to school (Liverpool Institute for Boys with George Harrison), having a smoke and going into class…it was a reflection of my schooldays. I would have a Woodbine (a cheap unfiltered British cigarette) and somebody would speak and I would go into a dream."

Lennon launches into another seduction, the *"Ahhhh"* portion, which could havebeen easily picked up from the sensual send up from the third line of the Beach Boy's "Good Vibrations," magnified four times over.

Lennon goes into another *"I read the news today, oh boy"* section, this time around about the discovery of 4,000 holes in Blackburn, Lancashire. This last verse was lifted from a *Daily Mirror* news item. One word was missing to connect "holes" with "Albert Hall." Lennon could not think of the verb for the missing word. Terry Doran, a Beatle assistant and referred to in "She's Leaving Home" as "the man from the motor trade," suggested the word "fill" as in *"how many holes it takes to fill the Albert Hall."*

Lennon launches into another seduction and proceeds to another crescendo, a devastating climax.

The run-out groove finishes with a gibberish that does not end, something like a mantra. This random decision on the part of the creative team works perfectly well, suggesting that life is indeed an endless repetition.

With impressionistic style, innovative production techniques and a complex arrangement, "A Day in the Life's" beauty rests in having multiple levels of meaning like every perfect work of art. While it recalls mundane events, there is the double take on drugs as recreation. On an even higher level, there is the Existentialist meaning of life. This song pulls together the art of derivation and shows that real art could come off it.

As if to mock themselves out of believing the serious of the act, conservative orchestra members wore costume party accessories such as red nose or fake stick-on nipples over their formal attire.

From beginning to end, the *Sgt. Pepper's* album is a complete departure, both in concept and content, from rock. From the way Martin arranged the track list, the album suggested a theme with the inter-connection of song topic and treatment. It starts with "Sgt. Pepper's Lonely Hearts Club Band" and ends with a reprise in abbreviated form of the same song. In between, the gamut of the working class condition is tackled in varying moods and methods. As for the predicament that humans find themselves in, the meaninglessness of life, the album suggests a solution through the finale song's souring climax: getting turned on.

Critic Kenneth Tynan noted the album's historical perspective by writing that its release is a decisive moment in the history of western civilization." Professor Langton Winner of the Massachusetts Institute of Technology concurred with Tynan. He wrote: "The closest Western Civilization has come to unity since the Congress of Vienna in 1815, was the week the *Sergeant Pepper's* album was released. For a brief while, the irreparably fragmented consciousness of the West was unified at least in the minds of the young."

Newsweek wrote: "*Sgt. Pepper's* is such an organic work...a rollicking, probing language-and-sound vaudeville which grafts skin from all of the three brows -- high, middle and low -- into a pulsating collage about mid-century manners and madness."

Richard Poirier and Geoffrey Stokes raved this album that by "listening to the *Sgt. Pepper's* album one thinks not of simply of the history of popular music but the history of this century."

John Mendelsohn did not agree with the superlative assessments. Outright, he said that it was the Beatles' "worst album."

Frank Zappa concurred. He opined in a *Rolling Stone* article that "they were only in it for the money," appropriating the aesthetics of the hippies for monetary gain.

NME's David Quantick was less harsh. He wrote: "It's not the greatest album ever made, as some people would have you believe. It's not even the best Beatle album. But it is the first example of recording technology being used as an instrument and it does contain enough traces of the old McCartney lyricism that it appeared to bringing us up against the future even as it tied us nostalgically to the past."

But the most prophetic assessment of the *Sgt. Pepper's* album came from Richard Goldstein in *The New York Times*. He wrote that the album is "dazzling but ultimately fraudulent" and has the "power to destroy rock 'n' roll."

With the *Sgt. Pepper's* album, the group achieved a musical synthesis that far exceeded the subject matter and musical content of pop. By incorporating relevant or interesting ideas, they accomplished in several years what classical music took centuries and jazz music several decades to achieve. *Stereo Review* critic Eric Zalman called them "the first poets of the technological age," crediting their influences in art and life as "irreversible."

Regardless of the mixed and contradictory assessment about this album, the Grammy Awards gave it the Album of the Year, the first rock album to win it, and Best Contemporary Album in the 1968 awarding ceremonies.

But even in this maturity period, the Beatles remained White Negroes. They might not be nicking obscure rock 'n' roll songs but classical music and the developed styles of their peers by them were still imitation. They just became more sophisticated plagiarists.

The clear winner of the Beatles vs. Beach Boys music battle: the White Negro Beatles.

Chapter 5
The decline phase

Rejecting the communal ownership

"It is necessary for us to go out of our minds in order to use our heads."

- Dr. Timothy Leary

The decline phase is that necessary transition period when artistry is in an agonizing changeover, neither a peak nor dip, unconscious or half-conscious, often in denial.

Soon after the release of *Sgt. Pepper's Lonely Hearts Club Band* album, the Beatles lost collective enthusiasm and started to pursue individual intentions, both personal and professional. The album's prolonged production drained creative energy. Distance from the recording studio seemed the only way to recover collective zest.

An artistic culmination that set a standard that the Beatles had to approximate or surpass to rationalize their eminence as a group, instead the reverse happened: They underwent an agonizing downfall.

While Lennon repudiated classical rock, McCartney continued to focus on it, adding a robust inflection of nostalgia to his art. Their artistic proclivities became diametrically opposed. Lennon rejected the upper-middle class sensibility that McCartney cultivated for himself.

Lennon desired to be less studied and wanted to restore rock's freer sensibility into Beatles songs. He wanted to implement this by following the dictates of its form and avoid the production method. He has lost his belief in synthesizing their individual skills and efforts.

By this time, Lennon accepted the fact that the Beatles had reached the highest point they could expect. He believed that the possibilities of classical rock in Beatle songs were exhausted. He was aware of the ruthless cycle of creativity and that, like any other artist, their group was not an exemption.

Despite his bravado, Lennon remained a coward at confrontation. When hurt, he lost his nerve to fight. His first scuffle in high school ended with him retreating when badly beaten up. With McCartney's artistic dominance that started with *Revolver* and fully exploited in the *Sgt. Pepper's Lonely Hearts Club Band* album, for him to stay on with the Beatles meant to succumb to this dominance.

This time, his cowardice translated into a desire to leave the Beatles. He preferred flight to fight. He embarked on a radical transformation of his role as an artist, expressed in the form of emotional independence from the other three Beatles.

Even before the Beatles embarked on the *Sgt. Pepper's* album project, he had started on launching a solo career. He accepted the role of Private Gripweed in *How I Won the War*. By shedding his moptop for a military and adopting wire-framed National Health spectacles, he started to sever his emotional ties with the Beatles.

At the same time, Lennon rejected his wife, Cynthia, who refused to participate in recreational drug use. This installed a mental barrier between them. Their perspectives took a damaging reversal. She spurned Lennon's psychedelic partiality; he ignored her with despicable silence.

By replacing old relationships with newly recruited associations, their pedestal came down. In replacing old alliances, the tested Beatle communal ownership became the easiest to disprove.

The Beatles' decline period started when Lennon rejected the concept of communal ownership. He realized non-ownership of the songs he created himself because of the composing agreement with McCartney, which gave both of them credit even if he did not have any contribution to such songs. He was without a personality in a composing tandem and as a group member. The concept became an emotional burden.

The decline was a product of their actions, not the influence of external factors. These actions provided the impetus to affect such a downturn. The downward route didn't start late into their career. It was a latent force even before they recorded their first song. It did not happen in an abbreviated time. Specific events toward this inevitability catalyzed the turnover.

Its first real indication was when anger directed at them started to permeate

Beatles songs. Inordinately interested in the Beatles financial issues, Harrison recorded "It's Only a Northern Song" during the *Sgt. Pepper's* album production (but Martin did not include it in the final track list) to protest the poor royalty arrangement as a contracted songwriter.

Having ceased live performances where the bulk of Harrison's earnings originated, he was deprived of a major source of income, which was greater than record sales. Subtly held down by Lennon and McCartney from producing more songs, he demanded greater record space to compensate his personal loss, which he was unable to obtain.

Dumping Dylan

When asked in a Q interview if he saw Dylan as a primary influence in his songwriting, Lennon denied it. He explained, "No, no. I see him as another poet, you know, or as competition. Just read my books which were written before I've heard Dylan or read Dylan or even heard anybody. It's the same, you know. I didn't come after Elvis and Dylan, I've been around always. But I see or meet a great artist, I love 'em, you know. I just love 'em. I go fanatical about them -- for a short period. And then I get over it! And if they wear green socks, I'm liable to wear green socks for a period, you know."

Lennon gave a mixed-up answer. He stated that as far as songwriting was concerned, he was original since he was capable of introspection even before he met Dylan as evidenced by his two books, *In His Own Write* and *A Spaniard in the Works*. But as competition, he stated that whatever Dylan did, he could also do, stated like a full-blooded White Negro.

Lennon was a glib talker. What he did not say in his claim as being co-equal to these artists was that he competed with them by imitating their creative output. As this book has pointed out, he did this individually or collectively with McCartney by being a White Negro. He rehashed partially or sometimes even in their entirety the works of these artists and other artists their art of selection, and having done this, their works became those of the Beatles.

McCartney was more circumspect. "He (Lennon) loved Dylan so much... John was like that. John liked gurus. John was always looking for a guru," he said. He recalled that Lennon would introduce to him a person he would call "my new guru." He had to accept whoever this new guru offered, knowing that it might not last. He correctly surmised that this need for a guru was out of Lennon's psychological need for a father figure. He explained, "You know, to understand John you have to look at his past. The father leaving home when he was three; being brought up by his aunt. And his mother, you know. It's extraordinary he made it to the age he made it to."

For McCartney himself, Dylan served as an inspiration. "Maybe he (Dylan) allowed us to go further. He allowed the Stones to go further, then we did 'Pepper' and we allowed everyone else to go further. It was like boot walking... we'd take a step, Dylan's taking a step, Stone's take a step, all of us have from time to time," he said.

Of course, he also conveniently forgot that the first step of a thousand miles happened when they started their art of rehashing, of turning White Negroes.

Perhaps the best assessment of Dylan's influence on Lennon, McCartney, and the rest of the Beatles came from Harrison. He stated: "You know the famous Beatles story: we cleaned up our act a bit. Because Brian Epstein could get us more work if we had suits. By the time Bob came along it was like, yeah, we all want to be more funky again, and please put a little more balls into the lyric of the song. There's a funny thing that I don't think anybody else has noticed and that is when John wrote 'Norwegian Wood.' It was obviously a Bob Dylan song, and right after that Bob's album out and it had a song called '4th Time Around.' You want to check out the tune of that -- it's the same song going around and around."

What Harrison implied was: Dylan copied the Beatles as much as the Beatles copied Dylan. It is a truism in rock's code of imitation.

As far as Lennon was concerned, however, Dylan had served his time. So he could move on as the perpetually evolving artist he pictured himself to be, Lennon rejected Dylan and with the rest of the Beatles, Epstein, and Martin.

Epstein's death

Also to receive scorn was their business manager, Epstein, who was an excellent marketing person, but a weak finance manager. What he lacked in business acumen, he compensated with hard work. He gave them total emotional commitment by protecting them from unproductive business concerns to allow concentration on artistic issues. But in the end, he practically didn't matter to them.

Lennon and McCartney wrote "Baby, You're A Rich Man," suggesting the acrimonious relationship between Epstein and the Beatles in which he benefited from monetary windfall, but rendered the Beatles disadvantaged due to his poorly negotiated royalty schemes.

As much as Epstein wanted to improve, business was slipping from his hands. As his original contract as their business manager neared expiration, his agitation was compounded by personal problems. His lonely bachelor's life was made even lonelier by the death of his father. He attempted suicide after his father's death. And being infected with hepatitis, obviously from promiscuous life he led as a homosexual, he was medically prescribed with tranquilizers and sleeping pills.

He began to lose self-confidence and self-esteem when he learned about McCartney's idea of hiring Allen Klein, business manager of the Rolling Stones, to co-manage the Beatles with Epstein. Epstein had to issue a disclaimer to this possibility to ward off its insidious implication.

At the time the Beatles were planning to go to India to study Transcendental Meditation, Epstein planned a holiday for his intimate friends in his country house. For some reason, most of his friends declined his invitation, prompting

Epstein to seclude himself in his London townhouse bedroom. When he failed to reappear in his usual haunts, a valet broke down his bedroom door and found his lifeless body on August 27, 1967.

The media reported Epstein's death as a suicide. This was corrected by a coroner's report that determined the death as caused by the "incautious" overdose of sleeping pills. The eminent position that Epstein occupied in popular music history was emphasized by *Newsweek*, which eulogized him as "the man who revolutionized pop music in our time."

The untimely departure of Epstein exposed the Beatles to the vagaries and realities of complex business issues for which they were unprepared and untalented. Detesting the appointment of Epstein's brother, Clive, as his replacement, the Beatles decided to be their own managers, with McCartney leading them.

Lennon summed up the turn of events, thus: "After Brian died, we collapsed. Paul took over and supposedly led us. But what is leading us when we went in circles. We broke up then. That was the disintegration."

Martin's demotion

Martin's role was greatly diminished by this time as the Beatles relied less on experimentation and classical instrumentation. McCartney emphasized Martin's dispensability when he asked another arranger to score and conduct "She's Leaving Home." Martin was unavailable when McCartney was fired up with an enthusiasm that led him to hire another producer.

McCartney's decision was also an emotional rejection of the familiarity that Martin's indelible style imparted on the Beatles' songs. But, then, nothing new was coming from that style, only the repetition of proven techniques. This made his usefulness as a collaborator subject to indirect contempt with the rejection of input. Like any artist harboring a self-image, he became unavailable during some recording sessions.

A critic commended the *Sgt. Pepper's* album as Martin's "finest work." This attribution certainly wounded McCartney's ego. Generally regarded as a McCartney triumph, this attribution forced him to prove his mettle at Martin's role.

Determined to disprove aspersions on his artistic supremacy, McCartney focused and unrelentingly pursued the competitor until he came out as the unqualified winner between them. In other words, Martin joined the infamous rank of McCartney's competitors like the defeated Lennon and the bruised Brian of the Beach Boys.

McCartney recognized Martin as a "sage," but reduced his importance in the creation of Beatle song when he stated: "I don't think he does as much as some people think. He sometimes does all the arrangements and we just change them."

This retrogression was partly due to the economic failure of the *Sgt. Pepper's* album. In fact, of all the so-called "intelligent" albums of the Beatles, *Sgt. Pepper's* posted the lowest initial sales among existing records. Although *Sgt. Pepper's* had comparatively higher sales than *Rubber Soul* and *Revolver*, its receipts still registered lower than *Please Please Me* to *Help!* album.

The dismal sales of *Sgt. Pepper's* album convinced Lennon that so much time, money, and effort did not translate into economic gains that gave equal returns to compensate for the input. The artistic success was insufficient to convince him of the album's worthiness.

But, then again, *Sgt. Pepper*'s poor financial yield despite its artistic merits gave the Beatles almost limitless power to undertake their artistic fantasies. If Mendelssohn practiced self-censorship by presenting only his best work for performance and publication or if Picasso selected only his best artworks and hid those that were below his personal standards, the Beatles lost this aspect of quality determination by relegating Martin to the background and virtually taking over his job.

Pop messiahs

The British Broadcasting Corporation (BBC) asked the Beatles to be Great Britain's representative in the first live global television event, a two-hour program called *Our World* which would broadcast simultaneously in 26 counties. They were asked to write a song that could be understood in any language. Lennon came up with **"All You Need Is Love"** (LENNON-McCartney), perfect for the theme as it conveys the love message, a popular catchphrase of the '60s anti-war movement.

Martin, who used extracts from popular pieces of classic and contemporary music, scored the song. It opens with an orchestral rendition of "La Merseillaise," the French National Anthem, followed by the main melody based on the "Three Blind Mice" nursery song, and closes with Johann Sebastian Bach's "2-part invention #8 in F" (not "Brandenburg Concerto" as popularly attributed), snatches of "Greensleeves," Glenn Miller's arrangement of "In the Mood," and The Beatles' own seminal hit "She Loves You" and Jeremiah Clarke's "Prince of Denmark's March" lilting off at the end. He wove these pieces of music into the score believing they were all out of copyright. He was wrong. "In the Mood," used twice in the song, was still under copyright. KPM, the song's publisher, won a royalty settlement from EMI. The Beatles rush-released "All You Need Is Love" flipsided by "Baby, You're A Rich Man" as a single on July 7, 1967 to take advantage of the sales demand created by "All You Need is Love's" international television hook-up.

The Beatles originally recorded **"Baby, You're A Rich Man"** (Lennon-McCartney) for the *Sgt. Pepper's* album, but it was deleted by Martin, ending up being unused. Lennon wrote "One of the Beautiful People" and McCartney the "Baby, You're A Rich Man" section. It was originally entitled "Baby, You're A Rich Fag Jew" in direct reference to Epstein, who was both gay and Jewish.

"A natural E" (in the lyrics *"...How does it feel to be / One of the beautiful people? / Tuned to a natural E / Happy to be that way…"*) refers to E that is the easiest to learn on the guitar for startup bands. Lennon and Harrison used to travel across Liverpool to learn the chord B7, the dominant chord in the key of E, which resolves to E at the end of a phrase.

The "beautiful people" referred to in the song were the hippies who had become a dominant force in western sub-culture by the time the song was written.

The *Magical Mystery Tour* project

Lennon lost Beatles leadership because his recreational drug use had turned into a dependency. Where he held veto power before, he lost it because he could not care less. Aware that the Beatles continued to be a money-making machine, he tolerated it because there was material gain in being a Beatle even if the artistic self-realization that he was consciously seeking was not there. By default, McCartney took over the leader position, taking it upon himself to hold artistic control of the disorganized quartet. He conceptualized new projects and exercised creative management of recording sessions as he took the role of conductor in an orchestra.

It was in this kind of setup the Beatles entered the decline phase of their creative cycle with the *Magical Mystery Tour* project.

McCartney stated their purpose for doing the project as: "We thought we would not underestimate the people and would do something new." Thus, the Beatles took it upon themselves to have total artistic control. The takeover brought an implicit acknowledgement of McCartney's leadership. Lennon, who had begun to be apathetic to the Beatles and was then already occupied by personal interests, implicitly ceded authority to him.

McCartney conceived an idea for a television film about a mystery coach tour during a trip to the U.S. in 1967. He developed the idea upon viewing on American TV Ken Kesey's *Merry Pranksters,* a psychedelic excursion across America in a school bus. He wanted to know how the counter-culture people would behave in such a tour where loud music would be played and their drinks laced with LSD. Tom Wolfe's *The Electric Kool-Aid Acid Test* retold Kesey's adventures and misadventures. For McCartney, it recalled fond memories of mystery tour rides of his childhood. But he wanted to do it without the drugs angle. On the return flight to London, he threshed out project details.

Cooperation reappeared under the direction of McCartney who emerged to assume the duties vacated by Epstein. He discussed the proposal with the other Beatles and agreed to do an hour-long special called *Magical Mystery Tour.* They agreed to air it on British TV over the 1967 Christmas holidays. A frustrated filmmaker, McCartney once showed to director Michelangelo Antonioni his film shorts reminiscent of Andy Warhol's time-lapse works.

On June 1, 1967, the Beatles returned to the studio without Martin and recorded pure instrumental music, designed to prove them as self-contained artists. Martin laid low and allowed them to have their vaunted artistic independence.

Principal photography commenced, a five-day romp that brought its participants and hordes of media people through a mad chase in Hampshire, Devon, Cornwall, and Somerset. As an indication of things to come, it took two weeks to shoot, one week for post-production and eleven weeks for editing. McCartney took it upon himself to do the editing job.

The movie is a Carroll-inspired fit of playfulness, a formless film of a bus ride through the British countryside. McCartney and Starr as main directors began work on the movie, premised on the concept of shooting it and seeing what happens.

Each Beatle contributed impromptu segments and starred in the unscripted portion where professional and amateur performers improvised after the concerned Beatle/s explained their role. It is an application of their songmaking formula into film that relied on chance and its opportunities. Marred by disorganization, the horror of spontaneous filmmaking easily reflected on the final output.

"Hello, Goodbye" / "I Am the Walrus" single

The group released "Hello, Goodbye" and "I Am the Walrus" as a single on November 24, 1967.

McCartney wrote **"Hello, Goodbye"** (Lennon-MCCARTNEY) to demonstrate to friend Alistair Taylor how he composed songs. Taylor recalls in *Yesterday -- The Beatles Remembered* that he and McCartney were playing a harmonium in the latter's Cavendish Avenue house. "He was saying come on Al anyone could write a song and I said if they could there would be a million Lennon and McCartneys. But we pumped some air into this harmonium and he said you hit that end and I'll hit this end and let's get a rhythm going. Then he said I'll shout out a word and you shout out the opposite. Black-White, Come-Go. A few weeks later he gave me a white acetate and said there you go that's the new single. It was a number one -- 'Hello, Goodbye'."

The "*hey-la, hey-la alohas*" ending is a version of a traditional Maori greeting and goodbye salutation, fit for the song's subject of opposites.

McCartney explained the song's meaning to *Disc*, "The answer to everything is simple. It's a song about everything and nothing. If you have black, you have to have white. That's the amazing thing about life."

Lennon hated the song because it was made the A-side of a single with his "I Am the Walrus" on the B-side. He would later describe it as "three minutes of contradictions and meaningless juxtapositions."

Lennon wrote **"I Am the Walrus"** (LENNON-McCartney) when boyhood friend and confidante Pete Shotton, an original member of the Quarry Men, picked up a fan letter telling how a Quarry Bank literature teacher interpreted Beatles' lyrics. Out of exasperation, Lennon created "I Am the Walrus" to beat fans at their own guessing games. He referred to them in the lyrics as "texperts." He did this by converting invented words and borrowed phrases to confuse listeners who were obsessed with looking for such hidden meanings and messages -- the technique a mishmash of Joycean punning and Dylan-like wordplay.

Lennon lifted its title from Carroll's *The Walrus and the Carpenter* from *Alice in Wonderland*. How he came up with it shows literary pretension. He recalled, "For me, it was a beautiful poem. It never occurred to me that Lewis Carroll was commenting on the capitalist and socialist system. I never went into that bit about what it really meant, like the people were doing with Beatles work. Later I went back and looked at it and realized that the walrus was the bad guy. I thought, 'Oh s---, I picked the wrong guy. I should have said, 'I am the carpenter'. But that wouldn't have been the same, wouldn't it? (Singing) 'I am the carpenter…"

The song's two-note rhythm came from a police siren, which Lennon heard while writing the song.

"*I am he as you are he as you are me and we are all together*" opening line is based on the British folk song covered by The Smothers Brothers entitled "Marching To Pretoria," which contains the lyrics, "*I'm with you and you're with me and we are all together.*"

"*Sitting on a cornflake*" is a nonsense lyric.

The refrain "*I am the Egg Man*" instead of "*I am the Walrus*" shows a dichotomy, an example of Lennon's use of Jabberwocky in the manner of Carroll's *Through the Looking-Glass*. The Animals and War's founding member and vocalist Eric Burdon claims in his autobiography that Lennon called him the Egg Man as a hilarious reaction to having intimated to him about cracking an egg over groupies while having sex with them.

"*Goo goo g' joob*" are the final sounds that Humpty Dumpty produced when he had his great fall and died.

"*Mr. city policeman sitting / pretty little policemen in a row*" refers to the police siren Lennon heard while at his home in Weybridge. He wrote these lines to the siren's rhythm.

"*See how they fly like Lucy in the sky*" is a reference to Lennon's song "Lucy in the Sky With Diamonds."

"*Yellow matter custard / Dripping from a dead dog's eye*" are lines were copied from "Dead Dog's Eye," the title of Lennon's favorite song as a Quarry Bank student. ("*Yellow matter custard green slop pie, / All mixed together with a dead dog's eye, / Slap it on a butty, ten foot thick, / Then wash it all down with a cup of cold sick.*")

"Texpert" from the lines "*Expert, texpert choking smokers / Don't you think the joker laughs at you*" is a coined word combining "text" and "expert."

"Semolina pilchards" refers to the type of pudding kids were forced to eat during Lennon's childhood and to a type of sardines fed to cats, respectively. It was coined after Scotland Yard's Drugs Unit Head Detective Norman Pilcher, who had arrested Lennon on a drug charge.

"Elementary penguin singing Hare Krishna" was the first Beatles song to incorporate "Hare Khrisna" in the lyrics, in particular reference to Allen Ginsberg who converted to the Hare Krishna religion. The line refers to the naïve practice of spirited chanting of Hare Krishna followers in public places. It mocks their blind belief of an idol. Lennon admitted in the 1980 *Playboy* interview, "I was writing obscurely, a la Dylan, in those days."

"Man, you should have seen them kicking Edgar Allan Poe" is a snide remark directed at critics who panned the American poet.

The *"umpa umpa / stick it up your jumper"* chorus came from The Two Leslies' "Umpa Umpa," the 1935 song by Leslie Sarony and Leslie Holmes.

Lennon recorded the song's other half with a live feed from a radio program that gives the impression of changing radio channels by flicking the radio's knob back and forth during the song's recording at Abbey Road. Voices such as *"Now, good sir, what are you?"* and *"A most poor man, made tame by fortune's blow"* float in and out of the mix. It came from a BBC radio program, a dramatization of William Shakespeare's *The Tragedy of King Lear, Act 5, Scene 6,* lines 249-259.

The lyrical obscurity of this song leaves it wide open for misinterpretation. Lennon intended to put one over listeners' habit of discovering unintended meanings in the lyrics of their songs. When he referred to "Lucy in the sky" in the song's lyrics, he did not aim for a connection with the song but was leading the listener to make a connection. When he dropped "with diamonds" from "Lucy in the sky," he beat the listener at his own game.

Lennon had invariably insisted "I Am The Walrus" as an original song, denying any link with "Marching to Pretoria" despite the remarkable similarity. Most likely, it was an unconscious recollection of the song during one of his acid trips that he took as an original streak of creativity. The lyrics were clearly in the technique that Dylan tutored him and McCartney, explaining his mindset about its origin.

Regardless of style, Lennon anticipated "I Am the Walrus" as A-side but it went to McCartney's "Hello, Goodbye" as decided by McCartney and Martin for its commercial quality. Their judgment proved correct as the song hit number one in US charts. But this issue further incensed Lennon whose songs were relegated to the less-favored side of the 45 rpm record. He felt that his best and most innovative songs were regarded as "unworthy" although he was willing to compromise if McCartney's song was a stronger material. He put this state of affair between him and McCartney right to the heart of the issue after the breakup, "I got sick and tired of being Paul's backup band."

The BBC screened *Magical Mystery Tour*, a Technicolor movie in black and white, on Boxing Day, December 26, 1967, thus losing much of its psychedelic appeal. Upon telecast, the British viewers reacted with ambivalence, but critics widely panned the movie.

The Daily Express called it "blatant rubbish," denouncing it as "lamentable," "a great big bore," "a colossal conceit," and a "tasteless nonsense." Others dismissed it as "appalling, naïve, puffle, non-sense, contemptuous." It became painfully obvious that nothing happened during filming. It came out as an amateurish home movie.

McCartney admitted the Beatles "goofed" at the project for not thinking it out thoroughly.

Conceived for color telecast, the absence of color and the television's small screen removed the visual excitement the movie predicated in its fantasy concept. This absence stifled the suspension of disbelief necessary to make its fantasy believable. Some songs bordered on weirdness -- such as "Flying," "Blue Jay Way," and "I Am the Walrus" -- that made perception laborious. Its disjointed narrative, the absence of cohesion between medium *vis-à-vis* content, and the avant-garde pretensions of some songs advanced an esoteric sensibility incompatible with Christmas holiday sentiments.

British TV sets were mainly black and white, but color was a main component of the movie's appreciation. Viewing this psychedelic movie in two-tone not only removed its attractiveness, but also rendered it flat and unexciting. The Beatles' failure to make a comprehensible movie overestimated the sensibilities of its target audience. A seasoned moviemaker could have anticipated the effect of the influence of drugs, but the Beatles were certainly not moviemakers with far-reaching insights.

It became apparent the movie failed to deliver viewers' expectation of matching the witticism and craft of earlier movies; they misunderstood its free form.

McCartney was to answer for this debacle to the rest of the Beatles. This came in the form of indirect skepticism to the viability of his ideas. If the *Sgt. Pepper's* album was his crowning glory, the *Magical Mystery Tour* movie was McCartney's thorny stigma. If *Sgt. Pepper's* was a financial debacle, the *Magical Mystery Tour* movie was an artistic failure *and* a financial debacle at the same time.

This case proved one thing: McCartney's leadership of the Beatles was defective. He was not Epstein at business organization; he was no Martin at record production; and without Epstein and Martin, the Beatles were four artistic musicians with a lot of credibility and money to waste.

Magical Mystery Tour album

As a gratuitous move, Capitol Record released the soundtrack of the movie in album form on November 27, 1967 in the US, also titled as *Magical Mystery Tour*.

Still in their fairground period, McCartney converted the shouted opening vocal of "Sgt. Peppers Lonely Hearts Club Band" into the Barker's shouted message in **"Magical Mystery Tour"** (Lennon-MCCARTNEY). It is about a typical coach tour with a tour guide enticing participants to join, entertaining them while on board. The opening *"Roll up! Roll up!"* is a reference for wrapping up marijuana leaves, an "invitation" to get high to start off the Magical Mystery Tour.

Contrary to popular belief, **"The Fool on the Hill"** (Lennon-MCCARTNEY) is not a potshot at the Maharishi. McCartney recalled, "His detractors call him a fool. Because of his giggle, he wasn't taken too seriously…I was sitting at the piano in my father's house in Liverpool hitting a D 6th chord, and I made up 'Fool on the Hill'."

But Alistair Taylor has a different account of the song's origin. In his book *Yesterday*, McCartney recounted a surreal meeting with a man on top of Primrose Hill while walking his sheepdog Martha there. They exchanged greetings and the man said that it was a beautiful view from the top of this hill that overlooked London. While McCartney tried to appreciate the view as the man described it, the man had vanished by the time he looked at him again. McCartney and Taylor were sure the vision was not because of a drug trip, as they had not used any. The talk led to the discussion of God's existence, prompting the song's writing.

All four members composed **"Flying"** (Lennon / McCartney / Harrison / Starr), their first instrumental number, originally entitled "Aerial Tour Instrumental." It was incidental music for the *Magical Mystery Tour*, used as background melody for a psychedelic segment. It is the only incidental music in the film included in the album. The jazz section was taken from other recorded works from Abbey Road's extensive library. For the movie, it was shortened to two minutes from the original length of 10 minutes. The original recording featured a fast-paced traditional New Orleans jazz-influenced coda but it was replaced by tape loops prepared by Lennon and Starr.

Harrison wrote **"Blue Jay Way"** (Harrison) while renting a house in Blue Jay Way, Los Angeles and waiting for friend and former Beatles press agent Derek Taylor and wife Joan, who had taken up residence in the area, to arrive. Taylor lost his way to Blue Jay Way, the heavy fog having decreased visibility in the area. To pass the time, Harrison started playing a little electric organ and managed to come up with this song. An engineer treated Harrison's vocal with ADT with choruses taped backwards to give it the misty atmosphere.

"Your Mother Should Know" (Lennon-MCCARTNEY) is a conversion of "When I'm Sixty-four." A tribute to Jim McCartney, McCartney's father, it's a music hall song conjuring Fred Astaire in his top hat and tail leading a group of dancers tiptoeing to its lighthearted melody. The film *A Taste of Honey* has a song that goes by the same title. This song was also McCartney's alternative for the *Our World* broadcast, which, of course, went to Lennon's "All You Need is Love."

The Beatles previously released "I Am the Walrus" and "Hello, Goodbye" as a single.

The quartet also released "Strawberry Fields Forever," "Penny Lane," "All You Need Is Love," and "Baby, You're A Rich Man" as singles.

Magical Mystery Tour started as a bad business proposition, reflecting the Beatles' indulgence after Epstein's death and Martin's demotion. The infallibility that the Beatles displayed until the *Sgt. Pepper's* album cracked in the *Magical Mystery Tour* blunder -- a monumental first failure.

By casting away their concept of communal ownership and believing the myths about themselves as created by tri-media, the Beatles seemed irretrievably doomed. Having remained White Negroes, they were quick to find a new guru. In the short term, they found the Maharishi; long term, Lennon found Yoko Ono.

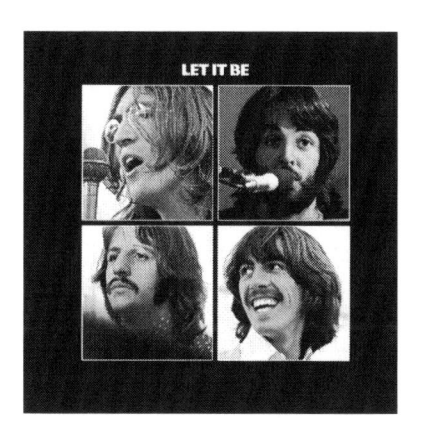

Chapter 6

The shift

"Art is anything you can get away with."

- Marshall MacLuhan

    The Beatles' art of derivation depended, to a large extent, on the personality Lennon idolized at the moment. This means theirs was no idle and unproductive adulation.

    When Lennon abandoned Donnegan & skiffle and embraced Presley & rock 'n' roll, the switch brought them to unprecedented fame. After some years, he replaced Presley with Dylan and recreational drugs and the switch brought the Beatles to the threshold of self-actualization.

    Lennon had always needed a new source of inspiration to give him the imagination to be creative. After Dylan and a brief fling with the Maharishi, Lennon undertook another renewal. He accepted Japanese artist Yoko Ono not only as a lover, but also as an artistic collaborator, turning out to be his new father figure. In effect, Ono and her avant-garde art were the replacements for Dylan, McCartney, Cynthia, and the Beatles.

    Ono did this by introducing Lennon to heroin.

    Lennon met the diminutive Japanese artist when he previewed her exhibit of conceptual art at the Indica Gallery. Through the association that followed, he learned that her small stature did not reflect her gargantuan determination. Her formidable self-image neither waned nor wavered even while she was in emotional pain.

Lennon severed his artistic ties with Dylan when he categorized him as a peer and a competitor. He reasoned out he had established his own writing style in *In His Own Write* as incontrovertible indication of his pre-Dylan originality, thus cutting the creative umbilical cord.

Ono convinced Lennon that succumbing to the bottled-up pressure of being a White Negro was prostituting his art. Of course, Ono did not state it this way. She talked in terms of being a Beatle and how expectations from such an image have made him less creative, contented with imitation and repetition rather than formulating new ideas about his art. As the most creative among the Beatles, Lennon was ready to do anything to improve this self-image, an attempt to get out of the White Negro mold. He found it by falling in love with Ono.

The relationship eventually reduced to a dependency issue, what Lennon called a "teacher-pupil relationship," where Ono became his educator, completing the succession of dominant female figures that punctuated Lennon's life starting with his Aunt Mimi. With a shattered ego as a result of constant acid use, Lennon required an emotional crutch to recover self-esteem. Ono answered this psychological need.

Ono produced anti-art, an informalization of art to make it accessible to common people. She was a member of Cage's avant-garde group, Fluxus. She called her art "mind games" to slow down the viewer's mind. Predicated on abstract communication theories, she stated, "We are just trying to make everyone communicate. An artist's role in society today is to communicate. We try to involve other people to open their minds, to share understanding and enlightenment. Everybody has an infinite interest. All they have to do is to be aware of it."

Declaring "the only thing we can do to make something worthwhile is to do something else," Ono thrived on originality, not imitation. Her art was anti-White Negro. So unique were her works that they repelled by the majority of the people with whom she wanted to communicate in the same way she was raved about by a minority for her uncommon genius. One of her film works was described as "the cinema's nearest equivalent to certain pieces of Bach." She maintained a reputation for originality, which necessarily subverted the White Negroes' ways of seeing, hearing, and feeling.

When Lennon sent his wife to a Greek holiday with friends, he invited Ono to his Weybridge House, determined to pursue her. After he had shown her his tape loop experiments, Ono prodded Lennon for them to produce electronic music. After the sound collage experiment produced the *Unfinished Music No. 1: Two Virgins* album, they made love to consummate their relationship.

Lennon's need for self-determination was impossible to achieve with Cynthia and the Beatles. He found fulfillment by affiliating with Ono. His need for a deep-seated emotional anchor became pronounced as his alienation increasingly made him detached from the rest of the Beatles. Ono somehow summarized Lennon's predicament by making him realize he had no personality while he remained with the Beatles. Until this time, nobody else had the guts to tell

Lennon this. Ono's acceptance of Lennon's drug habit made him accept her. She tolerated it because it was part of the art world from where she came. Ono's bohemian lifestyle allowed drug use, making her a willing accomplice. This influence limited itself to the extent that it secured Lennon's feelings about his self and what he wanted to be.

Understanding of the ambiguous relationship between Lennon and Ono entails several conjectural rationalizations. Ono was really a replacement for McCartney who contained Lennon's personality by covering up for its limitations and excesses. What Lennon and Ono recognized was reciprocity. Ono was the kindred spirit who could tell him the truth. Lennon was the masculine man who understood and accepted her art.

Despite the renunciation of imitation, Lennon did not totally leave his White Negro roots. He grew his hair in the same waterfall style that Ono wore hers. They became identical personalities wearing black or white clothes. As the most educated among the Beatles wives, she made the other Beatles terribly insecure. And they expressed this with outright rejection.

Without explanation, Lennon brought Ono into the control room of Studio Three of Abbey Road at the beginning of the recording sessions of "Revolution." On May 30, 1968, he quickly introduced her to everyone and she thereafter never left his side.

As the perennially mourning live-in girlfriend who had taken to wearing black clothes and never smiled, Ono nurtured the idea of social acceptance by building an impenetrable imaginary wall around her persona. Easily winning out in her pursuit of acceptance by rejection, she repulsed serfs, as well as their rulers.

Their relationship of dependency required Ono's constant presence wherever Lennon went, which inevitably led to the sanctum of the Beatles, the recording studio. Although Lennon termed Ono's presence as an inspiration, undeniably very real in his mind, she became a creative crutch. Together they became a formidable force McCartney had only a whimper of a chance to subjugate. But her presence did not translate to passivity, as the other Beatles had expected. Determined and outspoken about her ideas, Ono considered Beatles songs as substandard to her avant-garde works. She began participating in Lennon's work, suggesting ideas or ways to record new Beatles songs. Lennon had to silence the objection of the horrified Beatles by being cantankerous.

"Lady Madonna" / "The Inner Light" single

The quartet released the single "Lady Madonna" and "The Inner Light" on March 15, 1968.

"Lady Madonna" (Lennon-MCCARTNEY) has several attributions. The piano introduction was lifted from Humphrey Lyttlelton Band's '50s jazz classic "Bad Penny Blues," a minor chart hit in 1956 as produced by Martin. Its chorus is similar to the opening phrase of "Memphis, Tennessee." Overall, it resembles Duffy Power's "Day O'Brien (Leave That Baby Alone)," which was a hit in the

United Kingdom six months before the Beatles released "Lady Madonna." Power was an under-recognized British vocal artist who was a favorite rhythm-and-blues singer of the Beatles. McCartney also admitted that he copied the lead vocals' style from Fats Domino, for whom he originally composed "Lady Madonna." He picked the song's title from a *National Geographic* magazine photo of a nursing African mother entitled "Mountain Madonna." The "see how they run" line was contributed by Lennon. What appears like a brass sound were Lennon, McCartney, and Harrison blowing through their cupped hands.

Harrison adapted the lyrics of **"The Inner Light"** (Harrison) on the *Tao Te Ching (XLVIII)*. Juan Mascardo, a Sanskrit teacher at Cambridge University, watched Harrison and Lennon's appearance on *The Frost Report* during the Maharishi talk on Transcendental Meditation. Mascardo sent Harrison a copy of *Lamps of Fire*, which contains the poem *The Inner Light*. Harrison originally intended this track for the *Wonderwall* soundtrack, incorporating Chinese and Indian influences. To make the song universal, Harrison changed the original lines *"Without going out of my door, I can know the ways of heaven"* to *"Without going out of your door / You can know all things on earth."* Before proceeding to India, Lennon and McCartney decided on a recording session in which they added harmonies to the final line *"Do all without doing."*

"Hey Jude" / "Revolution" single

Although Epstein was dead, his company, NEMS, continued to exist as a legal entity and an on-going concern. According to the original contract with Northern Songs, Ltd., it should receive 25% of Beatles record royalties. Epstein's sibling, Clive, took NEMS chairmanship. As an initial advice, he asked the Beatles to engage in distribution to minimize tax payments, which continued to drain earnings. The Beatles, on their part, thought of opening a clothes retail stop, the Apple Boutique, which transpired on December 4, 1967 at London's Baker Street area.

Apple Corps was also appointed as the manager of the Beatles partnership according to the terms of a deed all the Beatles signed in April 1967. McCartney named the new company "Apple" from Harrison's favorite Granny Smith variety. Ono inspired the logo based on her 1967 exhibit of half household objects entitled *Half-A-Room* including an apple cut into half. Apple vinyl records (45 rpm, EP, and album) have the full apple logo on the A-side and the cut fruit on the B-side.

Lennon and McCartney launched Apple in a New York press conference on May 15, 1968 with divisions for electronics, movies, publishing, record, and retailing. McCartney declared his vision of Apple as "A beautiful place where you can buy beautiful things...a controlled weirdness...a kind of Western communism" while Lennon called it "a psychedelic Woolworth." They set out to establish a creative empire by artists for artists, but "without doing it like a charity and without seeming like patrons of the arts." With the Beatles' Utopian view of business management, Apple Corps. Was destined to fail.

After a long wait, the Beatles released what would turn out to be a monster hit song, "Hey Jude," flipsided by "Revolution" on August 30, 1968. The first single released by the Apple label simultaneously with Mary Hopkins' "Those Were the Days." "Hey Jude" was a token one because its copyright belongs to EMI and the catalogue number to the Parlophone label. "Those Were the Days" holds the distinction of being the first authentic Apple label release.

Originally entitled "Hey Jules" after Lennon's son by Cynthia, Julian, McCartney wrote **"Hey Jude"** (Lennon-MCCARTNEY) to console him when his father fell in love and started living with Ono. He recounted, "I was thinking of a nickname for Julian. 'Hey Jules, don't make it bad, take a sad song and make it better.' You know, don't be too brought down by this divorce, lad, it'll be all right, kind of style."

"Jules" eventually became "Jude," which McCartney considered as a better sounding name based on a character from the musicale *Oklahoma* named Jud. As McCartney placed it, the name was more "country and western." He finally called it "Hey Jude."

Such action suggested a close relationship between them. As a child, he was closer to McCartney than his biological father. Julian disclosed, "Paul and I used to hang about quite a bit -- more than Dad and I did. We had a great friendship going and there seems to be far more pictures of me and Paul playing together at that age than there are pictures of me and my dad."

Lennon indirectly helped McCartney finalize the song by advising him not to change the line, *"the movement you need is on your shoulder,"* which McCartney found stupid. Lennon rationalized it was the song's best line.

As the best application of Spector's production method in a Beatles song, McCartney constructed the instrument and vocal arrangement layer by layer. McCartney plays the piano, Lennon the acoustic guitar, Harrison the electric guitar, and Starr the drums. McCartney handles the lead vocals with the other Beatles providing backing harmonies.

Brilliant in its melody but pedantic in its message, the song uses a technique similar to "Yesterday" to build harmony. McCartney distilled the concept of "Yesterday," which is very much evident in the first musical phrase, "Hey Jude," sung *a capella* with melisma applied on the first word, joined in by piano notes from the second word.

For the first time in two years since they stopped live appearances, the Beatles sang this and "Revolution" on *The David Frost Show* in 1968.

This song is widely considered as the Beatles' biggest-selling 45-rpm disc at five million on first release. It made a popular music precedent with an exaggerated playtime of seven minutes and 11 seconds, more than double the three-minute standard. It almost equals the revolutionary length of seven minutes and 20 seconds of Richard Harris' "McArthur Park" by nine seconds and exceeds the six minutes and 13 seconds of Dylan's "Like a Rolling Stone" by 58 seconds.

McCartney disagreed about Harrison's answer to every line during rehearsal as it did not fit his idea of the song's arrangement and eventually rejected it. Driven to produce the best record at all costs, McCartney turned bossy, "oblivious to anyone else's feelings in the studio" as record producer Ron Richards observed.

McCartney considered "Hey Jude" one of his 10 best songs of the '60s together with the Lennon composition "Strawberry Fields Forever." He called it a "damn good song."

One month prior to the release of the *Sgt. Pepper's* album when the psychedelic band Tomorrow was mixing *The White Bicycle* LP in May, 1967, Lennon and McCartney visited them and admired their work. Tomorrow members influenced Lennon and McCartney with their musical concepts for future works. Vocalist Keith West later abandoned the British underground group for a solo career.

Tomorrow released the single "Revolution" in September, 1967 with the lyrics "*Have your own revolution NOW!*" In August, 1968, approximately 13 months after, the Beatles released **"Revolution"** (LENNON-McCartney) which has the lyrics "*You say you want a revolution*" that seems to respond to West's call for a personal revolution.

"Revolution" captures the revolutionary fervor of its time. Lennon created the song as a reaction to the spreading political activism in American and European universities in 1968. Change being the operative word, Lennon asks those who preach revolution to get their objectives through change.

It is a song through which Lennon thematically came to terms with himself. When still alive, Epstein prevented the Beatles from commenting about the Vietnam War. The more-popular-than-Christ comment of Lennon as misquoted by *Datebook* created unparalleled brouhaha in their public life. Common sense dictated that Epstein prevent another public relations debacle of that scale because the cancelled shows as a result of the public outcry caused huge income losses for the Beatles.

When Epstein died, Lennon felt relieved. He was then free to make political statements through his songs. After mulling over the idea in the hills of India, he began to open his views about war and revolution. "Revolution" is a distillation of these ideas and it served as a follow up to his pacifist idea in "All You Need Is Love."

"Revolution" is the speeded-up version of "Revolution 1," a perfect distillation of Lennon's ideas about the topic despite being forced to drastically alter its tempo. Lennon wanted to release the phlegmatic "Revolution 1" (originally entitled "Revolution"), previously recorded, but which McCartney and Harrison opposed. They insisted the song lacked the upbeat characteristic associated with a single release. To placate their fears, Lennon improved the beat to a point where it turned manic. With the Beatles playing their regular instruments, Lennon sang the frenzied lead vocals. It received overdubs of two distorted lead guitars, handclaps, two additional heavy drum tracks, and second manually tracked lead vocals, an electric piano, and a bass guitar.

The tremendous distortion was Lennon's answer to McCartney and Harrison's contentions. The engineers placed the two lead guitars through the recording console that overloaded the channel and produced the blistering sound. They also compressed and limited the drum tracks that squashed its hard and uncompromising sound.

The song opens with a fuzzed up lead guitar phrase, followed by one drum beat, after Lennon breaks in the manic scream, *"Aaaaahhh!,"* an expanded imitation of the introduction of Berry's "Let It Rock." This was an overdub. Lennon could not catch his scream to lead into the first verse. Nicky Hopkins played solo electric piano.

This single brought the Beatles back to the forefront of popular music, topping the U.S. musical charts for nine weeks and selling eight million copies worldwide on initial release.

Rock's crass commercialization

More than its intrinsic worth, "Hey Jude" provided the Beatles with the formula of a model product, which can be mass-marketed. After the *Magical Mystery Tour* flopped, the Beatles did not recover lost ground, even with the global telecast of *All You Need Is Love*. Something seemed irretrievably lost in the failed forays. When "Hey Jude" hit the airwaves, before becoming the largest selling single in their tattered career, the Beatles spearheaded by McCartney, bounced back with a vengeance -- the crass commercialization of Beatle songs.

By removing the classical strain and drug component of their previous songs, McCartney and Lennon simplified the formula of the Beatle song by deleting its art and retaining only its emotional appeal.

With "Hey Jude" and "Revolution," McCartney and Lennon reshaped the song into a formula-led approach that creates, sustains, and prolongs interest, emphasizes the beat and makes its disparate parts, oftentimes noises made by them, join, blend, and unify in a rhythmic combination that shapes its melody.

As they conceived it, the formula starts with an instrumental introduction that creates the mood. It is a redefinition, in musical terms, of the verse section of songs before the rock 'n' roll era. The Beatles consistently used this device to introduce raga rock in "Norwegian Wood" and "Love You To." The formula is an imitation of the drone concept of raga music to establish its emotional content.

The Beatles consistently used this derivation technique, which follows Spector's "Wall of Sound." They used anything to create this Wall to enclose, divide, support, or contradict its various sound components: electronic noises, distorted sounds, vocal improvisations, nonsense lyrics, and sound effects. The coalescence of design and chance tended to impart to the song intended and accidental importance and meanings. Instrumentation was layered and tended to mass at the mid-section. Depending on the emotional intention, the instrumentation might be reduced, limited to punctuations, or used towards the song's last portion.

At this stage of the Beatles' career, it did not matter to Lennon and McCartney what was eating away at individual members. It was not as important as converting the Beatles into a mass-production machine of disposable songs, the output of the ultimate White Negroes. After baiting their listeners with what sounded like "a damn good song," the Beatles were ready for the kill, to make their listeners shell out huge amounts of money for what was no more than dumping the tympanum with artistic rehashing.

Living up to its notoriety of being the least original of the mass arts, even relishing in the crime and definitely not minding the cash fallout, rock became nothing more than a rehash. Lennon declared matter-of-factly: "All music is a rehash. There are only a few notes. Just variations on a theme." By debunking claims of originality in popular music, he succeeded in propagating a fraudulent White Negro creative practice that made him its most compelling prophet. He explained the Beatles' rehashing code: "We're the receivers; we're just interpreting it as British kids." He was categorical in stating that there is nothing original in pop music, that any counter-claim is a deception.

Lennon vs. McCartney

Ill feelings among Beatle members gravitated toward McCartney as he had always been a perfectionist. Thus, this obsession with perfection resulted in a sense of isolation. But this did not hinder him from pursuing his ends. As the presence of Ono began to pose a problem, he became more determined to assert the glory of his perceived talents. It was his way of impressing upon the public that the Beatles was a self-sufficient group that needed an outsider to take it out from artistic ennui, as Lennon believed. Lennon's decision to let in Ono into the Beatles' career as recording artists was regarded as an unnecessary intrusion.

The Beatles was actually beginning to disintegrate, though McCartney failed to perceive it. Lennon, on the other hand, was able to recognize the malignant signs of Beatles' disintegration. He was even accusing McCartney of "subconscious sabotage" of his songs. McCartney continued to perpetuate the Beatles as a creative ideal to the extent that he believed he was the Beatles by himself. This was McCartney's motivation until he faltered at its impracticality.

This did not mean their artistic abilities had permanently sunk to an all-time low. Their individual capabilities to create songs had considerably improved. But then the absence of the Lennon-McCartney magic caused the decline of the quality and identity of their music. On the other hand, the quality of the Beatle songs as a whole could not be regarded highly because of their inconsistencies in terms of depth and range.

The decline of Beatle songs in quality was not immediately apparent. In fact, the quartet gave contradictory signs. Once they reached this point, their music started to manifest increased productivity, grandeur, and wide variations, belying the gradual disintegration.

The artistic inadequacy of the succeeding albums proved their failure to preserve or improve their standards to meet critical expectations. The general output was mediocre. A lack of common commitment diluted the potential of those works, aside from the fact that even the members constrained themselves with self-imposed limitations. Exceptions to the stream of mediocre songs, the *Abbey Road* album specifically, became sparse.

The inconsistencies in standards ranged from inconsequential manifestations to extensive discrepancies. It went on for three years, from 1968 to 1970, the longest phase in their creative cycle, manifesting their loss of direction. As they tried to adapt to their new situation, they seemed to contradict it at the same time. In the end, it made them realize that the situation seemed irreversible, as they became both the perpetrator and the prey of their predicament. The Beatles began to disregard quality and value as indispensable components of their output. This period saw Lennon and McCartney returning to unabashed adaptations of early influences and imitation of unrecognized works of British and American musicians who had not gained wide popularity. The Beatles committed copyright infringement for the unauthorized use of Glenn Miller's "In the Mood" in "All You Need is Love." The omission of quality control filled the succeeding LPs with copied and substandard works as a consequence. The inclusion of songs rejected in previous albums became predominant in the albums of the period.

Lennon and McCartney wrote songs on an individual basis as a practice. The convenience of avoiding confrontation, whether artistic or personal, proved more beneficial than the advantage in the proven strength of collaboration. They opted to compose individually, usually in the solitude of the studio or in the isolation of their respective homes. McCartney wrote complete songs while Lennon brought incomplete compositions, as he preferred to finish them in the recording studio.

For reactions and comments and to compensate for Lennon's unreliability, McCartney submitted half-finished compositions to persons he trusted. Lennon's coherence became a larger concern as his mind dallied on preoccupations outside areas of concern of the Beatles. McCartney's intransigence was not only destructive but also counter-productive.

Without the benefit of an equal creative mind to bounce off his compositions, McCartney bordered on emotionalism and idealism. On the other hand, left to his own devices, Lennon became overly entrenched in his ideas that were not subject to compromise for improved mass appreciation ("Revolution No.9," "I Want You (She's So Heavy")). As their egos became bigger than their creative minds, Lennon and McCartney's creativity proved inadequate. The extraordinary energy that worked for them very well dissipated and weakened. The robust creativity of the previous period turned lean, reduced to its elements of displaced perceptions. The Beatles, in turn, became fragmentized, freed from the bridle that Lennon and McCartney used to rein.

This disintegration extended to the recording studio sessions that slowly turned into an arena of conflicting ideals and intentions. The drift was not limited to the domain of Lennon and McCartney; it started to rub off on Harrison, Starr, and even Martin. Recording the music became an individual rather than a collective undertaking. The non-involvement of all the members in recording a song initiated by McCartney and Martin in "Yesterday" became a standard practice at this point.

Partly due to the mass production intentions, they broke up into smaller groups of three or less members to record songs in *The Beatles* and *Abbey Road* albums. Lennon and McCartney had become insensitive to the basic need for unity and cooperation among themselves; they no longer treated the other Beatles as indispensable parts of a whole. They resorted to using outside musicians, a less complicated set up that prevented clashes of egos among themselves. They regrouped only when the camera was present.

Quite ironically this period saw the widest release of songs for the Beatles. Four albums that contained 70 songs ((*The Beatles, Yellow Submarine, Abbey Road,* and *Let It Be*) and 10 single releases, doubled the number of songs they normally produced. This enormous output was not because they became more prolific. It became an exercise in songmaking that disregarded standards. As a consequence, the Beatles name became associated with mass production, literally making them a music machine. Any person directly associated with them could append the Beatles names to their individual work and duly claim it as the work of the Beatles. These are called "fillers," the collective term for musical pieces of substandard quality that are not discarded because they possess some characteristics that may prove useful to meet the required number of songs for new albums. The commercial success the Beatles enjoyed during this period was not based on quality, but the magic that their name spelled. Like any magic, it is good as long as it shows potency. For this, the Beatles had to enhance their name's magic that was greatly reduced by their successive failures. Their publicity machine did this by resorting to their mighty tool: the media.

The subsequent albums registered higher sales, proof to Lennon's claim that the market wanted ordinary quality.

The *Get Back* sessions

The last quarter of 1968 was troubling for Lennon. Cynthia won the divorce suit she filed against him on grounds of adultery. Ono suffered a miscarriage. Both Lennon and Ono were taken into police custody for cannabis possession, which Lennon owned up to in order to extricate Ono from responsibility.

The synergy of the communal ownership was sorely missing when the Beatles entered the Twickenham film studios on January 2, 1969 to begin rehearsing new songs for a live television show to be transmitted worldwide. While Lennon was perennially stoned, the Beatles commenced this undertaking with displaced objectives, poor interpersonal relations, and discontentment brought about by successive failed projects, money disputes, and contrasting ambitions.

McCartney theorized the root of their predicament: "I mean we've been very negative since Mr. Epstein passed away...That's why all of us in turn have been sick of the group, you know." He gave the solution to the problem: "It's discipline we need."

McCartney hypothesized if the Beatles could play live on film or stage with an audience, the shared loss of eagerness would be restored. McCartney began to rehearse the Beatles. The title of the project, *Get Back*, reflected the intent for the Beatles to return to their roots as a live performing group. The rest of the Beatles could not care less. A common lack of eagerness met the well-meaning proposal. Lennon suggested it was better to break up. Harrison rejected touring, but consented to the film idea.

The new songs would be played live before an audience. This excluded technical gimmickry exemplified by the extensive use of overdubbing to make the sound fuller. The songs must have a straightforward quality, reproducible for live performances and the public's expectation of the Beatles song must remain unchanged. Harrison recruited American organist Billy Preston to play the vital fifth instrument. He was there for a different implied purpose, to break the tension among members.

To organize the project, McCartney got more determined and domineering, which Martin referred to as McCartney getting "bossy" in getting them together and which the other Beatles greatly disliked. Wielding a superior attitude towards Harrison, McCartney nagged Harrison on his guitar technique. The latter had just come back from a U.S. trip (which should have invigorated him), but then the high morale he got from it could not extend itself to the studio as he became McCartney's object of put-downs. Harrison walked out.

When McCartney prodded the Beatles, "Come on, we've got this film to make," Lennon and Harrison would invariably dismiss him with a "Shut up!"

But the camera is merciless: it sees everything. In the *Get Back* footages, Lennon attempted to settle the score with McCartney's rejection of his moves to integrate Ono's artistic initiatives into Beatle songs. The camera captured Ono leading the Beatles in an electronic experiment, unceremoniously dropped as fast as they picked it up for its harshness and lack of melody.

When Lennon wanted to re-record the out-of-tune "Across the Universe," which he contributed to the *Nothing's Gonna Change My World* album, McCartney met his request with a yawn. To save face, Lennon suggested impromptu music-making, "Anyone want to do a fast one?" When McCartney began to play a boogie on the piano, Lennon realized McCartney's wanton inconsideration.

McCartney did not recognize he had aggravated Beatles relationships. He maintained an uncompromising attitude that excluded the other members and the people close to them in the blind quest to perpetuate the group.

Although the film was sanitized through editing, to hide the telltale signs of the missing communal ownership, the cameras managed to record the group's fleeting moments of harmonious kinship. It strongly contrasted what was happening to the Beatles while at work on the new album. This would turn out to be the *Let It Be* album. Outtakes showed the unsavory side of its proceedings.

The Beatles needed the camera's power to see what was apparent. They were obviously becoming separate parts and no longer a unit, their relationships hopelessly strained and splintered. The synergy was no longer there. Fragmentized intentions and efforts had taken over. The making of the album became a study in contradictions. The lack of complementation paved the way to perdition. McCartney's efforts had become counter-productive. No music playing could save them from themselves. Martin was conspicuously absent in many of *Get Back's* recording sessions. For unspecified reasons, Glyn Johns, hired as recording engineer, dispensed the responsibilities of a producer.

The ambitious worldwide telecast ended as an improvised concert on the rooftop of the Apple building. Exchanging the cellars of Liverpool for the rooftop of a London building met their basic need to sing in front of an audience. But it was a miserable exchange, totally inappropriate for supposedly great musicians who had changed the world.

Primarily because of the Beatles' lackadaisical attitude towards the project, the *Get Back* album was patched up from hundreds of hours of rehearsal tapes and 29 hours of documentary footages. Even the book component of the project encountered production delays. No longer wanting any part in the album's completion, Lennon and McCartney gave Johns the free hand to compile the *Get Back* album. Once completed, it failed to capture the excitement expected from a live concert, causing concerns of possible rejection from the buying public, leading to the freezing of the ambitious project.

The Beatles album

Instead of finding new inspiration in India where they collectively went to learn Transcendental Meditation in 1967, the Beatles discovered that they had become irretrievably divided. Just the same, they automatically returned to the studio to record songs they came up with in India. They needed to do a double album as each Beatle had been productive in rehashing and there was the need to finish off the Parlophone contract so they could release on their own label, Apple Records. What would they nick but the format of Dylan's two-set album *Blonde on Blonde*.

The Beatles had totally given up their artistic ambition and returned to the idea of the three-minute song recorded as quickly as possible, passing off throwaway numbers as masterpieces and thinking they got away with the corruption.

Their compositions at this time covered the spectrum of music genres, thus giving the impression the Beatles were still as productive as in their maturity phase. But in truth, such productivity did not leave the level of pretension. The White Negroes were no longer working as a group as McCartney fiercely wanted to be in control, about which Lennon, Harrison, and Starr could not care less.

The Beatles album, colloquially tagged by many followers as "The White Album" for its stark white cover, a mark of Ono's minimalist style who wore all-white (or all-black) attires which Lennon had copied by then, was released on November 22, 1969. It only had the embossed title and a stamped serial number as created by fine artist Richard Hamilton

Mike Love of the Beach Boys and Donovan went with the Beatles to Rishikesh, India to study meditation with the Maharishi Mahesh Yogi. Besides marathon sessions and prolonged meditations, they engaged in songmaking, one of their outputs being **"Back in the U.S.S.R."** (Lennon-MCCARTNEY), which McCartney called a parody of Berry's 1959 song "Back in the USA."

Based on British Prime Minister Harold Wilson's re-take the government campaign called *I'm Backing the U.K.*, McCartney converted it to "Back in the U.S.S.R." to sneer at the British establishment. Mike Love suggested to McCartney to use the melody of the Beach Boys' "California Girls."

The BOAC (British Overseas Airline Corp) reference was a joke. Early in their career, the Beatles exchanged free travel on BEA (the European arm) for the Beatles plugging the company. It became an inside joke on how they managed to fit the initials into the song.

In the Beach Boys style, McCartney wrote the *"Ukraine girls really knock me out"* partly with Love. It also incorporated the trademark Beach Boys scat *"Oooeeeeoooo"* for background harmonies.

The line *"Georgia's always on my mind"* is a wordplay. Georgia was one of the U.S.S.R. provinces and it is also the title of the Ray Charles' song "Georgia On My Mind" where McCartney nicked "Yesterday." McCartney even twisted the title into "I'm backin' the U.S.S.R." to show his political leaning.

If this song would have any importance in the floundering Beatles career, it was during its recording when Starr flared up because of McCartney's relentless perfectionism. Before walking out, he announced he was quitting the group. But this did not stop the recording session. McCartney played drums, completing the entire track with Lennon and Harrison.

"Dear Prudence" (LENNON-McCartney) referred to Mia Farrow's sister named Prudence, who was among those who went with the Beatles to learn meditation with the Maharishi. She would not come out of her chalet, having lapsed into a meditation-induced autism. That's why Lennon was assigned to coax her to come out and join the rest. He did this by nicking the tune of The Who's "Our Love Was" and singing it to her with a guitar plucking technique he learned from Donovan during the India trip. He nicked the line *"The sun is up the sky is blue"* straight from Holly's "Raining in My Heart," changing "up" with "out." McCartney also played drums in Starr's absence.

The lyrics *"The clouds will be a daisy-chain / So let me see you smile again"* were influenced by Carroll's *"...Whether the pleasure of making a daisy-chain would be the trouble of getting up and picking the daisies..."* in *Alice Goes Down the Rabbithole.* Of course, Lennon's writing does not match the depth of Carroll's text.

In **"Glass Onion"** (LENNON-McCartney), Lennon engages listeners in another challenge of finding hidden clues and meanings as he did in "I Am the Walrus." He pieced together phrases from Beatle songs such as "Strawberry Fields Forever," "There's A Place," "Within You Without You," "I Am The Walrus," "Lady Madonna," "The Fool On The Hill," and "Fixing a Hole." He created new ones like "bent-back tulips," from the table settings made of tulips with the petals pulled back at the London restaurant Parke's on Beauchamp Place; "a glass onion," the name suggested by Lennon to the group which eventually became Apple Records' contract artist called the Badfinger; "Cast-Iron Shore," the name of a real place; and "a dovetail joint," which is a kind of joint. He explained, "'Glass Onion' was a throwaway song, much like 'I Am the Walrus.' I threw the line in -- *'The Walrus was Paul'* -- just to confuse everybody a bit more. It could have been 'The fox terrier is Paul.' I mean, it's just a bit of poetry. I was having a laugh because there'd been so much gobbledegook about *Pepper* -- play it backwards and you stand on your head and all that."

"Looking through a glass onion" is clearly a re-arrangement of *Alice Through the Looking-Glass*. As *Popular Culture* critic Michael Roos observed, Lennon carried the influence not just the lyrics but to the musical production itself. Roos sees Lennon's experiments with backward music as derivative of the reverse looking-glass motif so abundant in *Alice Through the Looking-Glass*. But this was limited. He was influenced by drugs that made them available on request or recollection.

Acknowledged as the first white reggae song, **"Ob-La-Di Ob-La-Da"** (Lennon-MCCARTNEY), was derived from the Nigerian phrase which means "as life goes on." McCartney must have heard it from either amaican Jimmy Scott and the Ob-la-di Ob-la-da Band, whose leader was his friend, and/or Jimmy Anonmuogharan Scott Emuakpor, a Nigerian congo player, who played in a group called Bad Manners and whom he met in the Bag O' Nails club in Soho, London.

While in India, McCartney sneaked into a makeshift cinema packed with moviegoers. Going home, the line *"Desmond has a barrow in the marketplace..."* popped into his head as he remembered "Ob-la-di Ob-la-da" and used it extensively in the lyrics.

This novelty song was an early adaptation of reggae, the Jamaican sound popularized by Bob Marley, which is a fusion of rock, soul, New Orleans rhythm and blues, and traditional Jamaican folk music.

As usual, the White Negroes beat everybody else!

McCartney, as to be expected, did his borrowing imprudently, so Scott sued him for the unauthorized appropriation, thinking McCartney had nicked it from him. McCartney countered that it is a catchphrase among the Yoruba tribe. Nothing happened with the court case since Scott settled out of court. When Scott was jailed for his inability to pay the support being asked by his ex-wife, he ran to McCartney for help. McCartney agreed to pay a large part of the payment as long as he withdrew the court case against him.

McCartney wrote **"Wild Honey Pie"** (Lennon-MCCARTNEY) when Mike Love wrote "Wild Honey" for the Beach Boys in a fit of one-upmanship while in India. He was ready to discard the fragment of instrumental music he had inserted, but when Patti, Harrison's wife, voiced her liking for the odd piece, McCartney retained it and added the "honey pie" lyrics. Its brevity, regardless of its artistic merits, makes it a filler.

McCartney recalled, "We were in an experimental mode, and so I said, 'Can I just make something up?' I started off with the guitar and did a multi-tracking experiment in the control room...It was very home-made -- it wasn't a big production at all. I just made up this short piece and I multi-tracked the harmony to that, and built it up sculpturally with a lot of vibrato on the [guitar] strings, really pulling the strings madly -- hence 'Wild Honey Pie'."

Based on the tune of "Stay As Sweet As You Are" as written by Mack Gordon and Henry Revel for the 1934 movie *College Rhythm,* **"The Continuing Story of Bungalow Bill"** (LENNON-McCartney) recalls the short story written by Lennon with McCartney in his second book *A Spaniard In The Works* entitled *On SaFairy With Whide Hunter.*

Lennon combined Buffalo Bill and Jungle Jim, calling the main character Bungalow Bill because all meditators in India lived in bungalows. He mocked a young American college student named Richard A. Cooke III, the son of filthy rich Nancy Cooke de Herrera, who visited his mother during the India retreat to protest his action. Richard did go tiger-hunting with his mother, shooting and killing a tiger as the song goes. When they returned, he explained to Lennon and McCartney why he had to kill a tiger. He said, "It was either the tiger or us! The tiger was standing right in front of us." Lennon rewrote this as *"If looks could kill it would have been us instead of him."*

Ono sang the line *"Not when he looked so fierce,"* the first female vocal in a Beatles song.

The *I Ching, The Book of Changes* states the Eastern concept that whatever happens is meant to be, and there's no such thing as coincidence, that everything happens for a purpose. When Harrison decided to write a song based on this concept, he saw "gently weeps" on the book he picked from his mother's bookshelf and proceeded to construct **"While My Guitar Gently Weeps"** (Harrison) around the phrase.

Since the other Beatles did not show interest to record the song, Harrison invited Clapton to do it with him. Initially, Clapton did not like the idea countering that no name rocker had played in a Beatles song. But he agreed to play lead guitar to help out a dear friend. This provided Harrison the chance to play rhythm guitar. Harrison later clarified that Clapton played lead and not guitar virtuoso Casey Vail as rumored. He said, "So Eric played that, and I thought it was really good. Then we listened to it back, and he said, 'Ah, there's a problem though; it's not Beatley enough.' So we put it through the ADT to wobble it up a bit."

But Harrison had to be more assertive to have it recorded. He recounted,

"It wasn't easy, sometimes, getting up enthusiasm for my songs. We'd be churning through all this Lennon-McCartney, Lennon-McCartney, Lennon-McCartney. Then I'd say, 'Can we do one of these?' When we first started recording 'While My Guitar Gently Weeps,' it was just me playing acoustic and singing, and nobody was interested. Well, Ringo probably was, but John and Paul weren't. When I went home that night I was really disappointed because I thought, 'This is really a good song, it's not as if it's s---.' The next day I happened to drive back to London with Eric Clapton and I suddenly said, 'Why don't you come and play on this track?' He said 'Oh, I couldn't do that, the others wouldn't like it.' I finally said, 'Well, damn it, it's my song and I'd like you to come down.' Which he did. And everybody behaved and the song came together quite nicely."

Lennon adapted the title **"Happiness Is a Warm Gun"** (LENNON-McCartney) from an American gun magazine with the cover blurb, "*Happiness is a warm gun*" that Martin gave him during a recording session. The composition has three snippets of songs: The first part with an opening line created by Derek Taylor during an LSD trip with him; the second part about needing a fix, Yoko having introduced Lennon to cocaine in the summer of 1968; and the third part being a parody of the Everly Brothers' style, he decided to piece them together as "Happiness Is A Warm Gun." This explains the song's frequent shifts in time signature. This fragmented structure was copied by Lennon from the Incredible String Band's "A Very Cellular Song." He once claimed the song as a "sort of a history of rock and roll."

Derek Taylor suggested the line *"She's not a girl who misses much."* *"Velvet touch"* was about a fellow wearing moleskin gloves for sex. *"Multicolored mirrors"* was from a news story about a Manchester City soccer fan arrested for putting mirrors on his shoes to look up women's dresses. "Lying with his eyes while his hands were working overtime" was ostensibly about a shoplifter who had fake arms in his coat. Spike Milligan inspired the line *"A soap impression on his wife which he ate and donated to the National Trust."* "Donating to the National Trust" is slang for s---. *"Mother Superior jumps the gun"* refers to Ono because she was one jump ahead rabbitting on in the car.

"Martha My Dear" (Lennon-MCCARTNEY) refers to McCartney's Old English sheepdog named Martha. Based on two short and sweet tunes, "Martha My Dear" and "Silly Girl," McCartney wrote it in India, and which he combined in the style of "The Fool on the Hill," putting Noel Coward-type lyrics. The title might have been lifted from the 1939 movie *A Christmas Carol*. There is a character in the movie where Scrooge addressed a character as "Martha My Dear."

Lennon put into writing his feelings about the two daily mandatory 90-minute lecture sessions and prolonged periods of meditation in India in **"I'm So Tired"** (LENNON-McCartney). As he had to stay alcohol- and nicotine-free, he could not sleep at night, leaving him fatigued at daytime. "Stupid get" is an insult directed at Sir Walter Raleigh who introduced tobacco in England. "Git" is an English variant of "get," a cuss word similar to fool or bastard. *"My mind is set on you"* refers to Ono confirming Lennon's decision to continue his extra-marital relationship with her.

McCartney wrote **"Blackbird"** (Lennon-MCCARTNEY) either in India or on his Scotland farm. He told *Guitar World Acoustic Magazine* that he converted its music from the popular Bach piece "Bourree by Em," which George and Colin Manley taught him to play while a student at the Liverpool Institute. He admitted, "…it was the basis of how I wrote 'Blackbird,' the voicing of the notes…[with] the B string open and the bass G." He opens the song with a segment and repeated it throughout its duration.

The song is a metaphor for all Black women in the U.S. experiencing civil rights persecution. According to Martin, a guy who did birdcalls professionally performed the bird sounds.

"Piggies" (Harrison) is English slang for policemen, and the song is an acerbic commentary in the tradition of "Taxman." Harrison wrote it like George Orwell's *Animal Farm*, but in reverse. A satire about revolution, the book is about animals in Mr. Jones' farm staging an uprising against their human masters. Harrison represented the moral authority revolting against the metaphorical animals, the "piggies." Lennon improved the line *"Clutching forks and knives to cut them for chops"* to *"Clutching forks and knives to eat their bacon,"* suggesting to cannibalize the "piggies." The melody's Baroque flavor snugly fits its English character.

The phrase *"a good damn whacking"* came from Harrison's mother when he asked her something with which to rhyme "backing" and "lacking." When cult leader Charles Manson heard the phrase, he allegedly took it as a secret message from the Beatles for him to attack American policemen.

McCartney did not parody Dylan in **"Rocky Raccoon"** (Lennon-MCCARTNEY) but imitated him with a literary pretension. He copied Dylan in the *John Wesley Harding* album, particularly, "The Ballad of Frankie Lee and Judas Priest," almost perfectly but with defective artistry. If Lennon went all out to imitate Dylan in "You've Got to Hide Your Love Away," it was McCartney's turn to play the consummate White Negro in "Rocky Racoon."

As pointed out by www.morethings.com, McCartney begins the song with a no pause recitation of the lyrics (*"Nowsomewhereintheblackmountainhillsof-Dakota…"*), a typical Dylan way of singing. There are also hints of harmonica. And let us not forget the song also attempts Dylan's moralizing technique by mentioning Gideon's Bible, but it ends there, a mere mention. It is not a tribute to Dylan, but a triumph at shameless derivation.

Starr wrote **"Don't Pass Me By"** (Starkey), the first song written by him, in 1963, but did not get to record it. Cowboyish in tone, it was undoubtedly out of place in the so-called Beatles sound of the time. This free-for-all album provided him the opportunity to record it, four years later! If Starr was not as prolific as Lennon and McCartney, or even Harrison to a certain extent, it was because he was contented with being a drummer. Or at least until this designation as a songwriter was given to him in the group without censure or pressure.

"Why Don't We Do It on the Road?" (Lennon-MCCARTNEY) modifies

"Girl From Ipanema" done in the Little Richard-style. The rapid-fire copulation of monkeys in the mountains of Rishikesh, which McCartney observed during the India trip, inspired the song. He recalled, "I was up on a flat roof meditating and I'd see a troupe of monkeys walking along and the male just hopped onto her back and gave her one, as they say in the vernacular. Within two or three seconds he hopped off again, and looked around as if to say, 'it wasn't me,' and she looked around as if there had been some kind of mild disturbance but thought, huh, I must have imagined it. And I thought, bloody hell, that puts it all into a cocked hat, that's how simple the act of procreation is, this bloody monkey just hopping on and off. There is an urge, they do it, and it's done with. It's that simple."

McCartney adapted **"I Will"** (Lennon-MCCARTNEY) from the Beatles' own downbeat song "I'll Follow the Sun," the first love song McCartney wrote for Linda Eastman whom he was dating at the time. He recorded this song in an unprecedented 67 times before getting what he wanted, desiring perfection for the subject of his affection.

"Julia" (LENNON-McCartney) is a solo Lennon recording, the first time he did it as a Beatle. It is a tribute to the two important women in his life, although Lennon made it appear like it was only about his mother Julia when it was very much about his girlfriend Yoko. "Yoko" is a Japanese word which means "ocean child" in English. The song's modified lyrics came from Kahlil Gibran's *Sand and Foam* poem, transposing the Lebanese poet's point of view to the first person and adding matching words, similar to what he did in "Being For the Benefit of Mr. Kite."

The first person of *Sand and Foam* changed from the third person of "Julia." *"Half of what I say is meaningless / But I say it just to reach you, Julia…"* are direct quotations from *Sand and Foam* as highlighted: *"Half of what I say is meaningless; but I say it so that the other half may reach you."*

"So I sing a song of love, Julia" is a conversion of *"And the seventh time when she sang a song of praise,"*

"Her hair of floating sky is shimmering, glimmering / In the sun" from *"We are fluttering, wondering, longing creatures a thousand thousand years before the sea and the sea gave us words."*

"When I cannot sing my heart / I can only speak my mind Julia" from *"When Life does not find a heart singer to sing her she produces a philosopher to speak her mind."*

"Julia, sleeping sand / Silent cloud, touch me / So I sing a song of love, Julia" from *"The song that lies silent in the heart of a mother sings upon the lips of her child."*

Lennon learned the plucking guitar style, as earlier stated, from Donovan.

McCartney adapted two birthday songs, the Tune Weavers' 1957 "Happy Happy Birthday" and the traditional "Happy Birthday to You" song to come up with the electronic birthday song **"Birthday"** (Lennon-MCCARTNEY). He wrote it after watching his favorite rock 'n' roll movie *The Girl Can't Help It*, which featured songs from Berry, Cochran, Gene Vincent, Fats Domino, and others. Ono sings backup vocals in a Beatle song for the first time with Patti Boyd, Harrison's wife. Ono, Eastman and Patti Harrison provided backing vocals.

"Yer Blues" (LENNON-McCartney) is a sarcastic exaggeration of the blues music flourishing in 1968 with groups like Fleetwood Mac, Ten Years After, and the Chicken Shack as foremost proponents. Written in India, the song reflects Lennon's disenchantment with the Maharishi as suggested in the pessimistic phrase *"Trying to reach God and feeling suicidal. Just like Dylan's Mr. Jones."* "Dylan's Mr. Jones" refers to Dylan's protagonist in "The Ballad of the Thin Man" who is an intellectual but an emotional cripple. To re-create the cramped Cavern Club atmosphere that Lennon wanted, the Beatles recorded in a studio stockroom.

The Maharishi gave a lecture about the unity of man and nature during the Beatles' India trip. McCartney interpreted it as **"Mother Nature's Son"** (Lennon-McCartney) while Lennon wrote "A Child of Nature." The tune, however, is from Nat 'King' Cole's "Nature Boy." The authors embellished it with distillation of two Beach Boys' ditties, "Country Air" and "Friends." It took its texture from "Country Air," the whistling taking the form of "toot too too." Its ending even quotes fully the vocal leap of the "Friends" refrain. Lennon plucks the guitar. At this late period, the Beatles were still grappling with their musicianship.

Originally entitled "Come On, Come On," Lennon converted "Dizzy Miss Lizzie" to **"Everybody's Got Something to Hide Except Me and My Monkey"** (LENNON-McCartney). The idea came from a cartoon where Ono is depicted as a monkey chained to Lennon. The song is about his relationship with Ono and how they had nothing to hide about it; "monkey" refers to Yoko and "monkey on back" to cocaine. One of Lennon's attractions to Ono was her willingness to participate in his recreational drug habit, which Cynthia obviously refused to do. The lines *"Come on, come on"* and *"Come on, it's such a joy"* were Maharishi's catchphrases. The rest of the lyrics are positive statements from the Maharishi during the India lectures.

Lennon explained in 1980: "That was just a sort of nice line that I made into a song. It was about me and Yoko. Everybody seemed to be paranoid except for us two, who were in the glow of love. Everything is clear and open when you're in love. Everybody was sort of tense around us: You know, 'What is *she* doing here at the session? Why is she with him?' All this sort of madness is going on around us because we just happened to want to be together all the time."

Lennon whipped **"Sexy Sadie"** (LENNON-McCartney) in India immediately after he and a group of participants confronted the Maharishi about rumors that he allegedly attempted to rape Mia Farrow. Alexis "Magic Alex" Madras, the Greek electronic whiz who turned out to be a fake, spread the rumor among the Beatles.

With chordal and melodic arrangement similar to "This Boy," Lennon converted "Sexy Sadie" from Smokey Robinson and The Miracles' "I've Been Good to You" *"Look what you've done / You made a fool of someone"* to "Sexy Sadie's" *"What have you done / You made a fool of everyone."*

The song was originally entitled "Maharishi" and having some obscene lyrics (*"You little twit / Who the f--- do you think you are? Oh, you c---."*). Harrison convinced Lennon that he had to change the song's title and tone it down to prevent legal repercussions.

McCartney created **"Helter Skelter"** (Lennon-MCCARTNEY) out of envy of the great reviews The Who was getting for their kind of loud music. To negate the claim that The Who recorded the loudest piece of rock ever, McCartney encouraged The Beatles to record their most raucous song. What he did was exaggerate The Who's "I Can See for Miles," infusing it with the Jimi Hendrix style in "Manic Depression" and "Purple Haze." The title is based on the chutes and ladders of a spiral slide at British fairgrounds, but then McCartney claimed it is about a confusing nightclub. The lyrics *"Will you, won't you want me to break you"* and other variations were nicked from *The Lobster Quadrille* section of *Alice in Wonderland's "Will you, won't you, will you, won't you, will you, won't you join the dance?"*

Producing rock cacophony, a discordant maelstrom, the song ends with Starr screaming "I've got blisters on my finger!" He had developed finger blisters from non-stop and hard drumming during the recording sessions. By the end of one of them, he shouted his physical affliction at the song's end. The rest of the Beatles found Starr's proclamation good enough to be included in the song. It's one more evidence of the Beatles' drawn out affair with chance art to spice up their songs.

Harrison wrote **"Long Long Long"** (Harrison) in India. The "you" in the lyrics refers not to Harrison's wife Patti or any female for that matter, but God. With the working title "It's Been A Long, Long Time," Harrison lifted the sappy chords from Dylan's "Sad Eyed Lady of the Lowlands" off his *Blonde on Blonde* album as suggested by Dylan himself. The song expresses the conflict between Harrison's marital duties and religious beliefs that eventually led to the breakup of his marriage. The Wall of Sound in the recording includes a bottle of Blue Nun wine rattling on the piano's top.

This is the original lethargic version of "Revolution," now entitled **"Revolution 1"** (LENNON-McCartney) as Lennon wanted it. When the other Beatles opined it was not fast enough, Lennon sped up the tempo in exasperation. This fast version with the manic scream was released as a single.

Lennon wrote the song after watching on television the *Spring of Revolution* participated in by thousands of people who marched in protest to the American Embassy in London's Grosvenor Square. He expressed his pacifist views about revolutions. He wanted to know the plan of such revolutionaries as Jerry Rubin and Abbie Hoffman, and declared that if they were going to use violence, then they should count him out.

This song contains the lines *"When you talk about destruction / Don't you know that you can count me out"* which is opposite of "Revolution's" "in" and "out." Lennon explained he had not finalized his stand about revolutions when "Revolution" was recorded so he included both options.

McCartney grew up listening to songs in the style of **"Honey Pie"** (Lennon-MCCARTNEY). Written in the music halls songs of the Flappers from the '20s, "Honey Pie" is a tribute to his father James who loved such songs.

Harrison adapted the title **"Savoy Truffle"** (Harrison) from a Mackintosh's Good News Double Center Chocolate Assortment box. Upon checking out the names on the box, he decided to make a song out of them. As such, the song has the words Crème Tangerine, Montelimat, Ginger Sling, Pineapple Heart, Coffee Dessert, Savoy Truffle, and Apple Tart. Derek Taylor contributed the chocolate names Cherry Crème and Coconut Fudge and the line *"You know that what you eat you are,"* lifted from the title of a movie *You Are What You Eat* by friends Alan Pariser and Bart Feinstein, which he watched prior to Harrison composing the song.

To tease his friend Eric Clapton, whose dentist had advised him to stop eating chocolate, Harrison tempted him with the chocolate goodies he loved while composing the song. He wrote, *"You'll have to have them all pulled out after the Savoy Truffle."*

As usual, Lennon modified the idea of **"Cry Baby Cry"** (LENNON-McCartney) from the TV commercial "Cry baby cry, make your mother buy." Nicking the melody and the lyrics from a nursery rhyme of his youth, "Sing a Song of Sixpence" (*"The king was in the counting house...the queen was in the parlor...the maid was in the garden...down came a blackbird and pecked her on the nose..."*), he made up the King of Marigold from *Alice in Wonderland* (*"the King married to / in love with gold"*) & Marigold brand of rubber gloves, and the Duchess of Kircaldy with Donovan's help. (The Beatles played at the Carlton Theater in Kircaldy in 1963.) The last line *"For a séance in the dark / With voices out of nowhere"* came from a séance Lennon and Cynthia attended while filming *How I Won the War* in Spain.

Lennon disowned this song in a 1980 interview, calling it "a piece of rubbish," forgetting it's his own composition.

Lennon collaborated with Ono to come up with an aural interpretation of revolution in **"Revolution No. 9"** (LENNON-McCartney), piecing together tape loops, feedback, screams, vocal overdubs, sound effects, and noise. While the act of creating it did give a semblance of experimentation and giving Beatles music a new direction, it was nothing more than pushing the idea of the Whites Negroes to the limit. Lennon was not copying part of another artist's song and interpreting it in his ubiquitous style. He borrowed materials outright from various sources -- attracting Harrison to collaborate while McCartney and Starr stayed away -- and put them together in a form that he thought was avant-garde music. Harrison contributed such phrases as "upon a telegram" and "who's to know." It ends with demonstrators shouting, "Lock that gate! Lock that gate!" The words sounded like a premonition that Lennon was separating himself from the Beatles.

All these samplings on how "Revolution No. 9" came to be gave the appearance of a different kind of creativity, probably anchoring itself on the idea of chance art's "beauty of selection." The result was nothing more than a manic sound assembly, certainly neither music nor song -- an extreme departure from the Beatles' musical format. Lennon distanced himself from rock's mass appeal and was preparing to move to avant garde music's elitism.

As to be expected, McCartney and Martin rejected "Revolution No. 9" and did not want it included in this album. But Lennon had his way and it stayed. The White Negroes were irretrievably divided, not in creativity but in direction. At least for this brief experimentation period, Lennon had turned into a non-Beatle and solo non-White Negro. He would pursue it in solo projects with Ono such as the albums *Two Virgins* and *Life With the Lions*, missing out on both critical and commercial triumphs.

Grudgingly, Lennon would return to rock format and give up his Cage pretension, turning once again as a White Negro.

"Good Night" (LENNON-McCartney) is a lullaby written by Lennon as a bedtime song for his then five-year-old son Julian who was having a problem sleeping. Perhaps Julian recognized in his young mind the marital problem his mother and father were having. Lennon wrote it to sound in the McCartney style. Only Starr recorded the song with an orchestra backing him up. It ends with the line "Good night, children...everywhere," which is from Lennon's favorite radio program during his childhood.

Indeed, the song was ominous of Lennon's emotional mindset, that is, to bid the Beatles goodbye.

The pompous size of *The Beatles* album indicated the gnawing restlessness among the group's members. Evidenced by the lack of real Beatles music, each member produced songs in their individualistic styles. They were too varied and wide-ranging in subject and format songs that they are difficult to categorize. This led Lennon to sarcastically state, "There isn't any Beatle music in it.. It was John and the Band, Paul and the Band, George and the Band, like that."

Lennon seemed invincible with the quantity of his contribution and the range of themes he decided to tackle. The initial high of his relationship with Ono surfaced. McCartney wrote all types of music, from nonsense to inspirational songs, from 12-bar blues to metal rock. It was as if he was essaying to show the progression of rock 'n' roll music. Here was McCartney trying to prove his mettle as musicman. While succeeding to achieve this, the album did not merit the importance of the *Sgt. Pepper's* album. Martin advised the Beatles to trim the number of songs from 30 tracks to about half of it. The Beatles opted to ignore the recommendation but not entirely. Lennon's "What's the New Maryjane" and Harrison's "Not Guilty," which were supposed to be included in the album, were pulled out at the last minute.

The best that Jan Wenner could state about the White Album in his *Rolling Stone* review was that it is "the history and synthesis of Western music." Rock critic Lester Bangs perceived it as "littered by materials alike in temperament if not in quality." Tony Palmer of the *London Review* was more generous. He wrote: "If you think that pop music is Engelbert Humperdinck, then the Beatles have done it better -- without sentimentality, but with passion; if you think that pop is just rock 'n' roll, then the Beatles have done better -- but infinitely and more vengeful; if you think that pop is mind-blowing noise, then the Beatles have done it better -- on distant shores of the imagination that others have not even sighted."

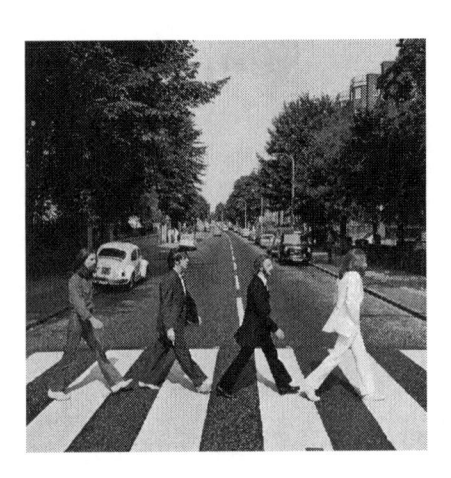

Chapter 7
The death phase

Art and artifice

*"And in the end, the love you take
Is equal to the love you make."*

- "The End," The Beatles

The Beatles had a contractual obligation with United Artists to do a third full-length feature after *A Hard Day's Night* and *Help!* While still alive, Epstein rejected various follow-up film projects because the principal photography required so much time from the Beatles. By then, the quartet became occupied with musical experimentations. So Al Brodax, producer of the ABC-TV cartoon series *The Beatles,* submitted a screenplay to be made as an animated movie. It required minimal effort from Lennon, McCartney, Harrison, and Starr. By relegating to other artists and technicians the completion of their work, it signaled entry into the death period of their creative cycle.

This final period of the creative cycle when discouragement or depression over lost creativity from self-doubt, worry over finances, etc. add stress & trauma and disrupt & bring this death phase.

Yellow Submarine album

With "Yellow Submarine" as the film's theme song, Lee Minoff wrote the movie's storyline based on the song's narrative. He, Brodax, Jack Mendelssohn, and Erich Segal, author of the sappy novel turned best-selling movie *Love*

Story, wrote the screenplay.

The Beatles could only manage a short appearance at the movie's end by showing off memorabilia from Pepperland. Such lackadaisical attitude came from the ego-busting experience of the *Magical Mystery Tour* disaster and the personal stress they were undergoing. Managing to resurrect rejected songs from previous recording sessions, they seemed to have been sapped out of the energy and the interest to put in longer exposure in the film. Professional actors were hired to dub their vocal parts. Due to time and budget constraints, the dazzling psychedelic colors intended for the ending scene was replaced with faster to do and economical hand-drawn images. Martin had to fill in, coming up with orchestral pieces based on Beatles song themes. The *Yellow Submarine* album was released at the same time as its movie version on January 17, 1969.

Although most parts of the *Yellow Submarine* film were borrowed (the Blue Meanies' ears were patterned after Mickey Mouse's), it nevertheless took a semblance of originality much like Beatle songs. The album opens with "Yellow Submarine." Having been rejected in previous albums, the rest of the remaining songs in the A-side of this album are substandard works except, of course, for "All You Need is Love."

"It's Only a Northern Song" (Harrison) is another piece originally recorded for the *Sgt. Pepper's* album but deleted by Martin because of its substandard quality. The song is a veiled commentary on Northern Songs, Ltd., the company owned by Dick James and the partnership of Lennon, McCartney, and Epstein (named as NEMS Enterprises) on a 50-50 sharing basis. The song is Harrison's public admission of disgust over the fact the company's ownership structure left him out of the profit-sharing arrangement from the company's income. The song title is a joke in relation to Liverpool being the Holy City of North England.

"All Together Now" (Lennon-MCCARTNEY) is a sing-along song in the style of "Yellow Submarine" originally sung by McCartney during their India trip. Recalling Music Hall performers asking the audience to sing along, he converted it from the nursery song "Jumping Round the Room" which has the lyrics *"lying on your backs, skipping round the room, jumping in the air..."*

With the working title "Hey Bullfrog," Lennon knocked off the quirky **"Hey Bulldog"** (LENNON-McCartney) during the making of the "Lady Madonna" promo clip at Abbey Road Studios and launched the song's impromptu recording. Having become a lazy White Negro, he converted its piano romp from, what else but, "Lady Madonna." At take 10, McCartney started barking like a dog, followed by howling as a joke. That's how it got its final title "Hey Bulldog."

Taken from a 25-minute jam session during the *Sgt. Pepper's* album recording sessions, Harrison adapted **"It's All Too Much"** (Harrison) from the trumpet of Jeremiah Clarke's "Prince of Denmark's March," according to www.beatlesdiscography.com. The line *"With your long blonde hair and your eyes of blue"* was lifted from the Merseybeat's "Sorrow," a 1966 hit. Merseybeats' members were old Beatles acquaintances.

A-side ends with "All You Need Is Love," a new version rearranged by Martin.

Seven instrumental tracks by the George Martin Orchestra make up the album's B-side. The Beatles was unable to deliver the so-called original songs. Using Beatle themes, the instrumental pieces are **"Pepperland," "Sea Of Time," "Sea Of Holes," "Sea Of Monsters," "March Of The Meanies," "Pepperland Laid Waste,"** and **"Yellow Submarine In Pepperland."** Lennon failed to appreciate Martin's effort to cover up for the group, calling it a "mistake," "Sea of Hole" as "s--t" and all his other compositions as "terrible s--t."

Apple of discord

From day one of Apple Corps operations, cash flowed from its coffers as a financier for obscure artists and lost causes. An audit of Beatles business affairs resulted in writing off three company motor cars and thousands of pounds representing advances to various people. NEMS' 25% share in Beatle record royalty earnings continued to pose a thorny question, as the Beatles no longer benefited from its provisions. With Dick James selling his stake in Northern Songs and the Beatles in a terrible money bind, Lennon and McCartney were eventually forced to sell the publishing rights to their songs except for the early ones like "Love Me Do" to ATV, the entertainment conglomerate owned by Sir Lew Grade. This meant that whenever they would like to perform or record their own compositions, they had to pay royalty.

What they stole as White Negroes, they lost as bad businessmen.

"Get Back" / "Don't Let Me Down" single

The Beatles hurriedly issued the songs "Get Back" / "Don't Let Me Down" on April 11, 1969 as a single, a customary act to prepare the market for an LP release. The single is a study in contrasts: "Get Back," written by McCartney, is a veiled rebuke of Ono; while "Don't Let Me Down," composed by Lennon, is a desperate plea to the other Beatles not to let him down simply because they dislike Ono. It is a curiosity, though, how Lennon initially overlooked the thinly veiled inference in McCartney's song.

McCartney borrowed the title of **"Get Back"** (Lennon-McCARTNEY) from a line of "Sour Milk Sea," *"Get back to where you should be,"* which Harrison wrote and produced for Jackie Lomax. He converted it to *"Get back to where you once belonged."* McCartney also rehashed it for the song's chorus.

Its verses are a conversion of the melody of the Creedence Clearwater Revival's hit single, "Proud Mary." Proud Mary is the name of a steamboat, which popularized what became known as "swamp rock" in the late '60s. An interpretation of an Afro-American musical tradition along the Mississippi river by the California-based group, swamp rock is an expression of Southland aspirations with its strong imagery, shouted vocals, and distinctive guitar style.

"Get Back" uses these elements, but eliminates its rural imagery. This unabashed imitation, plus the use of riffs from Perry Como, was given the distinction of a parody by McCartney. His derision alludes to Ono, an expression of the hostile attitude he subjected her to for intruding in Beatles territory. Ono posed not only an unnecessary encroachment as far as McCartney was concerned, but also served as a threat to his claim for leadership.

Lennon told *Playboy* in 1975, "I've always thought there was this underlying thing in Paul's 'Get Back.' When we were in the studio recording it, every time he sang the line 'Get back to where you once belonged,' he'd look at Yoko." McCartney, on the other hand, maintains that the song is a political satire about Britain's repatriation of immigrants, particularly Pakistanis.

Although the animosity between Lennon and McCartney was about to cause their separation as partners, the latter's antipathy towards Ono aggravated it, finding a subtle expression in "Get Back." The inference could not be avoided as Ono migrated to the U.K. from the U.S. and her masculine disposition reflects the song's man as woman predicament of the fictitious Loretta Martin.

The sporadic use of session musicians, including virtuosos like lead guitarist Eric Clapton, augmented the instrumentation required by a song as the Beatles' resources and talents proved inadequate. In the case of "Get Back," Billy Preston also served as emollient to buffer the on-going friction among the Beatles. As Harrison put it, "Straight away it just became 100 percent improvement in the vibe in the room."

Billy Preston is duly credited ("The Beatles with Billy Preston") on this single, the only time an outside musician received credit on a Beatles record.

"Don't Let Me Down" (LENNON-McCartney) is a personal plea for the other Beatles not to disappoint him because he loves Ono deeply. Although it is about Ono, the lyrics use the third person to refer to her. As such, it can only be addressed to the Beatles, as Lennon's candor required an intimate insight on his personality to bare his emotion. His rationale originated from his treatment of Ono as a kindred spirit. Harrison plays guitar similar to "Devil in My Heart," The Donays song which the Beatles covered in the *With the Beatles* album.

"The Ballad of John and Yoko" / "Old Brown Shoe" single

When Lennon married Ono in Gibraltar, Spain, he wanted to release a song recounting the happy event and some of its less-than-happy side issues. He composed "The Ballad of John and Yoko," released as a single in stereophonic format, a first, with "Old Brown Shoe" as B-side on May 30, 1969. This song turned out to be Lennon and McCartney's actual last collaboration under the Beatles name.

"The Ballad of John and Yoko" (LENNON-McCartney) narrates in a diary-like approach the circumstances surrounding his marriage to Ono as narrated by Lennon and how the media reported the event. Starting off with a series of

18 intervals similar to the intro of Dorsey and Johnny Brunette's "Lonesome Tears in my Eyes," (Johnny Burnette / Dorsey Burnette / Burlison / Mortimer) that Lennon sang at a BBC broadcast *Pop Goes The Beatles* on July 23, 1963, he proceeded to construct it as a "newspaper record." Lennon conceptualized it as "a newspaper of his life," a record that narrates a recent important event about his life. That is why this song tells of Lennon and Ono emerging from a canvass bag eating chocolate cake during the press conference. The song puts it as *"Eating chocolate cake in the bag."* The chocolate cake most likely refers to the famous Viennese cake *sachar torte* which the 16-year-old apprentice chef Franz Sacher created for Prince Clemens Lothar Wensel Metternich in 1832 out of leftover ingredients.

In a desperate act to release the song immediately after their return from honeymoon, Lennon telephoned McCartney and asked for his assistance to record the song. Harrison was on a holiday while Starr was filming *The Magic Christian,* his first solo movie. Putting aside his unfriendly attitude towards Ono, McCartney willingly obliged. McCartney prevented another public relations debacle for Lennon by making him realize that its original title "The Ballad of John and Yoko (Christ, They're Gonna Crucify Me)" unwittingly and unnecessarily called for public wantagonism.

This song is a mock ballad. Instead of being a slow, sentimental love song which is the true characteristic of a ballad, Lennon took liberties by telling a story in a song, more like a journal.

Lennon did lead vocals plus lead guitar and acoustic guitar while McCartney sang harmony vocals and played bass, drums, piano and maracas. McCartney's bass line resembles "Donkey Dong."

Several US radio stations banned this song for the use of the word "Christ" and "They're gonna crucify me."

"Old Brown Shoe" (Harrison) can be distinguished from Harrison's typical songs in its upbeat tempo and theme of romantic love. It is a turnaround song with Harrison casting off his old personality for a fresh attitude. It was written similar to McCartney's "Hello Goodbye." Explained Harrison: "Again it's the duality of things -- yes-no, up-down, left-right, right-wrong, etc."

Abbey Road

When Dick James informed Lennon of his intention to sell 50% stake in Northern Songs to Sir Lew Grade, Lennon and McCartney refused and engaged in proxy battle to gain control. But a proxy vote settled the fight. This galvanized a meeting of minds between Lennon and McCartney that the latter took advantage to bring the Beatles back into the recording studio.

With the objective of recapturing the Beatles' original sound, McCartney approached Martin to record an album in the old Beatle manner they had developed in the past. Martin replied that that would mean the Beatles should be what they used to be. The cooperation that pervaded the recording sessions reflected the common desire to produce a good LP that was to be their last.

Around September 1969 before the release of the *Abbey Road* album, the Beatles had a meeting where McCartney talked about the future of the Beatles. Lennon cut him off, saying, "I think you're daft. I want a divorce." This statement effectively terminated the Beatles as a group.

Abbey Road was released on September 26, 1969. It actually pre-empted the release of the *Get Back* album that was not culminated because it did not meet standards for quality. Originally to be called *Everest* from the name of the cigarette that Emerick used to smoke, the album title had to be altered because the cover concept called for the Beatles to have a photo shoot at the Himalayas!

McCartney suggested that the album's title be changed to *Abbey Road,* in honor of their favorite recording studio, as well as the album cover to show them in the middle of the pedestrian crossing and walking away from the Abbey Road Studios. Nobody knew among the Beatles that *Abbey Road* would be their last album but they felt it would be. Wearing their regular style of clothing during that time, they got photographer Iain MacMillan on a short notice to shoot. McCartney thought of doing something different like painting his ears blue but he settled for walking barefoot. As it was a hot day and fans were beginning to gather in the area, they hurried up.

Yet as it turned out -- chance art transformed into perfect art -- the jacket of *Abbey Road* portrays ominous imagery: Lennon leads McCartney, Starr, and Harrison in crossing Abbey Road, away from the studio where most of their songs were recorded. Lennon is in a white suit; McCartney in a black suit and barefoot; Starr in a black suit; while Harrison wears work clothes. The scenario is clear: with Lennon acting as the priest, McCartney as the deceased, Starr as a mourning relative and Harrison as the gravedigger, they are acting out a funeral procession. By all implications, the Beatles had reached the end, and they came to bury themselves. To further emphasize the point, the Beatles' name is painted on a cracked ancient wall at the back cover.

The on-going Lennon and McCartney disagreement in terms of musical direction was solved by a compromise. The A-side of the album is for rock-type songs, obviously to please Lennon; the B-side, with its *Sgt. Pepper's*-type of music, to suit McCartney. Lennon imposed this arrangement to proceed with the project that ended up as a collection of borrowed materials (most of them without permission), short tunes and fillers conjoined with heavy embellishments. It gave them a dazzling quality and mistakes used as chance art. Of course, *Abbey Road* has its high moments, but they are not tall enough in originality to equal the imitation at the respectable level.

Lennon copied **"Come Together"** (LENNON-McCartney) from Berry's "You Can't Catch Me." Not content with the shameless imitation of its lyrics (*"Here comes Old Flat Top / He was groovin' up with me"* to *"Here comes Old Flat Top / He comes grooving up slowly"*), Lennon proceeded with the use of gobbledygook similar to "I am The Walrus." Lennon rehashed "You Can't Catch Me" by slowing down its tempo, its lyrics substituted with wordplay and a middle-eight added. He purposely did this to hide the song's drug message (*"He shoots / Coca-cola / He says..."*).

"Come Together" is a campaign song similar to Plastic Ono Band's "Give Peace a Chance." Timothy Leary commissioned Lennon to write it during the bed-in with Ono in Toronto, Canada, which Leary attended. He intended to use it for his California gubernatorial campaign against Ronald Reagan in 1969 with the slogan "Come Together -- Join the Party." The phrase "come together" was supplied by Leary himself, coming from the *I Ching*. But before Leary could use it, he was jailed for marijuana possession, thus failing to continue his campaign.

Morris Levy, the publisher of "You Can't Catch Me," sued Lennon for the unauthorized use of a Berry song. Lennon settled by agreeing to record songs from the publisher's catalogue such as "You Can't Catch Me" and "Sweet Little Sixteen" which made up Lennon's *Rock & Roll* album as released in 1975.

Harrison distilled **"Something"** (Harrison) from the title and the first line of James Taylor's "Something in the Way She Moves" (*"Something in the way she moves / Attracts me like no other lover"*), using Ray Charles' "Georgia" strings line in the second verse. He wrote it during the While Album recordings. Taylor released his debut album on the Beatles' own record label, Apple Records. He narrated, "I had a break while Paul was doing some overdubbing so I went into an empty studio and began to write. That's really all there is to it, except the middle took some time to sort out. It didn't go on the White Album because we'd already finished all the tracks."

Was it inspired by wife Pattie Boyd as widely believed? Harrison dropped a bomb. He was thinking Ray Charles when he wrote it. He offered it to Jackie Lomax who previously recorded his song "Sour Milk Sea." But it was rejected by his management so he gave it to Joe Cocker who previously covered "With A Little Help From My Friends." This happened a full two months before the Beatles released their version.

During the recording, Harrison could not figure out entirely the lyrics -- as usual. He had a problem with the succeeding line he nicked from Taylor: "*Attracts me like...*" Lennon advised him to just say whatever came into his mind until he found the appropriate words. For a time, Harrison sang *"attracts me like no other lover"* as *"attracts me like cauliflower."*

Lennon considered it the best song off this album. The same with McCartney who passed the judgment, "For me I think it's the best he's written." For sure, these statements were self-correction of the long years they dismissed Harrison as a second-class songsmith.

For sure, Frank Sinatra's assessment that "Something" is "the greatest love song ever written" helped change their perception but Sinatra was equally guilty of putting down Harrison. He originally thought it as a Lennon-McCartney composition, of course, correcting the error. Harrison did not mind. True to his White Negro code, he borrowed Sinatra's alteration of "*You stick around now it may show*" to "*You stick around Jack she might show*" in his solo tours.

"Maxwell's Silver Hammer" (Lennon-MCCARTNEY) is a vaudeville-style song, a whimsical conversion of McCartney's earlier songs "With A Little Help

From My Friends" and "When I'm Sixty-Four" in the Beach Boys' style. But this time around it is as dark comedy. About a serial killer named Maxwell Edison, it tackles the law of karma (*"The moment you do something that's not right, Maxwell's silver hammer will come down upon your head."*)

The lyrics use the avant-garde word "pataphysical," a branch of metaphysics invented by French pioneer of the absurd theatre, Alfred Jarry. The use of a blacksmith's anvil was an imitation of a technique the Beach Boys used in the song "Do it Again" where a hammer continuously pounds on an anvil until the song ends.

In 1977, Harrison commented, "I mean, my god, 'Maxwell's Silver Hammer' was so fruity."

McCartney adapted the verses of **"Oh Darling!"** (Lennon-MCCARTNEY) from Fats Domino's "Blueberry Hill" in the 12-bar blues style. To achieve the Little Richard manic voice, McCartney kept singing it for an entire week before actual recording. In the 1980 *Playboy* interview, Lennon said, "'Oh! Darling' was a great one of Paul's that he didn't sing too well. I always thought I could have done it better -- it was more my style than his. He wrote it, so what the hell, he's going to sing it."

Starr wrote **"Octopus's Garden"** (Starkey) in Sardinia, Spain when he went there with his family after the brush with McCartney and resigning from the band during the White Album's recording sessions. (Yes, it produced this song.)

Starr narrates: "Peter Sellers had lent us his yacht and we went out for the day. We told the captain we wanted fish and chips for lunch (because that's all we ever ate, being from Liverpool). So when lunchtime came around, we had the French fries, but there was this other stuff on the plate. He said, 'Here's your fish and chips.' -- 'Well, what is this?' 'It's squid.' -- 'We don't eat squid, where's the cod?' Anyway, we ate it for the first time and it was OK, a bit rubbery. It tasted like chicken.

"I stayed out on the deck with him and we talked about octopuses. He told me that they hang out in their caves and go around the seabed finding shiny stones and tin cans and bottles to put in front of their caves like a garden. I thought this was fabulous, because at that time, I just wanted to be under the sea too. A couple of tokes with the couple and we had 'Octopus' Garden'."

What happened to Starkey's plan to quit? He returned after he got a telegram from the guys stating, "You're the best rock 'n' roll drummer in the world. Come on home, we love you." When he returned, Harrison had decked the drum sets with flowers.

"Octopus's Garden" is a conversion of "Yellow Submarine." There's a sequence in the *Let It Be* movie showing Harrison helping out Starr create this song on the piano. Starr having not developed into a full-time White Negro, Harrison rewrote a chord sequence.

Lennon repeats the line "*I want you*" in **"I Want You (She's So Heavy)"**(LENNON-McCartney), the last song recorded by the Beatles as a group, over and over. The vocal variations on each line are his way of declaring endless love for Ono. Dylan has a song entitled "I Want You" on the *Blonde on Blonde* album. McCartney credited music promoter Tony Bramwell for coming up with the subtitle "She's So Heavy." Bramwell commented, "It's so heavy" once he arrived at a Beatles' meeting and found the mood there dejected.

Lennon did this not because he had nothing to say. He kept repeating "*I want you*" because that's the only message he wanted to put across. He surrounded the minimalist message with a barrage of what is known as "white sound" to denote how "heavy" his feeling for Yoko.

Lennon's repeated rhythm is reminiscent of Donald Bailey Quartet's "Comin' Home Baby"(Bob Dorough). McCartney, on the other hand, played bass based on The Animals' "House of the Rising Sun."

Lennon operated the White Noise generator that increased the noise towards the song's end.

The BBC TV program *24 Hours* panned the song when its host sarcastically said, "'*I want you / she's so heavy.*' That's all it says," adding that it is a sampler of the "banalities of pop." This is not necessarily correct as it has a third line, "It's driving me mad" used as a counterpoint.

Lennon defended the song by stating that lyrics-wise, it is better than "I Am the Walrus" or "Eleanor Rigby" as it was a progression for him. He explained, "If I would want to write songs with no words or one word then maybe that's Yoko's influence. But when I get down to it, 'Bop-bop-a-lula's' great, that's what I'm getting around to."

McCartney adapted the idea of the operetta on Side B of "Abbey Road" from Mark Wirtz' *Teenage Opera* that used lush orchestrations and a children's choir but did not materialize as a completed work. It produced Keith West's hit solo single, "Excerpts from a Teen Opera" released in July, 1967.

Since many of the McCartney compositions in this side of the album are short tunes that he could not finish as full-length songs, they were no more than fillers. He came up with the idea of joining them together with elaborate orchestrations to bind them, giving it the semblance of complete songs.

Harrison explained that he wrote **"Here Comes the Sun"** (Harrison) "as a variation of the "Be My Baby" and "Don't Worry Baby" mold, the smooth-flowing songs by The Ronettes and The Beach Boys respectively about throwing worries away.

The Apple office had turned into a stressful environment. As Harrison put it, "Apple was getting to be like a school, where we had to go and be businessmen: 'Sign this, sign that. Anyway, it seems that winter goes on forever in England. By the time spring comes, you really deserve it. So one day I decided to sag off Apple and I went to Eric Clapton's house. The relief of not having to go and see all those dopey accountants was wonderful, and I walked around the garden with one of Eric's acoustic guitars and wrote 'Here Comes the Sun'."

The instrumental section was converted from "Badge," the song Harrison and Clapton wrote for Cream in April 1969. He capped his guitar with a technique he used in "If I Needed Someone."

"Because" (LENNON-McCartney) is Beethoven's "Adagio sostenuto" or "Moonlight Sonata" backwards. Lennon heard Ono play the first movement of the Beethoven opus, *Piano Sonata No 14 in C Sharp Minor, Opus 27 Number Two*. He asked her to play the same chords backwards. In a creative streak, he distilled the chord progression forward -- not backward as generally believed. He then resorted to wordplay by adding simple but double-meaning lyrics (*"Because the world is round / It turns me on"*), a stylistic borrowing from Ono's *Grapefruit*, with a three-way harmony recorded thrice by McCartney, Harrison and him. It turned out to be the perfect imitation, without traces of the original and nobody to sue Lennon because the composition is in public domain.

But Beatles song analyst Ian Hammond opines the likely source of the song's title was Guy d'Hardecourt's 1902 song, "Because Song" (*"Because, God made thee mine. I'll cherish thee, through light and darkness."*), and a possible source of this song is a slowed down version of Johann Sebastian Bach's "C Minor (BWV 9999)."

Lennon, McCartney and Harrison sing in triple-tracked three-part harmony, effectively producing a beautiful showcase of nine voices.

Martin plays a Baldwin spinet harpsichord.

McCartney converted **"You Never Give Me Your Money"** (Lennon-MCCARTNEY) from the title of Steve Howe's instrumental music, "You Never Stay in One Place." McCartney pieced together three short tunes ("You Never Give Me Your Money," That Magic Feeling" and "One Sweet Dream"), which he could not expand into full songs. Putting lyrics pertaining to personal circumstances in his life, he linked them together with beautiful orchestration and harmonies. The second part recalls the middle eight of "A Day in the Life." The last part is about leaving with Linda from one of the difficult meetings with Klein and driving away from problems. The song fades out with a chant similar to Ma Baker's nursery rhyme "All Good Children" (*"1, 2, 3, 4, 5, 6, 7 All good children will go to heaven"*) set to a guitar riff based on "Badge," the Cream song composed by Harrison with Clapton.

McCartney admitted that this song attacks Klein. He explained, "It was directly lambasting Allen Klein's attitude to us. No money, just funny paper, all promises and it never works out. It's basically a song about (having) no faith in the person."

Lennon used of dreamy reverb of Fleetwood Mac's "Albatross" as the starting point of **"Sun King"** (LENNON-McCartney). Originally entitled "Here Comes the Sun King," it was clipped to "Sun King" to avoid confusion with "Here Comes the Sun." Both start with the lines *"Here comes the sun"* so "king' was added to this song's opening line to strike the difference.

Lennon used exaggerated nonsense lyrics and wonderful harmonies. Using Latin-type lyrics that are a combination of Spanish, Portuguese and Italian words, the Beatles freely mixed them together. Lennon explained, "When we came to sing it, to make them different, we started joking around saying 'cuando para mucho.' We just made it up. Paul knew a few Spanish words from school, so we just strung any Spanish words that sounded vaguely like something. And of course we got 'chika fendi' -- that's a Liverpool expression, it doesn't mean anything, just like 'ha-ha-ha.'"

Here's translator Mario Giannella's interpretation of the dialects and languages towards the song's end. He translated the original lyrics of the chorus: *"Quando paramucho mi amore de felice corazon / Mundo paparazzi mi amore chica ferdy (verde) parasol / Cuesto obrigado tanta mucho que can eat it carousel (cara sole)"* as *"If (When for much, my love of happy heart / World paparazzi, my love, chica (girl) ferdy (green) for the sun / This thanks, very much, cake and eat it, carousel"*

A "paparazzi" is a person who takes pictures of celebrities in compromising situations and without their permission. "Parasol" is an umbrella, but literally translates to "para sole" as in "for the sun," or perhaps "pa re sole" for "sun king." "Obrigado" is Portuguese for "thank you." "Obbligato" is a musical term referring to secondary, yet necessary part. "Que can eat it" should be "que/ cake and eat it." "Carousel" is a popular chocolate brand in Britain.

It ends with a guitar style similar to Jimi Hendrix's *Are You Experienced?* album.

Sang in Scouse, the very strong Liverpudlian accent, Lennon put together two short tunes to come up with **"Mean Mr. Mustard / Polythene Pam"** (LENNON-McCartney) which were inspired by odd people the Beatles met in the course of their career.

A broadsheet article about an old miser who concealed his money wherever he could hide it to prevent others from spending it inspired "Mean Mister Mustard." A bag lady that used to keep her stuff in a plastic bag and sleep in Hyde Park also inspired the song. Lennon changed the original lines "S---s in the dark trying to save paper" to the incongruous substitute "Shaves in the dark trying to save paper" to ward off controversy.

"Polytheme Pam" also had two inspirations: one, by a girl fan who had the weird habit of eating from polythene, becoming known as Polythene Pat, during the Beatles' Cavern days; and two, by a girl Lennon met through a friend from Liverpool, the poet Royston Ellis. Lennon went to his Isle of Guernsey flat and found with Ellis a girl named Stephanie, who was dressed in polythene. He spent the night with them having an orgy. The line *"She's the kind of a girl that makes the News Of The World"* refers to the tabloid that publishes risqué stories.

By the way, Lennon credited Ellis as the original person who introduced the Beatles to drug by teaching them how to get high from the strips inside a Benzendrine inhaler.

Lennon changed *"His Sister Shirley"* to *"His Sister Pam"* to "Mean Mister Mustard" to make it sound that the song has something to do with the following song, "Polythene Pam."

McCartney adapted **"She Came In Through The Bathroom Window"** (Lennon-MCCARTNEY) from an experience with Margo Bird, a girl fan who propped a ladder on the bathroom window of his St. Wood's home and managed to break in. She was a member of Apple Scruffs, the group of girls who waited for the Beatles outside their homes and recording studios. After she opened the front door, she let other teenage girls come in and helped them get souvenirs from his household including a '30s tinted photo that was McCartney's favorite. Eventually, McCartney got it back with Margo's help, but the other items were never returned.

"Silver spoon" refers to the protection the girls have because they are still juveniles. *"Sunday on the phone to Monday, Tuesday on the phone to me,"* refers to McCartney's neighbors who saw the break-in and reported it to him. *"Quit the police department"* refers to LA cab driver Eugene Quits.

McCarftney and Harrison exchange guitars here: McCartney plays lead guitar while Harrison the bass.

McCartney rehashed **"Golden Slumbers"** (Lennon-MCCARTNEY) at the house of his father James in Heswell, England. He saw the piano book of his seven-year-old half-sister Ruth, opened it to the traditional "Golden Slumbers Kiss Your Eyes" lullaby, title and lyrics written in 16th century prose by playwright Thomas Dekker. It goes, *"Golden slumbers kiss your eyes / Smiles awake you when you Rise / Sleep pretty wantons, do not cry / And I will sing a lullaby."* Since McCartney could not read the chord sequence, he decided to modify it by putting his musical interpretation and writing additional lyrics. He retained only one verse by Dekker. He contemporized it by shortening the title to "Golden Slumbers" and changing the "kiss" in the line to "fill," and "wantons" to "darling." And voila! he churned out his own version of "Golden Slumbers." In true White Negro practice, nothing is sacred. The end justifies the means, or so the Beatles would like to think.

"Carry That Weight" (Lennon-MCCARTNEY) is reminiscent of the Scottish regiment's "Tune of Glory," and it is about McCartney's task of keeping the Beatles together upon Epstein's death. The end parts feature an arpeggiated guitar notes which Harrison had used in "Here Comes the Sun" and the Cream's "Badge."

In **"The End"** (Lennon-MCCARTNEY), Lennon, McCartney and Harrison engage in a grand guitar battle, the first and last time. Starr delivers his only drum solo in a Beatle song. They did this before conveying their final message: *"And in the end, the love you take is equal to the love you make."*

While working on the album, this line popped into McCartney's head. He recounted in a 1994 interview, "I just recognized that it would be a good end to an album. And it's a good little thing to say -- now and for all time, I think. I can't think of anything much better as a philosophy, because all you need IS love. It still is what you need. There ain't nothin' better. So, you know, I'm very proud to be in the band that did that song, and that thought those thoughts, and encouraged other people to think them to help them get through little problems here and there. So uhh...We did good!!"

Lennon, on the other hand, described this line in a 1980 interview as "a very cosmic, philosophical line -- which again proves that if he wants to, he (McCartney) can think."

The drum solo, however, was faked since Starr did not agree. The bass and guitar were muted to give a semblance of a drum solo according to Lewisohn's *The Complete Beatles Recording Sessions*. The *Rolling Stone's* John Mendelsohn calls "The End" as "a perfect epitaph for our visit to the world of Beatle daydreams."

"**Her Majesty**" (Lennon-MCCARTNEY), a filler, ends the album. The song is a conversion of "God Save the Queen," the British National Anthem. McCartney asked Abbey Road Studios tape operator John Kurlander to remove this song placed between the "Mean Mr. Mustard" and "Polythene Pam" tracks. Instead of discarding it altogether, he decided to place it as the album's last track. Yet when McCartney heard it, he decided to retain it. It was another accident ending up as perfect art. McCartney said it removed the terminal implication of the album's penultimate number, "The End."

The group largely submerged their animosity during the recording sessions to realize once again what the Beatles were about: music. Even if such a commitment was limited to recording the basic tracks and doing the overdubs by whoever composed the song. The album has a fragmented quality despite the grandiose spirit that it wanted to project. The sum of each member's parts was simply not evident in the album. The distinct separation of its two sides, what some critics expressed in positive terms, was a dead giveaway about the album's artistic success.

Lennon rated the album as "a competent album, like *Rubber Soul*." He liked the A-side, but not "the sort of opera" of B-side, describing it as "junk" and having "no life." *NME* rated the album as "slick, artificial and CD-friendly ahead of its time. *Abbey Road* may be the painted corpse of the Beatles, but it is also a monster album." As to be expected, McCartney was kinder in his assessment. When Tony Hicks of the Hollies opined to him that the album was "the same quality as *Sgt. Pepper's*, he countered, "I don't think it is as good as *Sgt. Pepper's*, but I do like George's song, I think that's the best. 'Something' is the best song George has ever made."

Abbey Road miserably failed to approximate a decent farewell album. Though technically brilliant in parts, the album's gloss -- the window-dressing technique used in many of its parts -- is insufficient to cover up for its defects. To top it all, the album was produced with several copyright infringements as shown above.

The Beatles issued "Come Together" and "Something" as a single on October 31, 1969.

"Let It Be" / "You Know My Name (Look up the Number)"

To promote the reworked *Get Back* album, now to be released as the *Let It Be* album, the Beatles released "Let It Be" and "You Know My Name (Look up the Number") as a single on March 6, 1970.

Out of desperation for the Beatles' imminent break up, McCartney converted the Everly Brothers' "Let It Be Me" into **"Let It Be"** (Lennon-MCCARTNEY) by removing the "me" in the title, speeding up the melody, following the phrases' structure, and changing the chorus similar to "Hey Jude." He coverted the first stanza of "Let It Be Me": "*I bless the day I found you / I want to stay around you / And so I beg you / Let it be me*" to the first stanza of "Let It Be" as: **"***When I find myself in time of trouble, / Mother Mary comes to me / Speaking words of wisdom, / Let it be."*

This was not a conscious rehash on McCartney's part. He pinched it unconsciously similar to "Yesterday." The lyrics speak about Mary, McCartney's dead mother who appeared to him in a dream. He recounted in Marlo Thomas' book *The Right Words at the Right Time*, "So in this dream 12 years later, my mother appeared, and there was her face, completely clear, particularly her eyes; and she said to me very gently, very reassuringly, 'Let it be.'" Upon waking up, he composed the song revolving around the three-word phrase: he came up with appropriate and meaningful lyrics.

But there's another version on how the title came to be. While meditating in India, McCartney was supposed to have visualized Evans standing before him, reciting, "Let it be, let it be." When McCartney finished writing a song with the title "Let It Be" a few months later, it had the line "*Mother Malcolm speaks to me.*" But he would change it to "Mother Mary" as listeners might misunderstand and cause a controversy.

"You Know My Name (Look Up the Number)" (Lennon-McCartney) is another throwaway number from the *Sgt. Pepper's* album recording sessions. Lennon lifted the song's title from the slogan on the cover of the British phone book company: "You know their name? Look up their number," which he found in McCartney's house. Used like a mantra, he repeats the line, a technique which Lennon would copy in future songs.

According to Pollack, the sleazy song sung in cabaret ambiance might have been influenced by the Rolling Stones' "Something Happened to Me Yesterday" and Mothers of Invention's "America Drinks & Goes Home," both issued in 1967. It could not have been influenced by Monty Python's Flying Circus because it started broadcasting on BBC only on October 5, 1969. Lennon might have been encouraged to revive it because the group's style closely resembled the Beatles song's, preempting it by a good two years!

When he wrote the song in 1967 during the *Sgt. Pepper's Lonely Heart Club Band* recordings, all four Beatles attended with the Rolling Stones' Brian Jones doing the saxophone part. It featured McCartney singing a la '50 crooner Vic Damone as The Master of Ceremonies and Showman in a mythical cabaret called Slaggers in the style of the Four Tops' "Reach Out, I'll Be There." The Dennis O'Dell mentioned in the lyrics was Apple's director of films and publicity.

Lennon originally wanted to release "You Know My Name (Look Up the Number)" in 1969 as a Plastic Ono Band single with "What's the New Mary Jane" as B-side. McCartney, however, liked "You Know My Name (Look Up the Number)" so much he vetoed Lennon's plan. In the midst of their personal and professional differences, Lennon and McCartney laid down the vocal tracks and additional sound effects with Evans. Harrison and Starr were not required to attend. Released a year later, it became the B-side of the "Let It Be" single.

Let It Be album

Badly needing to bring in cash to Apple coffers, the Beatles agreed with Klein to release the *Get Back* album. Instead of re-recording the album's songs, they relied on its substandard songs, many of them fillers, works-in-progress, throwaway numbers and studio chat and jamming passed up as "live recording." Lennon, Harrison, and Starr agreed to have other artists do the dirty work of putting them together in a releasable form, with Spector as chief mechanic. Only McCartney disagreed, and was, thus, outvoted. When the album was released on May 8, 1970, it was tagged as a "new-phase album"; but, then, for sure it marked their dying moments as a group, and the album was a tattered example of their art of rehashing.

The Beatles planned to record the album in front of a live TV audience, with another TV special about how the album was made. When Harrison protested, plans for the live show were scrapped and the album was assembled from various sessions. Spector was brought in to work with the tapes, and the album was finally released about a year after it was recorded.

"**Two of Us**" (Lennon-MCCARTNEY) is about McCartney and Linda Eastman and not about Lennon and McCartney, contrary to common belief. As proof, the song talks about the postcards McCartney and Eastman exchanged while they were still courting since Eastman lived in New York while McCartney shuttled between London and Scotland. McCartney wrote the song after driving outside London, pulling off into the woods, and Eastman taking a walk with him.

To give the song and the album a live feel, Lennon introduces it with the snide remark, "'I Dig a Pygmy' by Charles Hawtrey and the Deaf Aids...Phase One in which Doris gets her oats." Hawtrey was a famous '50s jazz bandleader while Deaf Aids is the nickname given to the Beatles' Vox amplifiers.

With strong "Peggy Sue" drum beats, the vocal harmonies of "Two of Us" are similar to The Everly Brothers' "Bye Bye Love." McCartney paid tribute to the duo of Don and Phil Everly, McCartney by referring to Lennon with the spoken words "Take it Phil." The song's guitar part resembles Johnny Thunder's "Loop de Loop."

Spector enhanced the original recording by beefing up the acoustic sound. He had the option to choose from the various takes from practice sessions held at the Twickenham Studios or from the live performance on the rooftop of Apple offices building, both of which were recorded and filmed.

For **"Dig a Pony"** (LENNON-McCartney), Spector used the rooftop version, passing it off as a stream-of-consciousness-type of song that was actually a song in progress by Lennon originally entitled "Con a Lowry." Clearly, Lennon sang words that came to his head, improvising them where he had not figured out the appropriate lyrics. He once called it a "piece of garbage."

The theme of omniscience of **"Across the Universe"** (LENNON-McCartney) is a tribute to the Maharishi after the group met him and was impressed by his spiritual power. In fact, the song's title was a straight lift from the greeting of TM disciples who were with the Beatles in India.

Notice how Lennon adapted Gibran's poetry in *Sand and Foam* in the way he Constructed the "Across the Universe" lyrics: *"Words are flowing out like that endless rain into a paper cup / They slither while they slip away across the universe / Pools of sorrow, waves of joy are drifting through my open mind…"*

Lennon mishmashed Gibran's words as follows: *"Words are flowing out like endless rain into a paper cup"* from the lines *"Words are timeless."* and *"When my cup is empty I resign myself to its emptiness,"* He improvised *"They slither while they pass they slip away across the universe"* from *"They spread before us their riches of gold and silver"* to connect the first line to the third line. *"Pools of sorrow, waves of joy are drifting through my open mind…"* are from the combination of *"Only great sorrow or great joy can ravel your truth. / Though the wave of words is forever upon us yet our depth is forever upon us yet our depth is forever silent."*

Lennon also refers to "*million suns*" in one verse, which Gibran wrote as "*countless suns.*"

"*Jai Guru Deva Om*" (meaning *"Hail Master Lord"*) was the mantra assigned by the Maharishi to Lennon. *"Jai Guru"* literally means *"Glory to the teacher," "The heavenly teacher is divine"* or *"Lift up your spiritual master"* depending on the interpretation of the Sanskrit from which it came. Since it refers to Guru Dev, who is the Maharishi's guru, it means *"Long live Guru Dev."*

The *"om"* is a one-word chant to invoke oneness with the universe.

In Lennon's mind, this appropriation must have come as a fitting tribute to the universe and its creator's omnipresence. In his 1970 interview with *Rolling Stone,* Lennon referred to the song as perhaps the best, most poetic lyric he ever wrote: "It's one of the best lyrics I've written. In fact, it could be the best. It's good poetry, or whatever you call it, without chewin' it. See, the ones I like are the ones that stand as words, without melody. They don't have to have any melody, like a poem, you can read them." Lennon in the 1980 *Playboy* interview, however, seemed to have erased the lyrics' origination from his memory. He stated, "The words [of *Universe*] stand, luckily, by themselves.

They were purely inspirational and were given to me as BOOM! I don't own it, you know; it came through like that [i.e. automatically]. I don't know where it came from, what meter it's in, and I've sat down and looked at it and said, *Can I write another one with this meter?* It's so interesting: *Words are flying out like* [sings] *endless rain into a paper cup, they slither while they pass, they slip away across the universe.* Such an extraordinary meter and I can never repeat it."

In *Alice Goes to the Rabbithole,* Carroll also wrote of Alice being "*in the pool of tears"* that she wept when she grew nine feet high.

These kinds of lyrics were unusual for Lennon before the *Magical Mystery Tour* album. He normally wrote in the first person and in straightforward, literal sentences. Using figurative and poetic language is a characteristic of Ono's poetry in *Grapefruit.* Lennon's suddenly turning poetic is, therefore, her influence. Where Lennon adapted specific lines of Gibran's poems in "Julia," he might have unconsciously rehashed the Lebanese poet in this song by modification.

Recorded during the "Lady Madonna" sessions, Lennon intended "Across the Universe" as its B-side (which eventually went to "The Inner Light"). He thought that McCartney tried to sabotage "Across the Universe" by getting fans -- two girls who were Apple Scruffs members, particularly Lizzie Brown and Gayleen Pease -- to sing the song's chorus instead of trained singers. In the 1980 *Playboy* interview, Lennon admitted, "The Beatles didn't make a good record of 'Across the Universe.' I think subconsciously we...I thought Paul subconsciously tried to destroy my great songs. We would play experimental games with my great pieces, like 'Strawberry Fields,' which I always felt was badly recorded. It worked, but it wasn't what it could have been."

This was a proof of how their working relationship had turned acrimonious, at least, during the song's recording sessions.

On the suggestion of Spike Milligan, he decided to give it to World Wildlife Fund for its *Nothing's Gonna Change My World* album. The track off this album -- and other bootleg copies of the song -- does contain the original version with its defective back-up harmonies.

Spector liked the song when he reworked the *Get Back* tapes and decided to include it in the *Let It Be* album. He edited out the opening overdubbed bird sounds, slowed it down a little, removed the off-key back-up vocals and added a choir of professional singers and full orchestra. This gave it a clearly lush feel that is more Spector than Beatles.

"**I Me Mine**" (Harrison) is a wry exposition about Lennon and McCartney's self-absorption, as Harrison was largely unable to record his new compositions at the time of this album's recording sessions. As a reaction to the ego clashes among members, he wrote this song about the ego in the Hindu context by lifting the theme from the *Bhagavad Gita* 2:71-72: *"They are forever free who renounce all selfish desires and break away from the ego-cage of 'I,' 'me,' and 'mine' to be united with the Lord. This is the supreme state. Attain to this, and* *pass from death to immortality."*

Blending folk and blues, Harrison adapted the waltz tune after listening to an Austrian marching band on television. This song replaced McCartney's "Teddy Boy" which he asked to be pulled out but eventually was included in *McCartney*, his first solo album.

Spector expanded its original play time by adding two "*I me mine*" choruses. After the line "*flowing more freely like wine,*" he stopped the tape and spooled back two verses, picking it up again with "*all through the day.*"

"Dig It" (Lennon / McCartney / Harrison / Starkey) is a modification of the infectious refrain of Dylan's "Like a Rolling Stone" in stream-of-consciousness style. They simplified his combination of two lines (*"How does it feel / How does it feel"*) as *"You can dig it."* The next three lines of Dylan's song (*"To be on your own / With no direction home / A complete unknown"* was simplified as *"Dig it / Dig it / Dig it."* In Dylan's idiosyncratic vocal delivery, Lennon exaggerated said line by singing it three times, adding names and acronyms as mock lyrics. B.B. King refers to the blues singer; Doris Day is the Hollywood movie actress; Matt Busby was the ex-Manchester United soccer team manager.

Spector clipped "Dig It" from the 12-minute jam session entitled "Can You Dig It" as a sort of introduction to the next album track, "Let It Be." He introduced it with the Lennon imitating Little Georgie Wood's high falsetto voice, "'Can You Dig It' by Georgie Wood. And now we'd like to do "Ark the Angels Sing.'" Wood is the 4'9" British music hall and novelty singer Little Gorgie Wood while 'Ark the Angels Sing' is a corruption of Mendelssohn's "Hark The Herald Angels Sing." Clearly, Spector was frantic to give the album a live feel and to break the serious undertone it had turned into by this part.

Previously released as a single, Spector sharpened the **"Let It Be"** (Lennon-MCCARTNEY) sound by increasing the tape echo of Starr's hi-hat. He edited a repeat verse into the song's end, extending its duration. He added a lead guitar solo overdub, omitting the April 30, 1969 recording and falsely imitating this guitar overdub to show that this version is different from the single release.

Based on an 1856 minstrel song by American Benjamin Russell Hanby entitled "Darling Nellie Gray," **"Maggie Mae"** (Arranged by Lennon / McCartney / Harrison / Starkey) is a 1957 song by The Vipers Skiffle Group about a sex worker named Maggie May, who lured sailors into dark alleys only to rob them. "Maggie" is the Liverpool slang for prostitute. As the Quarrymen, they played the coarse but cheerful tune when Lennon met McCartney in a church fair.

During the *Get Back* sessions, the Beatles used it as a breaker. Lennon improvised the lyrics. Both the album and the film versions use the song's chorus only.

The traditional lyrics go: "*Dirty Robin Maggie May / Did I've taken here the way / And she never walked down lounch beat anymore? / Oh, the Church he quilly pounder / Robin at home a bound / That dirty noke Robin Maggie May / To the port of Liverpool, they returned me to*"

The Beatles version was colloquialized as: *"Oh dirty Maggie Mae / They have taken her away / And she never walk down Lime Street any more / Oh the judge he guilty found her / For robbing a homeward bounder / That dirty no good robbing May Maggie Mae / To the port of Liverpool, they returned me to / Two pounds ten a week, that was my pay."*

"May" was changed to "Mae" for copyright purposes.

Having composed two short songs that they were unable to develop into full songs, Lennon and McCartney resorted to piecing together McCartney's blues piece in the Aretha Franklin-style called "I've Got A Feeling" with Lennon's ballad entitled "Everybody Had A Hard Year" to come up with **"I've Got A Feeling"** (Lennon-McCartney). The song reflects their personal situations during the recording, McCartney was about to marry girlfriend Eastman and Lennon was in the process of divorcing Cynthia. Ono experienced a miscarriage and was arrested for drug possession. The conversion worked favorably. McCartney's involved singing contrasts very well with Lennon's monotone recitation. This was the last Beatle song Lennon and McCartney co-wrote. Autobiographical, 1968 having been a difficult year for him, Lennon experimented with his part by beginning all lines with "everybody." It turned out a precursor of the campaign songs he would compose later ("Give Peace a Chance" and "Come Together").

"I've Got A Feeling" copied the "everybody" formula (*"Everybody's in despair, every girl and boy"*) from Bob Dylan's "Mighty Quinn (Quinn the Eskimo)," a song from his *Basement Tapes* recordings which Harrison distributed a copy of to all Beatles members. When Harrison pointed this out to Lennon and McCartney, they shrug it off, as if considering the imitation as immaterial to constitute plagiarism.

Lennon came up with **"The One After 909"** (LENNON-McCartney) in 1959. This is the earliest known song composition by Lennon, an artifact in his developing White Negro code. Written in Lonnie Donnegan's skiffle style, it is a rewrite of "Rock Island Line" which is discernible in their identical theme and rhythm. However, the guitar-plucking at the song's beginning is identical with the guiar lead in of Berry's "I Want To Be Your Driver."

Lennon revived "The One After 909" as a possible single in 1963. It was part of the juvenile bluff that he and McCartney had written "over 100 songs" before they could sign a record deal. But the plan did not materialize as Martin rejected it. It was re-recorded during the *Get Back* sessions to affirm the album's back-to-basics intent. Embarrassed with its sophomoric lyrics, he even volunteered to improve the shortcoming but did not get to it.

"The Long And Winding Road" (Lennon-MCCARTNEY), for sure, is a piano-based ballad with a sophisticated structure. Based on the hackneyed expression, the title came to McCartney from an actual long road that twists and turns into his Scotland farm estate, High Park. Known as B842, this 16-mile road runs from the east coast of Kintyre into Campbeltown, the area closest to his farm.

Again, McCartney adapted the tune from "Georgia On My Mind" which Ray Charles recorded in 1960 from a reworking of the Louis Armstrong '30s version of the '20s Hoagy Carmichael hit. McCartney explained, "'The Long And Winding Road' doesn't sound like him [Ray Charles] at all, because it's me singing and I don't sound anything like Ray, but sometimes you get a person in your mind, just for an attitude, just for a place to be, so that your mind is somewhere rather than nowhere, and you place it by thinking, 'Oh, I love Ray Charles,' and think, 'Well, what might he do then?' So that was in my mind, and would have probably had some bearing on the chord structure of it, which is slightly jazzy..."

More than the melody, McCartney also rehashed the lyrics. He converted the attitude of the "Georgia On My Mind" lines *"Other arms reach out to me / Other eye smile tenderly / Still in peaceful dreams I see / The road leads me back to you"* into *"Many times I've in love and many times I've cried / Anyway you'll never the many ways I've tried."* *"The road leads me back to you"* that end the model's verses had been adapted into *"I've seen that road before / It* (referring to road) *always leads me here / Lead me to you door."*

Spector reworked the original by adding 18 violins, four violas, four cellos, three trumpets, three trombones, two guitars, drums, and a choir of 14 women. McCartney hated this lush orchestration which Spector resorted to cover up Lennon's haphazard bass-playing. He formally complained to Klein about it who decided not to do anything. He asked him to dissolve the Beatles partnership, but again, Klein did not act on it. This gave McCartney legal basis to sue him and the other Beatles later, claiming "intolerable interference" by overdubbing the song "without consulting McCartney."

Harrison attempted to write a blues love song for wife Patti and came up with **"For You Blue"** (Harrison). He reworked Blues artist Elmore James' "Madison Blues" with a rock sensibility. While playing a lap steel guitar, something he learned from Donovan during the India trip, Lennon makes a reference to James by quipping during the song's adlib, "Elmore James got nothin' on this."

The album ends with "Get Back," previously released as a single.

At best, the Spector-produced *Let It Be* album is a shoddy work, patchy in quality and over-produced. Reportedly, Martin was shocked to hear what he had done to the *Get Back* tapes. Johns scorned his work. In fairness to Spector, he accomplished what Lennon and McCartney asked him to do without re-writing and re-recording the generally substandard songs.

Besides, it was the Beatles who destroyed *Get Back's* simple, straightforward concept with no overdubs, edits or orchestras by recording overdubs on April 30, 1969 and January 3 to 4, 1970, compiled at their request on January 5, 1970 which included overdubs.

Lennon opined that Spector "worked wonders" to the album and made it listenable. He told *Rolling Stone* in 1970 (though the interview was published in 1971): "He was given the s-------t load of badly recorded s--t with a lousy feeling to it ever, and he made something out of it."

He agreed with critic Joel Vance that the Beatles "didn't know what to do with their talent any more" in 1969 and 1970, echoing how Kaemfert assessed them in 1962: "They have talent but did not know how to use it."

Lennon thought the album would de-mystify the Beatles.

It did.

Let It Be, the movie

Klein sold the rights of the *Get Back* film project to United Artists as another measure to improve the finances of cash-strapped Apple. Envisioned as a documentary on how the Beatles made their music, the *Let It Be* movie became an incontrovertible proof about the White Negroes' patchwork creativity and how such kind of inventiveness has rendered them irretrievably divided. Instead of a proper performance arena as originally planned, the Beatles opted to play live on top of the Apple building, showing their options had turned very limited.

The only alternative was to become bad White Negroes. They settled on termination, after trying to cling on and being convinced there was no more hope. The documentary echoed this mindset.

Lennon ends the rooftop concert with a wry quip, "I hope we passed the audition!"

They did.

The sum of the parts

The Beatles' greatness can be credited to how they presented their art of derivation -- in some instances "beyond recognition" to use the words of Owens -- that gave their body of work a sense of newness with the aura and feel of originality. The Shakespeare and Beethoven comparison originated from this talent for derivation. And the good thing about Lennon and McCartney was that they did not have any pretensions of being great composers as initiated by Epstein and perpetuated by many publicists, critics, singers, and fans, although they did get carried away at ego-bloating points in their career.

Lennon had several times admitted he had knocked off songs based on other composers' works and interpreted them in what became known as the Beatles style.

Although he would not credit such style to Martin, Lennon knew -- in his heart and in his mind -- that Martin was a vital part of developing that style. In the several occasions he denied this, because of his insecurity that the credit for the Beatles' unparalleled accomplishment was going to Martin, not to him, or more correctly, to him and McCartney. He knew that without him or McCartney, Martin had nothing so it must be him or with McCartney. This mindset was correct, however, its degree of accuracy depends on the phase of creativity being referred to.

Of course, Lennon was also known for double talk. It was a sort of defense mechanism for him or being an opportunist then too, as a White Negro, he would say what was best for the moment. This was the same reason he would state almost frequently with derision about the greatness of the Lennon-McCartney composing tandem. One time he called it as "two f------ brilliant songwriters" while at another he termed themselves as "cons." McCartney agreed. He admitted in the 1982 *Playboy* interview: "Oh, yeah. We were the biggest nickers in town. *Plagiarists extraordinaires.*"

There is no doubt that Lennon and McCartney were aware of their patchwork creativity and did not hide this fact, although their publicists glossed over it while mass media largely ignored it. They even cherished the hyperboles presented to them. But they were also aware that through this deficient creativity, they produced some of the best songs of their time. They have gold record discs and trophies from music award-giving bodies to confirm this greatness, besides their own perception of the magnitude of their fame as artists. This extremism -- and the things that happened in between -- made the Beatles so exciting as personalities, enhancing their songmaking and turning up so worthy of copying: White Negroes breeding White Negroes.

But Lennon and McCartney's admission of deficient creativity effectively reduces the importance of the Beatles to the popularization of musical style of other musicians that established their White Negro character. Lennon did not disown this diminution but, in fact, admitted it. He once blurted out, "This is a load of crap at singer's or musician's claims of originality." Rock 'n' roll, for him, was totally derivative. Presley, Holly, Smokey Robinson and the Miracles, and the Motown sound were the real music. He unequivocally added: 'We're the receivers, we're just interpreting it as English kids. Don't let anybody ever kid you it's original. It's all a rip off!'"

With this admission of being White Negroes, the Beatles undertook their subversion of existing composition and recording techniques, extended the instrumentation language of rock, improved on the vinyl format, created the forerunner of music video, and set themselves as role models of new and current bands and solo acts. They proved to be effective role models because of the economic success and critical acclaim they reaped by being White Negroes, creating an endless succession of White Negroes or as Dr. Leary correctly put it, "laughing freemen."

But these admissions do not absolve the Beatles on the question of the importance of their body of work or their importance as artists. In fact, the issue about their imitated body of work makes the question of Lennon and McCartney even more important. Whether the composing tandem transcended this derivative character by breaking the mold that they unwittingly shaped for themselves questions the basic quality of their body of songs. They may have gotten away scot-free with all the superlative labeling they received through the years, but the responsibility for assessing their talent and contribution to music remains a contention that has to be closely and critically analyzed within the context of the image-building strategies initiated by Epstein and the reaction of the critics who agreed or dissented with this manufactured image.

What the Beatles could be credited for is having created a good body of easy-listening and fast-evolving songs -- by combining art and artifice -- that inevitably changed the cultural norms of their generation and the generations that followed. The greatness of the Beatles does not lie much on their music, as in their musical personalities. Their songs can be best described as their medium of expression as musical personalities. Their contribution is more cultural than musical. This must remain as the Beatles' historical and artistic significance.

Does such importance account as progress? The consensus is that it does. And it continues to do so five decades after. Much of the vitality of Beatles songs remains intact as they easily measure up with or go beyond the quality of the current crop of song productions.

They did this by being Whites Negroes in the entirety of their creative cycle; from the birth period to the death period, the maturity period distinguished by the amount of refinement their indiscriminate borrowings underwent. By being White Negroes minus the terminology, they -- particularly Lennon and McCartney -- proceeded to create a large body of songs that went on to open the youth's minds to alternative ways of doing things. This made their White Negro practices, regardless of the creative cycle the group was in, seep and spread into popular culture in an almost speed-crazy way. What used to be largely underground practices turned into mainstream manners. The Beatles turned the necessary bridge that popularized the pleasure-seeking vision of the Beat Generation which would have remained esoteric stuff had the Beatles not polarized them.

Ten best songs, one best album

As White Negroes, the Beatles' 10 most realized songs by order of release are:
1. "Please Please Me" (LENNON-McCartney)
2. "She Loves You" (Lennon-McCartney)
3. "I Want to Hold Your Hands" (Lennon-McCartney)
4. "Help!" (LENNON-McCartney)
5. "Yesterday" (Lennon-MCCARTNEY)
6. "Strawberry Fields Forever" (LENNON-McCartney)
7. "Lucy in the Sky With Diamonds" (LENNON-McCartney)
8. "A Day in the Life" (Lennon-McCartney)
9. "Hey Jude" (Lennon-MCCARTNEY)
10. "Something" (Harrison)

Does Lennon's four solo compositions and McCartney's two in the shortlist make him the more gifted composer? For sure, no, but it was an indication of a better predisposition at the art of derivation or being White Negro.

Their best album: *Sergeant Pepper's Lonely Hearts Club Band.*

White Negro power

Recall what Crow stated about the Beatles in the Introduction of this book. He accused the Beatles of being a communist plot to corrupt the youth's collective mind. He predicted that fans would turn to communism and perpetuate the Domino Theory throughout the free world.

For sure, Crow over-hypothesized. The exact opposite happened. The Beatles were not a communist plot as much as they were the communal conspiracy of Lennon and McCartney as White Negroes.

The Beatles have been called almost everything, but they have never been called White Negroes until this book. Even the Beatles -- through postmodernism -- individually and collectively, never referred to themselves as White Negroes, perhaps because they were not aware of such terminology. The term was largely used in the past to refer to Presley and the fathers of rock 'n' roll and members of the Beat Generation. I think the failure of Beatle historians and critics to label the Beatles as White Negroes was mainly due to their failure to recognize the terminology's cultural and social significance. But all the marks of being White Negroes were there -- indelible marks -- that determined what they were and what they had become. The Beatles as White Negroes is an overdue recognition, something not to put them down to lift what they are and what being White Negroes did to them and to this planet.

That is why Crow and his clique proved erratic in their reasoning. The reverse happened. Twenty-two years after the Beatles released "Back in the USSR," the Berlin Wall collapsed. Berlin used to be divided into the American, British, French and Soviet sectors by that tall concrete wall but it was torn down in 1990 when communism collapsed. The Cold War ended, both sides have turned capitalistic societies. In other words, the Beatles -- if it might be attributed to them in this simplistic way -- expanded democracy and killed communism, the exact opposite of Crow's charge against the quartet!

Pavel Palazchenko, Gorbachev's interpreter and foreign policy aide, confirmed this when he wrote in *My Years with Gorbachev and Shervardnadze*: "I am sure that the impact of the Beatles on the generation of young Soviets in the 1960s will one day be the object of studies. We knew their songs by heart...In the dusky years of the Brezhnev regime they were not only a source of musical relief. They helped us create a world of our own, a world different from the dull and senseless ideological liturgy that increasingly reminded one of Stalinism. The Beatles were our quiet way of rejecting 'the system' while conforming to most of its demands." As Yuri Pelyoshonok, a Soviet-born Canadian professor of Soviet Studies said in the ABC Television documentary, *The Beatles Revolution* which aired in November 2000: "The Soviet authorities thought of the Beatles as a secret Cold War weapon. The kids lost their interest in all Soviet unshakable dogmas and ideals, and stopped thinking of an English-speaking person as the enemy. That's when the Communists lost two generations of young people ideologically; totally lost. That was an incredible impact."

By showing how to break the holding pattern, the Beatles allowed receptiveness of new ways of doing things that satisfy pleasure-seeking humans. Is this not the White Negro code?

Through their songs and lifestyles, the Beatles managed to imprint them and themselves to contemporary mores and manners. As they were mostly unforced, they managed to sip into popular culture and influence highbrow art. And they did this by being White Negroes. By rejecting the cultural standards of their time as dictated by being White Negroes, they installed a fast evolving lifestyle among the youth where the only operating rule was difference. But like the White Negroes, this difference did not come on an individual basis but through a class of people. The youth turned out to be the most receptive among the class-stratified society to this kind of collective behavior. Their idealism and an inclination for peer group mentality determined this, in much the same way it affected the White Negro Beatles.

A borderless mindset

In a way, the Beatles were also the group that made the socialist designs of the communists acceptable. By being White Negroes, they turned classless and paved the way for the borderless state of mind. This would eventually lead to the downfall of communism and many "isms" that used to rule social systems.

In the book *The Rise and Fall of Popular Music*, Donald Clarke called the post-1970 rock music as "unchallenging and often unmusical 'art'." Clarke was indirectly questioning the importance of the Beatles being the main proponents of rock music before the period in question. He noted: "What was typical about it was skill combined with empty content...All the bits copied from all the musics had been liquidized and squirted into a dozen moulds of utterly uninspired songs, adding up to rock as elevator music."

With the Beatles dead, Dylan having made the crossover from folk to rock that demystified himself, and the Rolling Stones burdened by the Altamont concert deaths in the '70s, Clarke failed to recognize the Beatles' legacy in its quest for seriousness where there was none before. His theory's weakness is his failure to recognize the postmodern spirit -- and the White Negro code that bred it -- that Beatles' songs initiated.

Modernism, influenced by science, emphasized the individual's rationality and objectivity. In the arts, the discontent with outdated styles, contempt for the unsightliness of modern art and their derivations and the need to modify symbolism of the emergent new times, brought about modernism's death. An example of modern music is Stravinsky's music. It believes in the development of the scientific point of view.

These distinctions established its importance through the scientific ideals of the modern times.

The Beatles' use of mind-altering drugs which blurred the distinction between romanticism and modernism and established the wholeness of combined ideals. In turn, the blurring of visions established the relationships between the Beatles and its other parts. The Beatles' lead-bass-rhythm-plus-drum format and multiple classical instruments, individual and collective work, originality and derivation, western and eastern systems ushered the Beatles into multiple but binding relationships. It produced their mature songs.

Alvin P. Sanoff, author of the book *The Saturated Self: Dilemmas of Identity in Contemporary Life*, referred to the Beatles as "perhaps the first important indication of modernism's demise." Despite the tentativeness of the statement, which is expected from a responsible writer, the Beatles did usher in the age of postmodernism.

Postmodernism is the new age of the present. This is the age when the self is part of the whole, not separate and distinct. It is our relationship with others and the social groups around us that determine who we are. The importance of our identity is its relationships with the social groups that we interact with. The self is not as important as the collective consciousness. We are not only interested in what is happening to us. Our interests take a global perspective and they affect our views and values. Present relationships improve and refine future relationships.

Owens defines the postmodernism theory in a critical essay entitled "The Allegorical Impulse: Towards A Theory of Postmodernism" when he wrote that it is the new manner of artistic application, not directed by specific medium that describes "its own contingency, insufficiency, lack of transcendence and narrates of a desire that must be perpetually frustrated, an ambition that must be perpetually deferred."

In the arts, postmodernism adapts the vast array of influences from the arts, science and religion, as well as media, in a coalescence of relationships expressed in a new combination that is unique and familiar as it is separated and unified.

By casting off individuality and looking to the environment for input, the Beatles removed the distinction between originality and imitation, individual and collective undertaking, noise and music, East and West, reality and fantasy. The Beatles redefined our understanding of boundaries and demarcations by making pleasant combinations of what used to be irrevocably divided and separated. This rearrangement partly removed the world's cultural separations and doctrinal isolations by promoting liberalism, English as a global language, love and freedom as valued aspirations. In doing so, the Beatles converted the youth of the world into White Negroes, in the process making life in this planet more homogenous or, as we put it in current terms, people-friendly.

Glossary

Aeolian Referring to the sixth mode on the keyboard, which was in common use until the 15th century.
alliteration The repeated use of the some letters to produce poetic effect through sound.
ambience The reverberation characteristic of a room.
Artificial Double Tracking (ADT) The electronic method to simulate manual double tracking of a song element, particularly vocals. ADT is a process of recording a signal taken from the playback head of a tape machine. The signal records onto a separate machine with a variable oscillator that allows the alteration of the speed. The engineers feed the altered signal back into the first machine, thus combining with the original signal.
baffling The separation of percussion instruments by artificial contraptions to control leakage into the microphones of other instruments.
Baroque In music, this refers to lavish ornamentation of the basic melody.
Bouree A technique in guitar plucking in which the melody and bass notes are played simultaneously on the upper and lower strings.
bridge The B section of a traditionally constructed song. In the AABA form, the bridge is introduced after the A section has been repeated twice.
Caesura A sudden silencing of the sound; a pause or break, indicated by the following symbol: //
demo A demonstration cassette or CD made to audition a song or singer or both.
double-tracking A recording process that gives a richer texture and fuller presence to a sound. It operates on the principle of recording two separate performances of the same sound element on separate tracks. The performances are slightly different, thus reinforcing the sound element when the two separate performances are added. This is the manual method of double-tracking.
dry sound A sound with absent or minimal reverberation.
echo The repetition of a sound by the reflection of the sound waves.
Epiphone Fully known as Epiphone Casino, it was the brand of electric guitars used by Lennon and McCartney for recordings, live performances, television appearances and films. McCartney was the irst Beatle to use the brand.
fade A song's repeated final phrase or section that is repeated over and over with diminishing volume until it disappears.
harmonium An organ-like keyboard instrument that produces tones with free metal reeds actuated by air forced from a bellows
melisma The use of two or more pitches for setting a single syllable.
middle-eight Another name for bridge. (See definition.)
motive The basic germ of a music idea. A series of notes set in a rhythm that will be used repeatedly in various ways throughout the song.
Motown Abbreviation for "Motor Town," the small Detroit record Company label for Afro-American artists that Gordon Berry founded in 1959 and which he proceeded to build into a dominant force in the music industry.
multiple tracking Allows the placement of a particular voice, instrument or effect. Volumes of specific instruments can be equalized individually in its low, mid range and high frequencies. At pre-set minimum and maximum levels, volumes of specific sounds can be regulated. The use of the multi-tracking

recording system allowed the combination of resonant and discordant sound elements into a sonic hash without contradicting one another.

overdub The process of allowing erasure, editing or changing by placing a new sound element over an existing one, usually undesirable.

reprise Repeating a song in several parts to make its mode indelible.

reverb Short for "reverberation," the degree of ambience in a room.

riff A short improvised, usually virtuosic interlude.

scat Nonsense or wordless vocal improvisations in which the singer uses the voice as an instrument.

syncopation Accent on an unexpected beat.

tape loop A segment or sequence of segments of magnetic tape which have been spliced end-to-end to form a loop or circle. When played in this form, the taped sound is continuously repeated, as distinct from tape echo or tape feedback.

Tierce de Picardie (meaning Picardie's third) A major chord at the end of a piece of music in a minor key.

YSG!
Young, Sexy & Gorgeous!
By Joyce Peñas Pilarsky

THE BEATLES:
Extraordinary Plagiarists
By Edgar O. Cruz

Published by EXOM Publishing House
Visit @www.todoentertainment.com
Contact exom.ph@gmail.com

Printed in Great Britain
by Amazon